Black, White and Gray:

Law and Ethics in Business

Suzanne Cummins, JD

Published by DZ Publishing

For written permission, contact the author at the Department of Management and Policy, Eller College of Management, University of Arizona, Tucson, Arizona 85750; or e-mail: scummins@email.arizona.edu

ISBN: 978-0-9753660-1-1

Publisher: Samantha Zipp Dowd, DZ Publishing
Managing Editor: Barbara Fraps
Cover Designer: Jeff Neff

Printed in the United States of America

Acknowledgements

There are four people to whom this book owes its existence.

The first huge thank you goes to my editor Barbara Fraps, who tirelessly did the really hard work for this book. From graphics, content editing, and proof reading, to personal encouragement as I lumbered through writing the first draft; her support, skill, patience, non-judgmental kindness, and confidence, kept this project from being completely abandoned.

The second thank you goes to Samantha Zipp, my publisher, former student, and friend. Her "yes" to every request has pushed me to complete this often-stalled project. Given what she has on her plate, mine has seemed empty, but she has never dropped a single ball.

Thanks to Lisa Hammond, our operations backbone, for her support and hard work in keeping my previous book flowing to its customers, and getting ready to take on the distribution of this new book. Her wonderful work ethic never faltered through her own adversity this past year.

And of course as always, thanks go to my beloved husband Ken, who for 42 plus years has put up with me, the past two of which he has had to listen to me whine through this latest effort.

Contents

Chapter 4

Chapter 5

Chapter 6

Contents

Chapter 1
Corporate Social Responsibility

In a sense, corporations are like Frankenstein's monster without the ugly body. They are entities created out of the human imagination rather than from nature, and once they have been liberated, they take on a personality all of their own. And though they have the capacity to do amazing things that mere mortals cannot, they can turn on you.

In the 19th century Mary Shelley novel, *Frankenstein or the Modern Promethius,*(1) the main character Dr. Frankenstein was motivated to create "life" in his laboratory. He was driven by scientific curiosity coupled with a good dose of ego, as he challenged divine providence. Though ego may play a small part in corporate formation, the existence of corporate entities didn't evolve from such strong human emotion. They were created to encourage individuals to invest their capital into an enterprise, by limiting the risk to those investors to the specific amount of capital invested. In other words, corporations were created to allow investors to own all or part of a company (in the form of shares), without incurring any responsibility or liability for the conduct of the business should things turn ugly.

One might query why a society would want to create a business entity where the owners have limited consequences if the business acts badly. Dr. Frankenstein (and his family) paid a hefty price for his arrogance in creating his monster—the monster killed them all. One might assume that shareholders should carry consequences beyond their initial investment if harm has been caused by an entity that they have tried to or actually profited from. But that would be inherently contradictory to the primary function that corporations serve, which is to encourage investment by limiting risk. It would also be inconsistent with the role shareholders play in corporations. Shareholders are not creators or decision makers—they exercise their will by electing a board to watch over their interests. Although there are instances where shareholders can hold a variety of managerial hats as well as ownership rights, the actual power of ownership is very limited, especially in publicly traded corporations.

Ownership in publicly traded companies is different than any other type of proprietary interest. Shares can be distributed among tens or hundreds of thousands of shareholders who can acquire or divest their interests in a split second. There is a significant and intended disconnect between ownership and stewardship. Individual owners have barely a whisper of control in the firm, and it is understood that their interest may be extraordinarily short term.

Although these ephemeral owners—shareholders—are the focal point of corporate boards of directors who owe their highest fiduciary duty to them, society is the creator of the corporate form and holds the primary obligation (through law and regulation) to try and control the creature. The obvious problem is that without ethics and integrity on the part of those who run the corporation, law and regulation alone will leave society very vulnerable to the whims of a giant.

Corporations can live forever. (Frankenstein's monster had to take his own life for it to end.) Corporations can appear to be unstoppable at times. Once Frankenstein's monster broke free in the Mary Shelley version of the

story, the good Dr. F was its final victim. When we as society legally emancipate corporations, giving each the status of a legal entity and endowing these creatures with certain rights (as recently when the U.S. Supreme Court decided that corporations have certain political free speech rights under the First Amendment), there is always the possibility that they can dominate in a negative way until laws change to constrain them.

To summarize, while there are many similarities between Mary Shelley's imaginary monster and the fictitious corporate entity that society has created, Mary Shelley's monster stays in the pages of her book. The corporate creature (fictitious though it may be in its inception) has some genuine power to do both good and harm. Regulating the corporate entity and/or imposing social expectations upon it to insure it is more of a positive than a negative force is one of the biggest continuing challenges for society.

What is CSR

This first chapter will pose the impossible question about how, in a perfect world, corporations **should** behave. In recent years, various constituent groups (business leaders, academics, political interest groups) have put words to society's moral expectation, and say that corporations should be socially responsible. In business schools we use the term "corporate social responsibility" and truncate

that to the acronym CSR as the common term to describe that expectation.

Unfortunately, we do not have a consistent notion in the business community of what exactly CSR is, in order to evaluate it. In general, we think of CSR as corporations doing good things like donating money to charity, or being environmentally protective, or paying good wages with good benefits to its employees, or various other combinations of good acts for the benefit of society. Because the term CSR has largely remained unqualified, it is difficult to scientifically demonstrate that CSR is a good thing in the economic sense. It may be counterintuitive to think that something as altruistic as CSR could ever be a bad thing, but there can be significant problems when corporations divert their attention to society and away from their business mission. To get an overview, it is useful to consider the various perspectives on CSR that are generally cited in business literature.

Milton Friedman is often quoted as the progenitor of the "profit maximization" theory of social responsibility. In his opinion, in a free market economy, "there is one and only one social responsibility of business—to use its resources and engage in activities designed to increase its profits, so long as it stays within the rules of the game...."(2)

Although one cannot argue against the notion that businesses should try to be profitable, to call that social respon-sibility seems strange. A business that fails to make a profit may fail for good economic reasons. It hardly seems logical that in so failing, it has violated its social responsibility. In fact, in an aggressive, efficient market, it is a benefit that some competitors will die out as the best and most efficient take market share. Conversely, just because a business is profitable, it does not seem right to give it special credit for being socially responsible.

It is still important not to dismiss Friedman's notion out of hand. Generally, a free market can create value for every member of society and therefore serve society's needs effectively, so it is by definition socially responsible. Although we will examine ways free markets do not operate for the benefit of society later in this chapter, and we will look at other theorists and their views of CSR, consider the following case study about Steve and Barry's, a discounting retailer that challenged both big name brands and social norms, and tried to address the needs of the young and disenfranchised.(3)

STEVE AND BARRY'S

Steve Shore and Barry Prevor seem to have been born to be entrepreneurs. They started their first business together while in high school, acquiring or buying up surplus t-shirts from conventions and social gatherings, and selling them cheap at flea markets. They opened their first store in 1985 while Barry was still a student at the University of Pennsylvania (Penn) and Steve was finishing up at Tulane. That first store opened near Penn's campus and was an overwhelming success, selling collegiate-style sportswear at super-discount prices.

At the onset Steve and Barry seemed to know that they needed to offer more than great prices and high-quality merchandise to be successful. To compel Penn students to come to their storefront, they needed to persuade their market that they presented a *cool* way to shop. Steve and Barry's managed to build a reputation for being both frugal and trendy, a difficult mix to accomplish. They opened nearly a dozen more outlets near major universities over the next thirteen years. Then, in 1998, they widened their vision and opened their first mall store. By 2008, they had opened 276 stores in 39 states, and their mission statement carried overtones of a social revolution.

Steve and Barry's systematically attacked the notion that status must be associated with pricey branding. They created a retail movement designed to correlate coolness with intelligent, value-based shopping—one where being poor and being cool could coalesce. They were not merely offering low prices for competitive products, they were (in their own minds at least) offering a vision of social equalization.

Enter Stephon Marbury

Only devoted fans would consider former New York Knicks guard Stephon Marbury to be a role model. He has generally had fractious relationships with his coaches and teammates, and despite a wealth of talent—as of this writing, he plays basketball in China—unable to any longer find welcome in the NBA. But he presented the kind of counter-culture image that Steve and Barry's wanted for their status revolution. They wanted someone who could relate to the poor, but, at least on some level, impress the rich. They wanted someone to help them carry the flag against social disequilibrium correlated to wealth.

Marbury understood the social importance of this venture. He had grown up poor, just outside of Brooklyn in Coney Island, New York. In communities like the one in which he was raised, Nike apparel—most particularly shoes—had been awarded an ominous form of respect that was as destructive as it was ubiquitous. Kids who didn't wear clothing with the "swoosh" felt as if they were personally inferior, and kids who did have the swoosh were targeted by those who wanted what they could not afford. Shootings, stabbings, beatings were not uncommon—all for shoes or apparel with a brand identity and a hefty price tag.

STEVE AND BARRY'S

The following PRNewswire piece was released by Steve and Barry's upon the launch of the Starbury shoe line in August 2006.

PORT WASHINGTON, N.Y., Aug. 16/PRNewswire/

Growing up in a Coney Island household with parents struggling to make ends meet, Stephon Marbury knows first-hand the pressure kids, parents and playground basketball players feel to spend top-dollar on the latest clothes and sneakers. Today, as a high-profile NBA player, he's now in a position to realize a lifelong dream to "change the world" by eliminating that aspect of our culture.

Marbury has announced that he is teaming with national casual apparel retailer Steve & Barry's to introduce the Starbury Collection....The Starbury Collection features nearly 50 casual and comfortable items for men and boys, including jackets, jeans, hoodies, tshirts, athletic tops and shorts, lifestyle and performance sneakers, work boots, hats and other accessories, with nearly every individual item priced at an astonishing $10 and under.

Perhaps no item reflects the extraordinary value of the Starbury Collection more than the Starbury One, a new high performance basketball sneaker that Marbury will wear on NBA courts beginning this coming season. Available in a variety of colors and all sizes for adults and kids, the Starbury One found on Steve & Barry's shelves will be identical to those Marbury will wear during games. Incorporating a sleek design and the same technical features for comfort, stability and durability found in basketball sneakers sold by the nation's top brands for $100 to $150, the Starbury One will carry a price tag of just $14.98. It's believed to be the lowest price for an NBA quality sneaker during the modern era.

Stephon Marbury said: "Kids shouldn't have to feel the pressure to spend so much to feel good about the way they look. I'm blessed to be in a position to do something about it, to help change the world. I couldn't find a better partner to create the Starbury Collection with than Steve & Barry's...."

STEVE AND BARRY'S

During the launch of the Starbury collection, Marbury commented to media and a group of young African Americans, "They are going to be jealous of US." "They" referred to those who could afford to put the Nike logo on their feet. And Marbury was right, "they" were jealous. People of wealth ran to the stores to buy Starbury shoes as word-of-mouth about the brand spread. Young African-American boys were televised on news programs depicting themselves as smart for buying Starbury shoes, and mocking the foolish people who spent too much on Nikes. The mothers of those children were filmed tearfully thanking Marbury for giving their children this option. Even his own mother was quoted as saying that she wished someone had done this for her children when they were young. Marbury himself was filmed breaking into tears over the response he received.

The product flew off of the shelves to the hands of purchasers that crossed class and racial lines. Together with Steve and Barry's, Stephon Marbury helped create a new generation of value shoppers, manufacturing for many of them a powerful vehicle for self-esteem, uncorrelated with spending more than rational for their outward image.

Assuming Steve and Barry's was profitable, then by Friedman's definition they were acting socially responsibly. But their case deserves consideration within the constraints of other scholars who have opined about what CSR is or should be.

Professor Archie Carroll is famous for constructing a pyramid of corporate citizenship (4) that corresponds a bit to Maslow's pyramidical hierarchy of needs. Carroll's pyramid presents the hierarchy of social responsibility as follows:

Obviously at the base of the pyramid is the fundamental requirement for corporate survival which is profitability. To say that one has to achieve that before moving to legality and then to ethicality is a somewhat scary thought, and Carroll is quoted as never having intended that those priorities be sequential, so the point is more that before a company can be philanthropic, it must be profitable within the law and ethical construct of business. The question of whether Steve and Barry's meets Carroll's highest notions of being a socially responsible citizen is an interesting one. If the clothing chain is merely meeting a market need and building a profitable business, then nothing in their conduct can be considered philanthropic.

Another scholar, Dr. Paul Portney who served as Dean of the Eller College of Management at the University of Arizona, and who previously headed the Washington, D.C. think tank Resources for the Future, has a descriptive rather than prescriptive definition for CSR.(5) He defines it as going "beyond compliance" with the law to do social good. Steve and Barry's would not fit his definition since nothing indicates that they exceeded what the law would require of them in order to do social good. In fact, if their motivation for approaching this market as they did was that it would maximize profit, Portney would not give them CSR credit for that either. After all, all businesses want to maximize profit, and theoretically all businesses do good for society by providing the goods and services for which there is demand. Demand is not merely what people want—it is what they want and have the resources to pay for. Steve and Barry's merely have been addressing an unmet demand.

But in that process, Steve and Barry's unequivocally attempted to do social good. The chain enfranchised otherwise excluded buyers and gave them a venue to shop that boosted both self-esteem and availability. Friedman would argue that this is exactly what should happen in a free market, where supply finds demand and meets it. Theoretically, no consumer with a dollar should be disenfranchised if there is a possibility to provide a good or service that can be produced profitably to meet that consumer's demand.

The Steve and Barry's story has an ending, although not a happy one. Below is the rest of the story.

STEVE AND BARRY'S, PART B

Steve and Barry's found more celebrity partners to promote their vision. Sarah Jessica Parker of "Sex and the City" fame, who had been pursued by several retailers to give her television image and her name to clothing lines, signed with Steve and Barry's to manufacture and sell her "Bitten" line. Tennis great Venus Williams also became a member of this passionate team. Growth was extraordinary, especially given competitive retailers. Stores thrived in both indigent and middle-class environments, theoretically leveraging each other against economic ups and downs.

Consequently, it was unexpected that in July of 2008, twenty-three years after opening their first store and only two years after the launch of the overwhelmingly successful Starbury line, Steve and Barry's filed for bankruptcy. After a brief attempt at reorganization, the firm closed its doors for good, losing money for investors, creditors, mall owners, and suppliers.

Steve and Barry's put the following statement on their website.

> We deeply regret that our company has filed for protection under Chapter 11 of the U.S. Bankruptcy Code and the effect it has on so many dedicated people and organizations. Steve & Barry's opened its first store 23 years ago with the mission of providing affordable quality clothing to everyone. This mission has grown beyond our wildest dreams, providing our customers with 80 million units of affordable clothing and accessories during the past year alone. We have commenced this reorganization case only because we have exhausted all alternatives and have no other choice.

In retrospect, it would appear that despite the best of intentions, or maybe because of them, Steve and Barry's did not have sufficient discipline or adequate margins to survive.

Hindsight would indicate that the growth of Steve and Barry's was too rapid, and too leveraged. Going from 37 stores in 2004 to 279 stores in 2008 was ultimately unsupportable. Using debt and advanced payments from malls, the profit engine could not produce a revenue stream to accommodate the cost of capital. This was catastrophic when coupled with the stressed economic conditions in the country at that time. Though Steve and Barry's depicted a part of the problem as a "credit crunch," it is very unclear that, even with additional liquidity, the company could have survived under its voluminous debt obligations.

The fallout from the bankruptcy was substantial. Steve and Barry's workers all lost their jobs. The malls that had invested scarce resources into luring Steve and Barry's to their properties and building out space to suit lost all of their investment. Perhaps most tragically, Steve and Barry's failed to pay the factories in the most destitute regions of the world where their apparel was produced. Factories that were located in places like Pakistan, Bangladesh, India, and Nepal were left with nowhere to turn. One Nepalese factory employee posted the following on a blog where workers, creditors, customers, and others shared thoughts:

> "I work for a garment manufacturing plant in Nepal which supplies garments to Steve and Barry. We have been told that our factory has not received payments for the orders already sent to them. Salaries have not been paid and we do not know wether [sic] the payment is coming or not. I came to know from you news above that S & B is contempleting [sic] on full liquidation. How can my employer safeguard his payment from S & B? Is there any answer?
>
> — Posted by Bharat D.Suba"

There were no safeguards—none of the factories were paid.

Although one might rigorously disagree with Milton Friedman's perspective that the social responsibility of a company is to make a profit, it is indisputable that a corporation unable to sustain itself will ultimately harm people.

Profit Seeking Should Inherently Benefit Society

If a competitive free market functions as it should, businesses produce the widest variety of goods and services to the most diverse consumers. The interests of business and society are generally synergistic. Adam Smith characterized the "invisible hand" that creates this synergy well over two centuries ago.

If a business prices too high relative to competition, it will be put out of business. If a business creates supply that nobody wants, it will go out of business. In the sense that the expenditure of our dollars is a vote for what we are willing to purchase, business will strive to meet our needs at a price we are willing and able to pay, or they will be put out of business. Businesses consequently search for markets where there is unmet demand, thereby creating the widest range of supply for the best price. In theory, if Steve and Barry's had done their job, they would have been meeting an unmet need, and all would have been well. No matter how one views the social responsibility of business, making a profit would seem essential for any business to meet its primary responsibilities.

That said, most people will generally conclude that there are businesses or markets, when left unregulated, that will not function perfectly in the best interests of society merely on the basis of supply and demand, especially not with profitability as the primary responsibility a business has to its shareholders. As Milton Friedman implies, there needs to be "rules of the game." The question that society must answer is what the rules need to be.

Market Failures

Because profitability is a fundamental mandate in business (without which, as we noted with Steve and Barry, really bad things can happen), only law and conscience stand between producers and society when the interests of the two conflict. Therefore, a primary task is to figure out where, even with a well-operating invisible hand freely influencing supply and demand, the interests of business and society do not align.

Economists have identified "market failure" areas where the free market has no internal mechanism to either operate efficiently or protect the larger interests of society. In a market failure area, the free market will harm rather than help: either through inherent inefficiency, or by the lack of market forces compelling businesses to act in the best interest of society. Most economists would agree that market failure areas are the reason we need "rules of the game" imposed upon businesses.

The economic phrase market failure refers to attributes of a properly functioning free market that need to be regulated by the government to prevent harm to society. Although not all laws in a free market society relate to market failure issues, most business-related law and regulation does. Economists generally identify four areas of market failure:(6)

1) imperfect information,

2) monopoly,

3) externalities, and

4) public goods.

These four areas will not respond to the ordinary pressures of supply and demand, as will be explained in detail in the next section of this chapter. But before those explanations are explored, this section will conclude with what market failure is not.

The phrase market failure can be very misleading and it is important to distinguish the notion of market failure from that of human suffering. In the macro-economic sense, layoffs, personal financial struggles, and business failures are generally the result of how markets are supposed to function. They occur when the invisible hand is working to optimize efficiency by eliminating unnecessary production for which there is no demand, and forcing those resources (human and other) engaged in excess production to move to where there is unmet demand. If consumers do not create enough demand for both Nike and Aviva to survive, one of those two shoe producers will die. The workers from the company that goes under will be forced to go elsewhere. It is not pretty, but it is not a market failure.

It is equally important to remember that *not* all regulation relates to market failure. A significant number of laws relate to the social side of our political economy, where supports are put in place for particularly vulnerable members of society who might be unable to self-sustain under ordinary market conditions. Social security for the disabled and the elderly, and Medicaid programs that provide medical insurance for children in families that do not have adequate resources to provide medical care are examples of this type of social system legislation.

However, because business regulation is predominantly market-failure driven, this next segment will focus on an explanation of the market failure areas.

Imperfect Information

The first market failure area to consider is "imperfect information." A free market includes two types of fundamental players: willing sellers and willing buyers. The underlying assumption is that the buyer is able to make an informed decision about the purchase. The common-law doctrine of *caveat emptor* or "buyer beware" assigns the buyer the burden of finding out the requisite data about a purchase, and presumes that such data is attainable and discernible. A good, self-interested buyer would not buy something without determining all that could be reasonably ascertained about the product and its quality as well as about the seller and his or her reliability. Unfortunately, the information that a buyer needs to make an informed decision is often only readily available to the seller. Although the seller could efficiently provide such information to all potential buyers rather than compelling each to engage in his or her own road of discovery, the seller has little or no rationale to do so.

In other words, the market inherently fails to compel a "perfect" disclosure that includes all relevant information from the seller. Although sellers would be willing to disclose all positive attributes of their products, there is no market incentive to provide, and strong market incentive to omit, negative information. Therefore, without regulatory support, a willing buyer will be inefficient in ascertaining information readily available to the seller, and will often be compelled to make a decision with "imperfect" information. Regulation is what forces sellers to disclose more perfect information.

Monopoly

The second market failure area commonly acknowledged by economists is that of "monopoly." The theory of monopoly-based market failure is based on fundamentals of how efficient markets operate. Choice is what gives willing buyers equality with willing sellers, and choice is only a reality where there is competition. A monopoly, to the extent that it is pre-emptive and permanent, would eliminate competition and buyer choice. In monopoly situations, the willing buyer is coerced by the monopolist into a take-it-or-leave-it situation. There is no force to pull the seller to efficiency in production or distribution. Consequently, the market, when monopolized, does not use the nation's people or productive resources efficiently. The monopolist can control what is produced, and by pricing at supra-normal profit levels, not only limit who is able to receive the goods, but in some instances impact overall demand for other goods or services. In the extreme monopoly condition, the market forces of supply and demand are no longer the driving forces, having been replaced by the will of the monopolist.

The problem is that without government regulation all business eventually tends toward monopoly. As a business begins to grow, it garners market share by taking customers from competitors with more efficient production, higher quality relative to price, and better pricing. However, at the point where there is optimal efficiency, and competition must become cut-throat for any given firm to grab more market share, it is in the best interests of the competitors to collude, fix prices, and combine into a single trust or enterprise in order to insure survival and maintain optimal profits. The best interests of the competitors, at that point, are inverse to the best interests of competition itself. Because it is not the survival of individual competitors, but the survival of competition itself that is the foundation of a free and healthy market, this paradox comes into play as any given market matures. Markets will tend toward monopoly if left to their own devices, and markets will fail when the interests of competitors are adverse to the interests of competition. It is for that reason that regulation is required to protect the free market from its own inclination toward monopoly.

Economists virulently disagree as to whether or not the assumptions made in the previous paragraphs about monopolies are true in today's high tech environments, but most would agree that to the extent that monopolies are maintained through means other than competition (such as coercion, collusion, or bribery), they should be prohibited.

Externalities

The third area of market failure to examine is "externalities." In this text, the focus will be on negative externalities as an area of market failure, because it is more difficult and less relevant to speak about positive externalities harming markets. In the most basic definition, a negative externality shifts a cost of producing a good or service from the producer onto society. For example, a company that produces chemicals and then dumps the resulting toxic waste into a nearby watershed shifts the cost of that pollution to society. The chemical producer makes the mess, but society suffers the illnesses from the waste and/or pays to clean it up.

There are economists who would argue that the solution to the problem of toxic wastes being dumped into watersheds is to make all watersheds "private," i.e., owned by individuals and not governments. Those economists assert that the negative externality is actually created by a "nonmarket failure" because government owns the watershed, and that is how the pollution cost is transferred to society. Those economists would argue that if the watershed were owned privately, then the individuals who own it could charge for the use of the watershed, or in the case of unauthorized use, bring a private cause of action (civil nuisance suit) against the chemical producer to force that producer to pay the cost of the cleanup. In fact, such a nuisance suite would theoretically bypass the need for government regulation. This position ignores the reality of the costs of lawsuits to litigants as well as to society, their imperfection and to some degree randomness, and the laborious and slow manner with which they proceed through the judicial system. Law-

suits are very risky, burdens of proof for specific damages require extensive use of experts and are often the subject of legitimate debate, and the courts that provide infrastructure for such suits are paid for by the taxpayer. Lawsuits are also reactive rather than proactive and can only be brought when the damage has already occurred.

The notion of "privatizing" away the problem of pollution has other serious limitations. Although we can privatize the watersheds that supply the nation's drinking water, it is unreasonable to believe that we can privatize the air that we breathe. At some point, there is the likelihood that a producer will create pollution that travels beyond the borders of its production facilities to public areas. When that happens, there are no market forces that will compel the polluter to clean up its mess, but there are market forces that will deter it from doing so. Absorbing the costs of clean-up would be inefficient for the producer when that cost can be shifted to society.

The self-interest of the competitor is in direct conflict with the interests of society in that situation. The market will fail because it will "give away" resources unfairly. The polluter will usurp clean air or water, converting it to less valuable air and water without paying for that devaluation. Most economists would agree at least to some degree that regulation is required to compel polluters to clean up their messes, because the natural functioning of market forces will not compel that outcome.

Public Goods

The final area of market failure is "public goods." Often the words "public goods" are misinterpreted to incorporate anything that is done for the good of the public. So, for example, one might believe that certain welfare entitlements are "public goods." This is, however, a misinterpretation of the meaning of the term as it was envisioned to categorize market failure.

Consider, for example, the system of Medicare. If one were to assume that Medicare was enacted to regulate the market failure area of medical care, then one would have to assume that the free market could not efficiently provide medical care. That is an incorrect assumption. Left to its own devices, the free market can supply medical care to willing buyers. The problem is not market failure, but human frailty that compels regulating payment by the government for medical care. There is no doubt that the free market can produce supply for the demand that our citizens have for medical care. The problem is that those who generally need the most medical care cannot afford to pay for it. That is not a market failure, but a human and social one.

In a purely free market, if someone cannot afford a resource, he or she just cannot have it. Nobody would argue that it would be a market failure if half the people of driving age could not af-

ford to purchase new automobiles. Some will never achieve that level of productivity, many through no fault of their own. The market has not failed; it has functioned properly in allocating the supply of new cars with the demand for new cars, at an efficient price, in the presence of substantial competition. The ability of an individual to buy a car is then solely dependent on the value of that person's productivity (as measured through wages, etc.) and his or her allocation of personal resources.

People don't die, however, if they don't have a new car. People do die without necessary medical care. The consequence of the free market functioning properly with respect to the distribution of medical services is that it leaves lots of older and disabled people vulnerable to death for lack of money. Medicare is a social safety net to avert that outcome. It does not remedy market failure, but instead intervenes with a socialistic response to free market function. Medicare bypasses the market altogether and uses a command economy solution by taxing the general working population and using those funds for the ones who are likely to have the greatest need for medical care. Medicare is actually an anathema to those who believe in a completely free market. Here is how the thinking goes. Everyone knows that he or she will, if lucky, get old. Everyone knows that he or she, if lucky, will survive long enough to retire. The incumbent obligation on all of us in a free market is to prepare for that eventuality with savings. Medicare removes accountability from individuals and shifts it to the government.

There are, on the other hand, public goods that are funded by the government because the free market cannot efficiently or appropriately provide them. Generally, economists accept that such things as military and police protection are market failure goods, because the free market cannot reasonably allocate them. For example, assume that private enterprise owned the military. There would be no way to refuse protection to those who would want to free-ride, while still providing payers with adequate services. Of course, if nobody paid, there would be no military and no national defense. Assuming most people recognized the need for a military and agreed to pay, those who refused to pay would still have the same protection as those who did pay. If competition were introduced, an armed struggle for market share might even develop. At the very least, there would have to be regulation, but if the only armies were those owned by the private companies, it is unclear how government could coerce or enforce such regulation. No free society has ever allowed a purely private army to serve as the guardian of the national defense. The theory of market failure simply offers an explanation as to why a free market cannot substitute for the government in that arena.

Similarly, police and fire departments are generally presumed to be more efficiently paid for by government than by the private sector. The argument for government run police departments mimics the argument for government controlling the military and is not worth repeating. Fire protection is worthy of consideration because it is not as obvious or straight forward as police protection. Unquestionably, the private sector could sell fire protection. However, if a property owner had to pay for fire protection service or go without, one can assume some owners (depending upon their personal assessment of risk and their financial condition) would not pay. In strict market terms, where there is a non-payer, a fully private fire company would theoretically be compelled to wait to fight a fire until a payer suffered some harm or damage before taking action, allowing non-payer properties to burn unfettered, and payer property to be put at greater risk as a result.

In lieu of using the tax base, some municipalities allow privatized fire departments to offer alternatives to citizens, providing that citizens can pay in advance for services as they would pay for other insurance. For those that do not pay, should they need fire protection service, regulations allow the private provider to collect a significant fee for services rendered. This would still not be a fully private solution because it requires regulation to both set the rates for the insurance equivalent and to allow for collection against the uninsured who is then provided the services. It also includes some risk to payers. If most people decided not to pay until and unless their own property catches on fire, it would be difficult for the private company to stay in business in years where fires are few, leaving those who have paid virtually unprotected.

In part because of the varying risks over time, in areas where there are large concentrations of homes and humanity, using the tax base for basic fire protection has economically been shown to fund fire protection more efficiently than other models, although variations on the models are always likely to be tested to save taxpayers money and limit waste.

When it comes to education and road building, the debate over whether the market or the government is most efficient widens.

The argument that education is a public goods market failure area relates to efficiency and fairness. Market failure, defined by Weimar and Vining, includes those instances where "private interest does not lead to…a fair distribution of private goods."(7) The private sector can certainly provide education to those who can pay for it, so one could argue that education is not a market failure area at all, anymore than Medicare is. However, the fact that the market can supply education does not paint the entire picture. We generally educate children who have not yet begun to produce value. Without government intervention, society would have to rely on parents with sufficient means to bear the costs of a child's schooling. The failure to ensure an adequate education for children would leave markets with a significantly less educated employment base. It also would operate to exacerbate inequalities in a free society. Paying for education through taxation is, from a social and economic perspective, the most efficient use of society's resources. It is certainly arguable that the free market fails to be as efficient as the government in this regard.

It is important to remember that debates over privatization of certain goods or services are tangential to whether or not the area to be privatized should be considered a market failure area. Privatization debates generally center on whether production of the relevant good or service (e.g., education) should be managed by the government (e.g., public schools) or delegated to the private sector (e.g., charter schools or school vouchers). The question is not whether or not the tax base should support education, but whether the government should run the business. In confusing the theory, some argue that the "nonmarket failure" or government failure to provide good public schools proves that the private sector can do the job more efficiently. That is only true with respect to the implementation component of the market failure area, not the funding source. There is the implicit admission in such arguments that the private sector cannot efficiently educate children unless the government intervenes by levying tax and guaranteeing the right to a free education to all children. That side of the debate is not about whether education is a market failure, but, rather, whether the proper level of government intervention includes having government operate the schools after the money is collected and the rights to education codified.

Society's Needs

As noted above, there are regulations for social supports that do not relate to market failure theory at all, including such things as Social Security, state-controlled unemployment insurance, welfare, and Medicaid. However, much regulation that does relate to market failure pushes the theory to its edge in order to meet perceived social needs, and to protect the society.

Under a purely market analysis, if the cost of "curing" any given market failure exceeds the benefit imposed, it would be irrational to regulate in that manner. Assume that the social cost of a given pollution source is $50,000 in added medical cost to the community in terms of health and human impact. Assume further, that the costs imposed on the market by regulation are in the millions of dollars. It would, at least theoretically, not be rational to impose that regulation. Determining rationali-

ty in a given situation (and understanding the political use of market failure evaluation) requires analysis concerning who is imposing the burden on society, who is paying the cost of regulation, and who is getting the benefit.

Sometimes, however, regulators simply act inappropriately under all standards, addressing a perceived harm without addressing the costs of the "cure." In McAdams' survey book, a quoted table illustrates the regulatory burden per life saved for various regulations related to negative externalities. According to that data, the cost of regulating DES cattle feed was $178,000,000 per life saved. There is a likely negative externality underlying the need for those regulations, but any regulatory scheme should include an analysis of how much market harm is imposed by the market failure cure. The trade-offs are quite direct.

Notes

1. Shelley, Mary. *Frankenstein or the Modern Promethius*, 1818, London

2. Friedman, Milton. *Capitalism and Freedom*, University of Chicago Press, 1962.

3. Cummins and Gilliland. "Steve and Barry's: A Case Study," 2010.

4. McAdams, Tony. *Law Business and Society*, McGraw Hill 2004, page 94, quoting Archie Carroll's "The Pyramid of Social Responsibility"

5. Portney, Paul R. "Corporate Social Responsibility An Economic and Public Policy Perspective." Copyright by Resources for the Future. Except for brief quotation in a scholarly article or paper, no part of these contents may be downloaded, copied, or retransmitted by print, electronic, or other means without the written permission of the publisher.

6. McAdams, Tony. *Law Business and Society*, McGraw Hill, 2004

7. Weimer, David L. and Vining, Aidan R. *Policy Analysis: Concepts and Practice*, 2nd ed., Prentice Hall, 1992.

Chapter 2
Ethics, American Ideology, and the Constitution

The first section of this chapter looks at two very different moral and ethical philosophies, and gives purpose to both perspectives in a business environment. In the end, we will use conventional wisdom to interpret these ethical paradigms and give them application in the business world, but in deference to the notion that critical analysis is an essential skill, we will at least peek at the original sources for insight. For those readers who have studied philosophy and have explored the intricacies of the works of Immanuel Kant and John Stuart Mill, let me just apologize in advance. I am certain that any assertions I make about these philosophers are at best a weak approximation of their vision.

Formalism and Deontology

In 1790, Immanuel Kant completed a philosophical work entitled *The Science of Right.*(1) In this work, he asserted that there is a system of "rights" in nature—a built-in natural order that is inherent in the world. From this natural order, "man" can derive "juridical" or legal rights, but Kant carefully distinguishes the law of man from the law of nature. In the natural order there are absolutes of what is right and what is wrong. These may or may not be consistent with legal constructs, so Kant emphasizes the distinction between what is moral and what is punishable under the law.

Kant's school of ethics is known as formalism, and the theory that morality can be scientifically discerned in nature is known as deontology. Deontology's root comes from the Greek word *deon* meaning duty or that by which we are bound. Deontology is the science of duty—what Kant calls the science of "right." Business ethics books consistently point to Kant as the source of the notion that a moral person acts morally irrespective of the consequences, and not based on fear of punishment. A moral person acts on good will. Kant is also credited with philosophically asserting that what is right is right, what is wrong is wrong, and the judgment about what constitutes moral behavior is to be made without regard to the outcome of the moral decision—only with regard to the decision itself.

This has become the conventional wisdom referred to in the introductory paragraph above. However, reading Kant directly is likely to demonstrate how simplifications can distort original work or reflect bias. Toward this end, the deceased philosopher shall speak for himself, at least momentarily. The first brief excerpt from Kant's work as translated by W. Hastie follows:

…Universal Division of Rights.

I. Natural Right and Positive Right.

The system of rights, viewed as a scientific system of doctrines, is divided into natural right and positive right. Natural right rests upon pure…principles…; positive or statutory right is what proceeds from the will of a legislator.

II. Innate Right and Acquired Right.

The system of rights may again be regarded in reference to the implied powers of dealing morally with others as bound by obligations…. Thus viewed, the system is divided into innate right and acquired right. Innate right is that right which belongs to every one by nature, independent of all [legislative and court-made law.] Acquired right is that right which is founded upon such [legislative and court-made law].

Innate right may also be called the "internal mine and thine"…for external right must always be acquired.

There is only one Innate Right, the Birthright of Freedom.

Freedom is independence of the compulsory will of another; and in so far as it can coexist with the freedom of all according to a universal law, it is the one sole original, inborn right belonging to every man in virtue of his humanity. There is, indeed, an innate equality belonging to every man which consists in his right to be independent of being bound by others to anything more than that to which he may also reciprocally bind them. It is, consequently, the inborn quality of every man in virtue of which he ought to be his own master by right…. There is, also, the natural quality of justness attributable to a man as naturally of unimpeachable right, …because he has done no wrong to any one prior to his own [lawful] actions. And, further, there is also the innate right of common action on the part of every man, so that he may do towards others what does not infringe their rights or take away anything that is theirs unless they are willing to appropriate it…. But all these rights or titles are already included in the principle of innate freedom, and are not really distinguished from it….

[The following distinguishes legally "excusable" conduct with conduct that is "right."]

The so-called right of necessity…is the supposed right or title, in case of the danger of losing my own life, to take away the life of another who has, in fact, done me no harm. It is evident that, viewed as a doctrine of right, this must involve a contradiction, For this is not the case of a wrongful aggressor making an unjust assault upon my life, and whom I anticipate by depriving him of his own…. It is a question of the allowableness of using violence against one who has used none against me.

It is clear that the assertion of such a right is not to be understood objectively as being in accordance with what a law would prescribe, but merely subjectively, as proceeding on the assumption of how a sentence would be pronounced by a court in the case. There can, in fact, be no criminal law assigning the penalty of death to a man who, when shipwrecked and struggling in extreme danger for his life, and in order to save it, may thrust another from a plank on which he had saved himself. For the punishment threatened by the law could not possibly have greater power than the fear of the loss of life in the case in question. Such a penal law would thus fail altogether to exercise its intended effect; for the threat of an evil which is still uncertain—such as death by a judicial sentence—could not overcome the fear of an evil which is certain, as drowning is in such circumstances. An act of violent self-preservation, then, ought not to be considered as altogether beyond condemnation…it is only to be adjudged as exempt from [death penalty] punishment…. Yet this subjective condition of impunity, by a strange confusion of ideas, has been regarded by jurists as equivalent to objective lawfulness.

The dictum of the right of necessity is put in these terms. "Necessity has no law…." And yet there cannot be a necessity that could make what is wrong right [lawful]. [In other words under Kant's standard necessity does have law– you cannot be said to be acting lawfully just because you have taken actions against another to survive.]

As you will note, there is one basic right in nature according to Kant, and that is "freedom." Therefore, if actions are consistent with the freedom of the actor and the freedom of everyone else, it is, scientifically speaking, moral. Kant asserts,

> "Every action is right which in itself…is such that it can coexist along with the freedom of the will of each and all in action, according to a universal law."

In other words, since everyone has this right to freedom, the logical limitation on that right must be that the freedom which one individual exerts must not impinge on the freedom of someone else. All natural laws of morality come from this basic construct in Kant's vision. Not all legislative laws come from the same construct, because legislative laws are constrained by practical considerations, where natural laws are not. The act and not the outcome is what determines moral behavior.

Most interesting, however, is the use of Kant's name to identify conduct that is ostensibly immoral under current values. For example, Kant has been used to decry conduct engaged in by the Enron executives who argued that they were following the law when they established the off-book partnerships that misled the shareholders re-

garding corporate earnings. Many business ethicists have responded that whether legal or not, the conduct was "deontologically" immoral. Kant would not necessarily see things in those terms. Although Kant certainly sees the protection of property rights as a part of freedom that emanates from a natural right, it would seem that fraud is not as wrong in the natural order as are other forms of theft. The listener to the fraud has the choice of whether or not to believe it. In the latter section of *The Science of Right*, Kant states:

> [Taking another's property against his will is different than] "…merely to communicate thought, to narrate anything, or to promise something whether truly and honestly, or untruly and dishonestly…, for it rests entirely upon these others whether they will believe or trust in it or not."

Kant is presenting the notion that since one person has the freedom to believe or not believe the communications of another, there is less of an obstruction to the natural order when a victim has had some choice in a matter, even when that choice is uninformed and manipulated. This would be more of a philosophical justification for the notion of *"caveat emptor"* or "buyer beware" than an argument for moral certainty. What underlies this perspective is probably the natural tension that freedom brings (both in nature and society) between free choice and personal accountability. If we are given free choice, we are generally held responsible for the choices we make.

This is not to say that Kant would support the right to defraud. He would not. Nor is it reasonable to assert that he is a moral relativist. He is not. He does, however, appear to be more complicated than is indicated in the generic books on business ethics.

We may adopt conventional wisdom for ease of comparing ethical theories. But as we do that, we are reminded that, in any context, conventional wisdom may be based on inaccurate or at least arguable assumptions that require independent analysis if those assumptions are important to our (ethical or other) decision-making.

Teleology and Utilitarianism

There are those who teach that the Utilitarian theory of ethics supports the notion that "the ends justify the means." These ethicists attribute to utilitarianists a moral "school" that espouses if the overall outcome is better for most people, it does not matter how you get there. This simplification is further interpreted to mean that it is the most moral to benefit the most people and harm the fewest. Most people would see the danger such a notion would carry. Enslaving a small minority to the benefit of the majority would be moral under such a system. And certainly stealing property from the rich and giving it to the poor (per Robin Hood) would be ethically compelled. Killing one person so that several might share his food and avoid starvation would also be warranted. These are interesting ideas, but they have little to do with the philosophy presented by the utilitarianists of the 18th and 19thcenturies who are credit-ed with establishing the "teleological" or utilitarian school of ethics.(2)

Utilitarianism was proposed in 18th century England by Jeremy Bentham and expounded by John Stuart Mill in the mid 1850s. It is Mill's famous work, *Utilitarianism*, that is most generally referenced when speaking of that ethical paradigm in America.(3) It is also most generally misunderstood.

Mill certainly adopted the notion that morality was inextricably tied to utility, or the benefit to the greatest number. As a result, he is properly credited with a moral theory that is directly tied to the outcome rather than the conduct that created that outcome. However, in his article *On Liberty* (4), he clarified as follows:

> "I regard utility as the ultimate appeal on all ethical questions; but it must be utility in the largest sense, grounded on the per-

manent interests of man as a progressive being. Those interests, I contend, authorize the subjection of individual spontaneity to external control, only in respect to those actions of each, which concern the interest of other people. If any one does an act hurtful to others, there is a *prima facie* case for punishing him...."

This "utilitarian" notion of optimizing good was constrained to a much larger picture of "good" than would support those examples given earlier involving harming a small number of people to help many. One can see by Mill's strong language that any harm by one to another is outside of the utility theory in the largest sense in which it was proposed. In this respect only, the assessment of morality in terms of the outer limits of acceptability would be the same for Kant and for Mill. Confusing opportunism with utilitarianism is the largest error made in both business and the literature on this subject of utilitarianism.

Since Mill, many other contemporary ethicists have refined notions of utilitarianism, so that today there are basically two theories of utilitarianism offered in most business ethics books.

Act Utilitarianism: Act utilitarianism espouses that whatever has the most utility or value to an individual is the highest value, short of harming or restricting the freedom of others. On a more global scale, the act utilitarian philosophy requires that all decisions made for an institution or group be considered on a case-by-case basis to determine whether the act benefits more people than it harms with the same limitations in terms of impingement on freedom.

To some extent every choice that has influence over others can be perceived as limiting freedom, but the idea for the utilitarianist is to limit the restraint imposed on the liberty of any person in order to benefit the whole.

Rule Utilitarianism: This form of utilitarianism adopts the political views espoused by Mill and others with regard to the role of government in a free society. This theory directs how governments should act as opposed to individuals or individual institutions. Under a rule utilitarian paradigm, the law is an optimized version of the utility model. A lawmust, under this ethical theory, act in the permanent interests of humankind and benefit more people than it harms. However, because the primary value underlying utilitarianism is freedom, rules that curtail freedom should only be imposed when absolutely necessary to protect the freedom of others.

Under a rule utilitarian model, once the optimized rule is in place, it *must be followed*, irrespective of the outcome. In this paradigm, the utilitarian application *cannot* be outcome-based, which differentiates it from act utilitarianism. The rule is set in place in anticipation of the outcomes, both good and bad, and the bad are to be accepted with the good to maintain the integrity of the law.

Examples of rule utilitarian moral application are readily found in American law. Take, for example, our exclusionary rule, which prohibits the courts from admitting or considering evidence that was taken in violation of the constitutional rights of the accused. The Fourth Amendment of the Constitution protects Americans from unreasonable searches and seizures. However, until 1961, there was little motivation on the part of policeto observe the constraints of the Fourth Amendment. The U.S. Supreme Court was concerned with the lawlessness of police officers who violated the constitutional rights of citizens and, in the case *Mapp v. Ohio* (5), imposed the exclusionary rule to remove the motivation for such unlawful conduct. This rule was not imposed to protect crimedoers, but to protect the rest of us who would be vulnerable to such searches if there were no disincentives to the use of unlawful search mechanisms.

However, there is a huge cost imposed by the exclusionary rule. If an officer makes a mistake, the accused may well go free. Leaving a dangerous criminal on the streets and a victim without redress is an undesirable outcome. The court understood that this could occur with the exclusionary rule, but believed the greater good (more freedom from police invasion into the privacy of our own homes) compelled this result. So, there is an optimization of utilitarian value. For the greatest good of everyone, our law will permit certain scumbags to go free. Here is the case that established the precedent:

Mapp v. Ohio (1961)

Supreme Court of the United States (367 U.S. 643)

Justice Tom Campbell Clark delivered the opinion of the court.

On May 23, 1957, three Cleveland police officers arrived at [the] appellant's residence in that city pursuant to information that "a person (was) hiding out in the home, who was wanted for questioning in connection with a recent bombing, and that there was a large amount of policy paraphernalia being hidden in the home." Miss Mapp and her daughter by a former marriage lived on the top floor of the two-family dwelling. Upon their arrival at that house, the officers knocked on the door and demanded entrance, but [the] appellant, after telephoning her attorney, refused to admit them without a search

warrant. They advised their headquarters of the situation and undertook a surveillance of the house.

The officers again sought entrance some three hours later when four
or more additional officers arrived on the scene. When Miss Mapp
did not come to the door immediately, at least one of the several
doors to the house was forcibly opened and the policemen gained ad-
mittance. Meanwhile, Miss Mapp's attorney arrived, but the officers,
having secured their own entry, and continuing in their defiance of
the law, would permit him neither to see Miss Mapp nor to enter the
house. It appears that Miss Mapp was halfway down the stairs from
the upper floor to the front door when the officers, in this highhanded
manner, broke into the hall. She demanded to see the search warrant.
A paper, claimed to be a warrant, was held up by one of the officers.
She grabbed the "warrant" and placed it in her bosom. A struggle en-
sued in which the officers recovered the piece of paper and as a result of which they handcuffed [the] appellant because she had been
"belligerent" in resisting their official rescue of the "warrant" from
her person. Running roughshod over appellant, a policeman
"grabbed" her, "twisted (her) hand," and she "yelled (and) pleaded
with him" because "it was hurting." [The a]ppellant, in handcuffs,
was then forcibly taken upstairs to her bedroom where the officers
looked into a photo album and through personal papers belonging to
the appellant. The search spread to the rest of the second floor including the child's bedroom, the living room, the kitchen and a di-
nette. The basement of the building and a trunk found therein were
also searched. The obscene materials for possession of which she
was ultimately convicted were discovered in the course of that wide-
spread search.

At the trial no search warrant was produced by the prosecution, nor
was the failure to produce one explained or accounted for. At best,
"There is, in the record, considerable doubt as to whether there was
any warrant for the search of [the] defendant's home."

* * *

"However much in a particular case insistence upon such rules may
appear as a technicality that inures to the benefit of a guilty person,
the history of the criminal law proves that tolerance of shortcut
methods in law enforcement impairs its enduring effectiveness...."

There are those who say, as did Justice (then Judge) Cardozo, that
under our constitutional exclusionary doctrine, "(t)he criminal is to

Mapp v. Ohio (1961)

go free because the constable has blundered." In some cases this will undoubtedly be the result. But as was said in Elkins, "there is another consideration—the imperative of judicial integrity." The criminal goes free, if he must, but it is the law that sets him free. Nothing can destroy a government more quickly than its failure to observe its own laws, or worse, its disregard of the charter of its own existence. As Mr. Justice Brandeis…said…, "Our government is the potent, the omnipresent teacher. For good or for ill, it teaches the whole people by its example. If the government becomes a lawbreaker, it breeds contempt for law; it invites every man to become a law unto himself; it invites anarchy."

[The court went on to reason that "the purpose of the exclusionary rule is to deter—to compel respect for the constitutional guaranty in the only effectively available way—by removing the incentive to disregard it," citing *Elkins v. United States*, 364 U.S. at 217.]

Although we have examined some of the nuances of deontology and teleology, for convenience and to align with the rest of those people who study business ethics from textbooks that seem to uniformly adopt the same simplifications, we will generally refer to these philosophical paradigms with the following summary shorthand:

Deontology: A theory that there is a natural order in which rights and what is right are scientifically ascertainable (*The Science of Right*). In application, once one knows what is right, one acts in accordance with that, irrespective of the outcome.

Act Utilitarianism: A theory that mankind is best served by acting according to that which provides the highest utility for the most people, so long as those actions do not infringe upon the freedom (or by corollary, the property rights) of others. In application, one looks both at the act and at the effect of that act on others (its outcome) to determine its moral soundness.

Rule Utilitarianism: A theory that applies to how governments should approach the passing of laws. Laws must provide the highest utility for the most people, with the limitation that those laws must not infringe upon the freedom of any individual except to protect the freedom of others. In application, the law must be crafted to anticipate the effect it will have on its citizens, however once the law is in place, it must be followed irrespective of whether the outcome is good or not. In this way, rule utilitarianism joins deontology in that the law must be followed even when sub-optimal or bad consequences occur at that particular time.

These theories provide a useful gauge when trying to understand the theoretical underpinnings of the law—what motivates the law, how it is likely to be applied, and how it should be approached. Laws about such controversial issues as abortion or right-to-die are clearly values-based and generally are motivated by deontological or absolute values. Laws about business regulation generally are based in practicality and fall within the rule utilitarian model.

Converting Moral Thought to Political Ideology

America's Mixed Economy

To begin this section, we will look at the free market political ideology that underlies our basic economic system. To do that, it will be necessary to consider the socialistic reforms that have evolved our economy into one that mixes capitalism with a complex social safety net. At the conclusion of this discussion, we will hopefully see the application of values that drive both the command and decentralized components of our society.

Morality of a Free Market

There are many who exalt the American free market and its role in protecting democracy in America, but few are as passionate or extreme as Ayn Rand, whose philosophy despises any imposition of a social system on a free society. Studying Ayn Rand is fun, so for an introduction into the principles of a free market, we will take a look at Rand's life and her vision.(6)

Ayn Rand (born Alice Rosenbaum) left her family and came to the United States when she was a teenager to escape Russian communist tyranny. She changed her name to one of her own invention and grew to become the voice of American laissez-faire capitalism in the 1960s in direct opposition to the "hippie" movement of that period. Her philosophy supported an unfettered market, without government intervention in either business or individual lives.

Rand died in 1982, but her novels, essays, and legend are vital parts of the contemporary American perspective. Her two major novels, *The Fountainhead*(1943) and *Atlas Shrugged* (1957), continue to sell hundreds of thousands of copies each year. Through these novels and other writings, Rand brought her "Objectivist" philosophy to the public, and that philosophy made its way to TV talk shows, college campuses, and political party platforms. Alan Greenspan, former chairman of the Federal Reserve Board, was at one time a committed member of Rand's inner circle of friends.(7) Her influence remains pervasive in American society today.

Ayn Rand's personal story is more intriguing than a novel, and less believable. By 1954, Rand was 49 years old, *The Fountainhead* had been published, and she was gaining popularity among young people who were intrigued with her contrarian perspectives. Some of those young people sought her out because they found her work inspiring. She eventually initiated a love affair with one of them, Nathaniel Branden, who was then a married man 25 years her junior. She used her intellectual gift for moralizing to compel both her own husband and her lover's wife to agree to the affair and to maintain its secrecy. After more than a decade of this strained relationship, when Branden was 38 and Rand was 63, Rand found out her lover was "cheating" on her with another woman—not his wife. In the confrontation following her discovery, Rand physically assaulted Branden, and then set about to virtually destroy the Nathaniel Branden Institute that had become the vehicle through which she promoted her Objectivist ideology. Subsequent efforts to promote her ideology have been less vigorous but still continue. Leonard Piekoff, Rand's cousin, still promotes her work and is the steward of her intellectual property. Nathaniel Branden remains connected with the "Objectivist" world with an iconic position as a resource to The Objectivist Center, an institute that exists to some degree to confront the relatively stagnant Ayn Rand Institute. There are countless Internet chat rooms, resource sites, and spokespersons either articulating or railing against the Rand message.

Although her philosophy in its entirety has more complexities and arguable inconsistencies than would be appropriate to discuss in this text, the political component of her perspective is addressable. As Dr. Kelly Ross writes:

> "Rand was an inspiring advocate for the free market and for the creativity of the autonomous individual. With her intimate, personal knowledge of the Russian Revolution, and all the loathing that it inspired in her, Rand will always be an invaluable witness to the practice and folly of totalitarianism. She is also a useful one-person test to distinguish libertarians from conservatives. Her atheism alienates most conservatives, who may even speak of her bitterly and dismissively."(8)

While taking a stance that an Objectivist society with a free market is the only free society, Rand flies in the face of a significant set of conventional values. For example, when we refer to a person's spirituality, most of us would assume we refer to a positive attribute. When Rand uses the word "spirituality," it is likely to appear as ridicule. For her, objective rational thinkers know what they know. Belief in the unknowable (i.e., God) goes against human nature. There is no divine hero from whom to seek guidance in her reality.

Likewise, when we refer to someone as altruistic, we are generally complimenting that person's values. One college dictionary defines altruism as "motivation for the good of others, rather than for one's own gain." This value is strongly supported in Western religions, and in general, we as a society admire qualities of selflessness, benevolence and philanthropy. When Ayn Rand refers to someone as altruistic, she is speaking with contempt. Altruism, for Rand, is a self-destructive personal value, and, when it aggregates among large numbers of people, it signals the beginning of the downfall of a capitalist society and the emergence of communism or some other form of dictatorship. The only positive value she recognizes in individual morality is selfishness. That is somewhat counterintuitive, so in order to understand that perspective, it is necessary to walk through Rand's logic and to identify what she sees as the Objectivist's "top values."

According to William Thomas of The Objectivist Center:

> "The heroes of Objectivism are achievers who build businesses, invent technologies, and create art and ideas, depending on their own talents and on trade with other independent people to reach their goals."

In summary, for Rand, the heroes of society, those who exemplify moral virtue and success, are the ones who build successful businesses.

In 1961, in the *Objectivist Newsletter*, Rand published an essay entitled "Man's Rights."(9) The essay was written in response to the Democratic Party's platform during the Kennedy election campaign. Her political philosophy naturally railed against Kennedy's liberal social vision. She says:

> "If one wishes to advocate a free society—that is, capitalism—one must realize that its indispensable foundation is the principle of individual rights."

Rand's ever-present presumption is that a "free" society is a completely capitalist one. She has no tolerance for the "mixed" components of a society that impose a social system onto the backs of productive workers and entrepreneurs. She accepts the negative consequences thatsuch a free society might leave those who do not adequately produce or save to depend on the whims of private charity or to suffer the consequences—unemployment, starvation, death from lack of medical care, etc.

In "Man's Rights," Rand defines "individual rights" according to her political philosophy. She says:

> "*Individual rights are the means of subordinating society to moral law.*" [Emphasis in original text.]

By this she means that when a government genuinely confers onto its citizens political rights, the rights of those individuals are *greater* than the rights of "society." The government cannot force the individual to act according to its whim because the government itself is the subordinate. This is the only moral way, according to Rand, for a society to proceed. Any other way allows the government to "enslave" individuals, and that can never be a morally acceptable outcome.

Rand labels a government that subordinates individual rights to the society's as a "statist tyranny" (tyranny by the state). Altruism is dangerous because it can cause the majority to vote to give money or resources away that were produced or earned by others—especially the "heroes" of society—those who have built businesses. According to this logic, the graduated income tax is a means by which the majority exercises tyranny over the wealthy. Rand argues that this is intrinsically immoral, and goes back to her fundamental objection to altruism. If you want to give money away, that is your choice. If your motivation is that you should sacrifice your own interests for someone else's, you are walking a dangerous moral platform because this perspective may lead to you voting to take away money and associated rights from those who would not voluntarily give them up for the benefit of others. In her opinion, you would be voting to give the government permission to steal and enslave.

Even the most benevolent of intentions leads to social destruction, if one follows this perspective. Assume the majority of citizens in a society want to help the elderly who no longer have sufficient resources to care for themselves. Through its voting power, that majority confers on the government the ability to levy a tax to address this problem, i.e., to take money from some individuals in order to give that money away to others (the elderly). Although the intention is clearly a kind one, to care for those who can no longer care for themselves, Rand finds intolerable the ability of the government to decide to take property away from one citizen and then give it to another. Altruism, she opines, is how all totalitarian regimes begin.

Rand argues that if moral law is the law of individual rights, then any state that puts itself in a position higher than the rights of individuals is inherently immoral. When the Democratic platform of 1960 supported such things as the right to decent jobs, housing, medical care, social security, and education, Rand asked the single question, "At whose expense?" If such rights are enacted by the majority, that majority has given government the right to take money from the achievers and give it to the non-achievers. Rand says:

> "If some men are entitled by right to the product of the work of others, it means that those others are deprived of rights and condemned to slave labor."

Rand may be extreme in referring to the imposition of taxation as the creation of slavery, yet the notion has been very persuasive, and many support the position today. The argument is as follows: If the product of your efforts is taken by the government (through taxation) to give to other people, then you have been condemned to work as a slave by a "statist" bully who gives you no choice but to hand over your pay for the good of someone else. Those who have experienced actual slavery in societies that tolerate it probably would not see it this way, but many Americans do.

Rand concludes her essay on Man's Rights with the notion that the rights to a minimum wage or to a free education are not properly rights of a free society, but rather "economic rights." Economic rights, she asserts, are not rights at all, but instead are the usurpation of individual rights. Today we would call the rights Rand rejects "entitlements" and these remain extremely controversial. By Rand's logic, economic rights (or entitlements) destroy individual rights, because if you have true individual rights, nobody else can have an economic right to your property. In summary, according to Rand the term "individual rights" is what she calls a redundancy, because she argues that in the moral sense, there can be no other kind.

Socialism in America

For those like Ayn Rand who openly advocate economic (as opposed to political) anarchy, it is an unpleasant notion that the economic system in the United States is both a free market, and to a lesser extent, a command economy (government controlled). We provide a certain amount of social system support to indigent populations for medicine, food, housing, and general subsidies through Medicaid, food stamps, rent support programs, and welfare. We also provide supports for disabled and retired people (Social Security and Medicare) based on a national insurance paradigm. Our entitlement programs are generally aimed at targeted and vulnerable populations, although in this respect, our safety net is not intended to be comprehensive.

Many people bemoan the fact that the middle-class members of our society will often "fall between the cracks" in our system and find themselves unable to get adequate medical care or housing, etc. This viewpoint takes the opposite of a free market perspective. A market perspective would not concern itself with the middle class falling between the cracks of socialistic supports, it would object to the existence of governmental social supports for any class. More socially minded people would say that vulnerable populations need to be protected from the whims of a free market.

When looking at ethical decisions, understanding the context in which you are exercising your judgment is all-important. What is ethical in a free market may be very different in a socialist economy. We live in a somewhat schizophrenic world in the United States, where our mixed economy produces very mixed values. The result is that we may have conflicting ethical viewpoints, all of which are supportable within their own fundamental paradigms. In a business environment, we generally frame our ethical judgments in the context of a functioning free market, but we must be vigilantly aware that we are not always judged by the public in that context. When making ethical decisions then, we need to always consider both the values and ethics of our decision, along with how the outcome will be perceived by the public. Considering the alternative political/economic (including free market and command economy) perspectives can provide insight into how public perceptions may vary and give us some ability to either disarm opposition or otherwise tailor outcomes appropriately.

The Constitution and Fundamental Values

The Constitution: Our First Statute

It is not necessary to consult with a historian to understand what was on the minds of political leaders in the United States after the American Revolution or after the Civil War. The Constitution and its Amendments clearly reflect the values and motives that propelled our country's leaders during those crucial periods in our history.

According to recorded history, the framers of our Constitution had not planned to create a constitution of such complexity and comprehensiveness during that summer in 1787 when they convened in Philadelphia.(10)(11) They had come because the Confederacy was faltering, and the problems of the states needed redress. Conflicts had arisen over currency (with different states printing their own money), judicial enforcement, and practical matters like who had the right to dam rivers that traveled through several states. National stability and national security were underlying concerns.

The framers, 55 delegates ranging in age from 26 to 81 years old, were men of insight and perseverance. Perhaps because the revolution had been fought so recently, and at such great cost, idealism was not readily abandoned despite the unforeseen complexities that arose when the constituents tried to solve the problems that had brought them together.

Of great concern during the post-Revolutionary-War period was insuring that safeguards were in place to control federal power once it was established. The states did not want to "reinvent" King George III by developing a domestic federal government that had the potential to become a tyrant. The Constitution addressed these concerns in two ways:

1) In order to prevent power from concentrating in a single person or group on the federal level, the Constitution adopted the French notion of "separation of powers," creating three co-equal branches of government: executive, judicial, and legis-

lative. In our particular adaptation of that political structure, the powers do not operate completely independently. Instead they are structured so that together they create a system of "checks and balances" on each other. This simply means that each branch has some ability to contain the other two, with no federal entity being able to usurp more power than the founders intended.

2) In addition to limiting federal power as a whole, the founders made significant effort to insure that each state maintained a voice in the new government, which served to prevent the large-population states from controlling federal law (in terms of the numbers of votes cast).

State power was protected against the "tyranny of the majority" by the creation of a Senate in which each state would have equal representation irrespective of size, and which would function as a co-equal branch of the legislature without whose approval laws could not pass. The House of Representatives was put in place to give voice to the popular sentiment. Individual freedom was certainly a fundamental value, but not the exclusive focal point of our foundational document in 1787.

In high school government classes students are taught that the legislative branch creates the laws, the judiciary interprets them, and the executive enforces them. This 12th-grade rendition of Constitutional law does more than over-simplify—it misrepresents. On a

variety of different levels, each branch of government has a hand in creating law, and a hand in limiting that creation. Consider that the president can veto the legislature's proposed statute, the legislature can (with two-thirds vote) overrule the president, and the judiciary can quash a statute or enjoin the president when it perceives that constitutional boundaries are violated. The interlocking powers of these co-equal branches are extraordinarily complex.

This chapter will proceed next with how Congress, the legislative branch of American government, makes laws. We call this kind of law "statutory." Statutes are also known as bills, codes, rules, and acts. The passing of statutes is a laborious and often an extraordinarily contentious process.

Statutory Law in the United States

The job of writing laws is delegated to the Congress in the first article of the Constitution, but the process of law-making has become significantly more complex than what the few paragraphs in Article I would imply. Today, the procedures involved in bringing a law to enactment reflect two centuries of political evolution. Proposals, sub-committee and committee meetings, hearings, and debate precede every congressional vote, and the process by which federal statutory law comes into being is anything but simple. In fact, most proposals for new laws never make it out of committee, and the Senate can use the modern adaptation of the filibuster (a process called cloture) to prevent a law from ever being voted upon even if it does get to the Senate floor.

Using portions of the document prepared by the House of Representa-tives' Parliamentarian (12) for a sum-mary description of the legislative pro-cess, the following material describes how federal statutes are "born."

How Our Laws Are Made

Revised and Updated January 2000.
By Charles W. Johnson, Parliamentarian
U.S. House of Representatives

* * *

I. Introduction

This brochure is intended to provide a basic outline of the numerous steps of our federal lawmaking process from the source of an idea for a legislative proposal through its publication as a statute. The legisla-tive process is a matter about which every person should be well in-formed in order to understand and appreciate the work of Congress.

It is hoped that this guide will enable readers to gain a greater under-standing of the federal legislative process and its role as one of the foundations of our representative system. One of the most practical safeguards of the American democratic way of life is this legislative process with its emphasis on the protection of the minority, allowing ample opportunity to all sides to be heard and make their views known. The fact that a proposal cannot become a law without con-sideration and approval by both Houses of Congress is an outstand-ing virtue of our bicameral legislative system. The open and full dis-cussion provided under the Constitution often results in the notable improvement of a bill by amendment before it becomes law or in the eventual defeat of an inadvisable proposal.

As the majority of laws originate in the House of Representatives, this discussion will focus principally on the procedure in that body.

II. The Congress

Article I, Section 1, of the United States Constitution, provides that:

All legislative Powers herein granted shall be vested in a Congress of the United States, which shall consist of a Senate and House of Representatives.

The Senate is composed of 100 Members—two from each state, regardless of population or area—elected by the people in accordance with the Seventeenth Amendment to the Constitution…. The term of office is six years and one-third of the total membership of the Senate is elected every second year.

* * *

Each Senator has one vote.

As constituted in the 108th Congress, the House of Representatives is composed of 435 Members elected every two years from among the 50 states, apportioned to their total populations.

* * *

Each Representative has one vote.

In addition to the Representatives from each of the States, a Resident Commissioner from the Commonwealth of Puerto Rico and Delegates from the District of Columbia, American Samoa, Guam, and the Virgin Islands are elected pursuant to federal law. The Resident Commissioner, elected for a four-year term, and the Delegates, elected for two-year terms, havemost of the prerogatives of Representatives including the right to vote in committees to which they are elected. However, the Resident Commissioner and the Delegates do not have the right to vote on matters before the House.

* * *

Unlike some other parliamentary bodies, both the Senate and the House of Representatives have [fundamentally] equal legislative functions and powers….

III. Sources of Legislation

Sources of ideas for legislation are unlimited and proposed drafts of bills originate in many diverse quarters. [Members of Congress are the most likely to propose legislation.]

In modern times, the "executive communication" has become a prolific source of legislative proposals. The communication is usually in the form of a message or letter from a member of the President's

Cabinet,…transmitting a draft of a proposed bill to the Speaker of the House of Representatives and the President of the Senate. Despite the structure of separation of powers, Article II, Section 3, of the Constitution imposes an obligation on the President to report to Congress from time to time on the "State of the Union" and to recommend for consideration such measures as the President considers necessary and expedient. Many of these executive communications follow on the President's message to Congress on the state of the Union.

* * *

The drafting of statutes is an art that requires great skill, knowledge, and experience. In some instances, a draft is the result of a study covering a period of a year or more by a commission or committee designated by the President or a member of the Cabinet. The Administrative Procedure Act and the Uniform Code of Military Justice are two examples of enactments resulting from such studies. In addition, congressional committees sometimes draft bills after studies and hearings covering periods of a year or more.

IV. Forms of Congressional Action

The work of Congress is initiated by the introduction of a proposal [and] the most customary form [of proposal] used in both Houses is the bill.

* * *

V. Introduction and Referral to Committee

Any Member, Delegate or the Resident Commissioner from Puerto Rico in the House of Representatives may introduce a bill at any time while the House is in session by simply placing it in the "hopper," a wooden box provided for that purpose located on the side of the rostrum in the House Chamber.

* * *

In the Senate, a Senator usually introduces a bill or resolution by presenting it to one of the clerks at the Presiding Officer's desk, without commenting on it from the floor of the Senate. However, a Senator may use a more formal procedure by rising and introducing the bill or resolution from the floor. A Senator usually makes a statement about the measure when introducing it on the floor. Frequently, Sen-

How Our Laws Are Made

ators obtain consent to have the bill or resolution printed in the Congressional Record following their formal statement.

* * *

Perhaps the most important phase of the legislative process is the action by committees.

* * *

Each committee's jurisdiction is divided into certain subject matters under the rules of each House and all measures affecting a particular area of the law are referred to the committee with jurisdiction over that particular subject matter. For example, the Committee on the Judiciary in the House has jurisdiction over measures relating to judicial proceedings....

Membership on the various committees is divided between the two major political parties. The proportion of the Members of the minority party to the Members of the majority party is determined by the majority party.

[It should be noted that a bill cannot get to the full House if the committee doesn't report it—which means that bills can languish and die simply by never making it out of committee. This gives committees inordinate amounts of power that were likely not anticipated by the founders. Although there are by-passes possible, for the most part, the committees do control the legislation that is considered by the full Congress.]

* * *

XVII. Enrollment

When the bill has been agreed to in identical form by both bodies,...[the House and the Senate, then presidential action is required].

XVIII. Presidential Action

Article I, Section 7, of the Constitution provides in part that:

> Every Bill which shall have passed the House of Representatives and the Senate, shall, before it becomes a Law, be presented to the President of the United States.

Veto Message

By the terms of the Constitution, if the President does not approve the bill "he shall return it, with his Objections to that House in which it shall have originated, who shall enter the Objections at large on their Journal, and proceed to reconsider it." [Congress then has the opportunity to over-ride the veto with a two-thirds vote of both the House and the Senate.]

* * *

Statutes at Large

The United States Statutes at Large…provide a permanent collection of the laws of each session of Congress in bound volumes. A legislative history appears at the end of each law.

* * *

Under the provisions of a statute originally enacted in 1895, these volumes are legal evidence of the laws contained in them and will be accepted as proof of those laws in any court in the United States.

The Statutes at Large are a chronological arrangement of the laws exactly as they have been enacted. The laws are not arranged according to subject matter and do not reflect the present status of an earlier law that has been amended.

United States Code

The United States Code contains a consolidation and codification of the general and permanent laws of the United States arranged according to subject matter…largely in alphabetical order. [The order in which statutes appear in the U.S. Code is somewhat ironic. The first set of statutes regulate and are "Armed Forces" and the last is "War." A "bill" is generally split up among several sections of the U.S. Code, to fit where it is most appropriate. For example, parts of the Civil Rights Act of 1964, as amended in 1991, appear in the labor code, housing code, and education code.]

How Our Laws Are Made

The United States Code is available on the Internet and is free. Statutory law is more accessible today with the help of the Internet than it has ever been in the history of our country. It is also more voluminous andless decipherable than it has ever been in our history.

The Sources of Conflict

Despite the abundance of federal statutory law, only a tiny percentage of the number of bills proposed are ever voted upon, and those that are can appear irrationally compromised due to the divided interests in Washington. This is most evident when budgets are being passed, or when appropriations are being allocated.

However, even when a statute does get past the political process—and this would include statutes from the municipal level all the way through the U.S. Congress—there is a final test that every law must pass, which is whether or not the law is constitutional. The decision of whether a contested statute offends the Constitution is generally decided by the nation's highest court, the U.S. Supreme Court. The consequences of a statute being unconstitutional can be quite far-reaching, and no case illustrates this more clearly than the controversial *Roe v. Wade*.(13)

Everyone knows that abortion is, at least at a certain point during a woman's pregnancy, legal. What many people are unaware of is how the *Roe v. Wade* decision caused this to be the case.

Most states up until 1973 had laws against abortion. The laws generally made having an abortion a relatively minor criminal offense, but performing an abortion was a felony that could cause a physician to lose his license to practice medicine. A few states like California had come to authorize therapeutic abortions where the life of the mother was jeopardized—and California liberalized the "life of the mother" standard to include suicidal ideation and less obvious forms of health risk.

However, Texas (consistent with Arizona), had continued to consider physician-assisted abortion to be a felony on the part of the physician, and prosecuted it as such. When Roe became pregnant and wanted an abortion, she could not get one legally in the state of Texas, and so she gave birth to the baby and relinquished it for adoption. But she pursued her claim, which would ordinarily be considered "moot" in the courts—meaning there was no longer a genuine controversy, and no abortion could be had at that point.

The U.S. Supreme Court astutely recognized that it would always take too long to get an abortion issue up to the highest court, and thus would always be moot, and the matter would never be formally decided unless an exception was made. It made that exception, and the *Roe v. Wade* case was decided and has been a subject of debate ever since. The language is complicated, so in the syllabus below, the more difficult legal terms are in bold print, and contextual definitions for those words are at the end of the case.

Roe V. Wade

Syllabus

Supreme Court of the United States

410 U.S. 113

> No. 70-18 Argued: December 13, 1971
> Reargued: October 11, 1972,
> Decided: January 22, 1973

A pregnant single woman (Roe) brought a class action challenging the constitutionality of the Texas criminal abortion laws, which **proscribe** [emphasis added] procuring or attempting an abortion except on medical advice for the purpose of saving the mother's life. A licensed physician (Hallford), who had two state abortion prosecutions pending against him, was permitted to **intervene**.... [emphasis added] A three-judge District Court, which consolidated the actions, held that Roe and Hallford, and members of their classes, had **standing to sue** [emphasis added] and presented **justiciable** [emphasis added] controversies. Ruling that **declaratory** [emphasis added], though not **injunctive, relief** was warranted, the court declared the abortion statutes void as vague and overbroadly infringing those plaintiffs' Ninth and **Fourteenth Amendment** rights....Appellants directly appealed to this Court on the injunctive rulings, and appellee cross-appealed from the District Court's grant of declaratory relief to Roe and Hallford.

Held:

* * *

2. Roe has standing to sue....

 (a) Contrary to appellee's contention, the natural termination of Roe's pregnancy did not **moot** her suit. Litigation involving pregnancy, which is "capable of repetition, yet evading review," is an exception to the usual federal rule that an actual controversy must exist at review stages, and not simply when the action is initiated.

* * *

3. State criminal abortion laws, like those involved here, that except from criminality only a life-saving procedure on the mother's behalf without regard to the stage of her pregnancy and other interests involved violate the Due Process Clause of the Fourteenth Amendment which protects against state action the right to privacy, including a woman's qualified right to terminate her pregnancy. Though the State cannot override that right it has legitimate interests in protecting both the pregnant woman's health and the potentiality of human life, each of which interests grows and reaches a "compelling" point at various stages of the woman's approach to term.

(a) For the stage prior to approximately the end of the first trimester, the abortion decision and its effectuation must be left to the medical judgment of the pregnant woman's attending physician.

(b) For the stage subsequent to approximately the end of the first trimester, the State, in promoting its interest in the health of the mother, may, if it chooses, regulate the abortion procedure in ways that are reasonably related to maternal health.

(c) For the stage subsequent to viability the State, in promoting its interest in the potentiality of human life, may, if it chooses, regulate, and even proscribe, abortion except where necessary, in appropriate medical judgment, for the preservation of the life or health of the mother.

[Case glossary:

Declaratory relief: When a litigant (party in the suit) asks the court to basically "declare" something—in this case, that a law is unconstitutional. This is one of the requests that is rarely given, and must relate to a question of law that doesn't depend upon a specific set of facts.

Injunctive relief: When a litigant (party in the suit) asks the court to enjoin (stop) a behavior—in this case, to stop the Texas prosecutor from pursuing the criminal complaint against Dr. Hallford.

Intervene: In this case, it basically means join in the lawsuit.

Justiciable: Something that is a claim a court has the right to decide upon.

Moot: This means the subject of dispute is no longer in controversy. In this case, Roe was no longer pregnant, so the state made an argu-

Roe V. Wade

ment that the case was now moot—and as is obvious from the case, that argument failed.

Standing to sue: A person who has an interest in the claim that can be resolved by the court. If you do not have "standing" you cannot be the party to bring the case, even if the case itself has value. For example, if a person observes bullying, but is not a victim, that person has no standing to sue the bully, even though he or she was a witness and was upset about it.]

It would not be a surprise to most students that the biggest sources of contention in the law surround three fundamental areas: taxes, entitlements, and basic values. Abortion is today, almost 40 years after *Roe v. Wade*, still one of the most divisive issues in America, and it has influenced battles on the floor of Congress during every session. One of the obstacles to a 2011 appropriations bill was that the majority in Congress wanted to exclude Planned Parenthood from any appropriation because Planned Parenthood does abortions (though these are not federally funded). Eventually this proposed exclusion was conceded.

On the other hand, when values coalesce, Congress has shown it has the power to act swiftly and with unity. In a matter related to but quite distinct from abortion, Congress passed the Born Alive Act in 2002, which protects infants from harm who are born alive, even if they are born as a result of a failed abortion attempt. This was a matter upon which there was virtually no dispute, and the act passed with rare unanimous support in the Senate. Of course as of yet, nobody has tested the constitutionality of the Born Alive Act.

Notes

1. Kant, Immanuel. *The Science of Right*, 1790. Translated by W. Hastie, T. & T. Clark, 1887.

2. Labor Law Talk Web site, encyclopedia entry for *utilitarian*, http://encyclopedia.laborlawtalk.com/utilitarian.

3. Mill, John Stewart, "Utilitarianism" 1863

4. Mill, John Stewart. *On Liberty*, *Readings in the Philosophy of Law*, Keith Culver, Editor; Broadview Press, 1969.

5. Mapp v. Ohio, 367 U.S. 643 (1961)

6. Ayn Rand Institute Web site. http://www.aynrand.org

7. Branden, Barbara. *The Passion of Ayn Rand*, Doubleday, 1986.

8. Ross, Kelly. "Ayn Rand: 1905-1982," http://www.friesian.com/rand.htm

9. Rand, Ayn. "Man's Rights." In McAdams, *Law, Business and Society*, 6th edition, McGraw Hill, 2001. (p. 8-10)

10. Constitutional Law Center Web site, Findlaw.com. http://supreme.lp.findlaw.com/documents/consthist.html.

11. National Constitution Center, nationalconstitutioncenter.org, http://www.constitutioncenter.org/explore/BasicGoverningPrinciples/SeparationofPowersandaSystemofChecksandBalances.shtml

12. Johnson, Charles W., Parliamentarian. "How Our Laws Are Made," Revised and Updated 2000. DOCID: f:hd093.108, from the House Documents Online via GPO Access [wais.access.gpo.gov].

13. *Roe v. Wade*, 410 U.S. 113, 1973

Chapter 3
Statutory versus Common Law

The Court System and the Anatomy of a Case

Most people understand what statutes are. They can readily accept that when the legislature passes a bill and the president signs it, there is a law. Whether statutes are called bills, codes, or acts, they are understood to be social mandates regarding behavior that the system will enforce with its courts and its power.

Understanding "common law," the law created through court-made precedents, is less intuitive and more difficult than understanding statutes. As mentioned earlier, if an American Government teacher told you, "Courts don't make law, they merely interpret the law that the legislative branch of government makes," you were told a fib, or at least given an oversimplification. Courts make substantially more law than do local, state, and federal legislators. Common law takes a bit of insight to understand. To garner that insight, one needs to learn the language of the courts and how they operate.

The significance of precedent in the realm of constitutional law cannot be overstated. It is the judicial branch of our government (the court system) that often makes the most sweeping and dramatic changes in our laws, when the U.S. Supreme Court considers the constitutionality of government conduct or legislative enactment. For example, as might be inferred after reading Chapter 2, there is no statute giving women the right to have an abortion. The "right to choose" is exclusively the result of the U.S. Supreme Court's 1973 decision in the case of *Roe v. Wade* (1), which struck down existing anti-abortion statutes on the grounds that such laws violated a woman's constitutional right to privacy. Statutes that make abortion unlawful may still appear in legislative codes in various jurisdictions, but those that pre-date *Roe v. Wade* are unenforceable in the wake of the monumental privacy right established in *Roe v. Wade*. Few statutes have been as controversial or had as much impact on American society as this precedent.

How Courts Work

When a "lower" or trial court hears a case, it does its best to apply the laws to the facts. Judges give juries instructions describing the law, and juries (or the judge if the case is being heard by "court trial") apply that law to the facts as they determine them. The adjudication of facts occurs *only* at the trial level. If evidence is improperly excluded, there may be cause for a new trial, but no appellate court can listen to additional evidence beyond what was in the trial record.

A case goes "up on appeal" when a party disagrees with the trial outcome *and* formally asserts that the trial judge erred (made a mistake) about the law. Grounds for appeal generally are based on whether the trial judge improperly admitted or excluded evidence, wrongfully instructed the jury about the law, or incorrectly applied the law to the case.

When the appellate court hears a case, it decides whether the trial court was right or wrong. This decision sets a precedent by further defining how evidence should have been handled, or what law should have governed that fact situation.

The hierarchy of the court system is simple, and an outline of the federal and state systems can be found later in this chapter.

States may differ from the federal system in what they call their courts, and how their courts (including the state Supreme Courts) operate. In the great state of New York, the trial court is called the "Supreme Court." It takes a state with a great deal of confidence to name its lowest court "supreme," then build up from there. Most other state trial courts of general jurisdiction are called "Superior Courts" or "District Courts."

Who Is Who in Litigation

A civil action ordinarily commences when somebody files a complaint in a trial court. Certain types of cases such as divorce begin with a pleading called a Petition, but, in general, the first pleading filed is the Complaint.

The person who files the Complaint is called the Plaintiff. The person who is being sued is called the Defendant. Those two titles only apply at the trial court level. There is no such thing as a Plaintiff or a Defendant on Appeal.

Once there is a final judgment or some other ruling from which an appeal can be taken, the disappointed litigant filing the Appeal is called the Appellant (or in certain types of actions, a Petitioner). The person responding to the Appeal is called either the Appellee or the Respondent. These names apply in both the middle Courts of Appeal and at the Supreme Courts (final courts of appeal).

Jurisdiction

Although it has been used several times in this textbook, the word jurisdiction has not yet been defined. In its basic legal meaning, jurisdiction is "power." If a court does not have "jurisdiction" over a party or a cause of action, it has no power to adjudicate (try) the claim. There are a variety of different types of judicial jurisdiction.

Personal Jurisdiction

Courts must be able to compel people to appear before them. Courts are constrained constitutionally with regard to whom they may compel to appear. If a New Jersey resident is sued in an Iowa court, and that resident has no contacts with the state of Iowa, Iowa has no constitutional right to exert power over the New Jersey resident. The reason for this is that the U.S. Supreme Court says that such an exercise of power by the Iowa court would be a denial of the New Jersey resident's substantive due process. It defines "substantive due process" as that process which is due. No help? OK, it just would not be fair to make the New Jersey resident go all the way to Iowa to defend himself or herself when he or she has no nexus (connection) to that state.

Big businesses generally do business in all states, and therefore can be sued in all states. In addition, personal jurisdiction can be agreed to or waived. A person can bring an action in a forum state that is not one in which he or she historically had a connection, and a person can agree to defend in a state that would not otherwise have jurisdiction over him or her.

Subject Matter Jurisdiction

Subject matter jurisdiction involves the kinds of cases courts have the power to hear. There are courts of special jurisdiction that are specifically designated to hear certain kinds of cases. In the federal courts these would include cases such as those heard in bankruptcy court and tax court. In the state courts these would include such cases as those for small claims or divorce. General jurisdiction courts are those that hear the cases for which there is no special jurisdiction court. The concept of subject matter jurisdiction is complicated and not worthy of inordinate amounts of attention, except to note that subject matter jurisdiction *cannot ever* be waived. If a court enters an order or judgment that it did not have the power to make over the subject matter, that order is, and always will be, invalid. For example, a small claims court award for a million dollars is and always will be an invalid award. Even if both parties stipulate that the court can hear the matter, the judgment is not legal.

The Setting of a Precedent

The *Beard* case that follows (2), though simple in appearance, contains a great deal of complexity in terms of process, political structure, and legal effect. A line-by-line analysis of the meaning and importance of each term and segment of the condensed case follows the text.

Royce and Debra Graff, Robby and Betty Hausmon v. Brett Beard and Dorothy Beard (1993)

Texas Supreme Court (858 S.W.2d 198)

Justice John Cornyn delivered the opinion of the court.

We are asked in this case to impose a common-law duty on a social host who makes alcohol available to an intoxicated adult guest who the host knows will be driving....

Houston Moos consumed alcohol at a party hosted by the Graffs and Hausmons, and allegedly left in his vehicle in an intoxicated condition. En route from the party, Moos collided with a motorcycle, injuring Brett Beard [and killing his wife Dorothy]. Beard sued both Moos and his hosts for his injuries. The trial court ultimately dismissed Beard's claims against the hosts for failure to state a cause of action [prior to which time Beard had settled his claims with Moos]. An *en banc* divided court of appeals reversed the trial court's judgment and remanded the case, holding for the first time in Texas jurisprudence that social hosts may be liable to third parties for the acts of their intoxicated adult guests.

Under the court of appeals' standard, a social host violates a legal duty to third parties when the host makes an alcoholic beverage available to an adult guest who the host knows is intoxicated and will be driving. In practical effect, this duty is twofold. The first aspect of the host's duty is to prevent guests who will be driving from becoming intoxicated. If the host fails to do so, however, a second aspect of the duty comes into play—the host must prevent the intoxicated guest from driving.

The legislatures in most states, including Texas, have enacted dram shop laws that impose a statutory duty to third parties on commercial providers under specified circumstances. We have recently held that when the legislature enacted the Texas dram shop statute it also imposed a duty on the provider that extends to the patron himself. Because the dram shop statute applies only to commercial providers, however, it does not govern the duty asserted in this case.

We think it significant in appraising Beard's request to recognize common-law social host liability that the legislature has considered and declined to create such a duty. A version of the bill that eventually became our dram shop statute provided for social host liability. Although that version passed the Senate, the House rejected it. The Senate-House conference committee deleted social host liability from the bill the legislature eventually enacted.

The highest courts in only four states have done what we are asked to do today: judicially impose a duty to third parties on social hosts who make alcohol available to adult guests. In two of these states, California and Iowa, the legislatures subsequently abrogated the judicially created duty. Neither of the two remaining jurisdictions, Massachusetts and New Jersey, had dram shop statutes when their courts acted. Rather, their courts first imposed a common-law duty to third parties on commercial establishments and then extended the duty to social hosts.

* * *

Deciding whether to impose a new common-law duty involves complex considerations of public policy. We have said that these considerations include "'social, economic, and political questions,' and their application to the particular facts at hand." Among other factors, we consider the extent of the risk involved, "the foreseeability and likelihood of injury weighed against the social utility of the actor's conduct, the magnitude of the burden of guarding against the injury, and the consequences of placing the burden on the defendant." We have also emphasized other factors. For example, questions of duty have turned on whether one party has superior knowledge of the risk, and whether a right to control the actor whose conduct precipitated the harm exists.

* * *

Ideally, guests will drink responsibly, and hosts will monitor their social functions to reduce the likelihood of intoxication. Once a guest becomes impaired by alcohol to the point at which he becomes a threat to himself and others, we would hope that the host can persuade the guest to take public transportation, stay on the premises, or be transported home by an unimpaired driver. But we know that too often reality conflicts with ideal behavior. And, given the ultimate power of guests to control their own alcohol consumption and the absence of any legal right of the host to control the guest, we find the arguments for shifting legal responsibility from the guest to the host, who merely makes alcohol available at social gatherings, unconvincing. As the common law has long recognized, the imbiber maintains the ultimate power and thus the obligation to control his own behavior: to decide to drink or not to drink, to drive or not to drive. We therefore conclude that the common law's focus should remain on the drinker as the person primarily responsibly for his own behavior and best able to avoid the foreseeable risks of that behavior.

We accordingly reverse the judgment of the court of appeals and render judgment that Beard take nothing.

Dissenting Opinion—Justice Gammage joined by Justice Doggett

I respectfully dissent. The majority errs in holding that the legislature must "create" the duty for social hosts not to send intoxicated guests driving in our streets to maim and kill. Logic, legal experience and this court's own earlier decisions dictate a contrary result.

* * *

All culpable parties should be liable—the social host who knowingly intoxicated the guest and the guest who drunkenly caused the accident. I am persuaded that both should be liable to the extent of their responsibility for the accident. "Friends don't let friends drive drunk." That is sound public policy. But today the majority says "Intoxicate your friends and send them out upon the public streets and highways to drive drunk. Don't worry; you won't be liable." That is, in the kindest term I can muster, unsound policy.

This case seems straightforward on the surface, but the devil is in the details. The "gist" of the case is easily understood—social hosts are not responsible for the consequences if their guests get drunk and drive. It is the subsurface that contains information that gives us insight into the process, to whom the law applies, how it will apply, and what its limitations are.

Title of the Case and Citation Information

Any appellate opinion will generally be printed with caption information. A lot can be discerned from that information, even without formal training. In the title for this case, the Graffs' and Hausmons' names go first. If the case is properly titled, this would indicate that at this stage of the proceedings, the Graffs and the Hausmons are the ones bringing the action. Beard is defending, because his name is second. Sometimes titles are incorrect, or there are subtleties that cannot be readily understood by someone who has not thoroughly studied civil procedure; however, generally the party asserting the action goes first in the title.

Below the names of the parties, there is a reference to a reporter in which the case can be located (e.g., 858 S.W.2d 918). This means that this opinion can be found in volume 858 of the Southwest Reporter 2nd series, on page 918. In this case, the text shows the court writing this decision is the Texas Supreme Court. If court information is not provided, but you happen to know the reporter system, you can often determine if the matter is state or federal and the level of court in which the case is being heard.

It is important to understand the implications of that simple fact. It means that this case binds all the courts in the state of Texas, but does not bind courts in the state of Arizona, or anywhere else for that matter. This precedent binds all courts in Texas because the supreme court of any state is the highest authority under which all lower courts of that state, including its appellate courts, are bound. The Texas Supreme Court has no jurisdiction or power, however, over the courts of any other state. An important component of learning to look at case law is to determine where that law would be applied, and where it would not.

Common-Law Duties

The case opens with the statement, "We are asked in this case to impose a common-law duty on a social host who makes alcohol available to an intoxicated adult guest who the host knows will be driving."

The first question you should be asking yourselves is, "What is a common-law duty?" A common-law duty is one created in the courts, not by the legislatures. The fib your American Government teacher told (referred to in the introductory paragraphs of this chapter) is now revealed. In this case, the courts are considering whether or not to impose a civil law that holds social hosts liable for the conduct of their drunk guests, and the type of law they are being asked to impose (actually create) is *common* as opposed to *statutory*. A statutory law is created by the legislature. A common law is one the court creates by applying historic precedents to new situations. Each time the court imposes a new duty, it creates a new precedent and a new law, without any need to confer with the voting public regarding its will.

Common law is the law of court precedent, applied on a case-by-case basis. But, do not be deceived by the case-by-case nature of common law. A precedent is not a flexible rule. Once a precedent is set in a given jurisdiction, that precedent must be followed in similar cases that come before all the courts in that jurisdiction. In that respect, common law is as binding, once established, as any statute.

You might ask whether or not courts can change their minds about precedents. Of course that can happen, but it does not happen very often. Just as legislatures can change their minds and write new laws that change old ones, appellate courts can set new precedents by overturning old ones, but this is a rare exception rather than the rule. Overturning a precedent is, statistically, a long shot, and the highest court that set the precedent is the lowest court that can overturn it. If a circuit court of appeal in the federal appellate system sets the precedent, then a federal district trial court in that jurisdiction must follow it, and cannot overturn it. Only the circuit court that set the precedent, or the U.S. Supreme Court, can overturn it. It is certainly something a litigant should not count on. The costs of litigation are too high and the likelihood of a different outcome too low to make the gamble worth taking in most cases.

You also might ask whether the legislature can change precedent. This can happen (and such an example is cited in this case, as we will see later) when the courts overstep and impose new common law with which the legislature disagrees. It also happens when precedents and statutes need to be revised to make them modern and more consistent with each other. States often have law revision commissions to update statutes and integrate precedent and statutory law into more cohesive legal schemes.

Now that you have a clear picture of common law (I hope), the next question you might ask is, "What is a duty?" In ordinary English, a duty is an obligation, or a moral responsibility. In the law, it is a bit more onerous. A duty in the law is a legal responsibility to a person you may or may not know. If a legal duty is breached, the one who breaches it will have to pay if an injury is caused as a result. Every time you drive a car, you assume a legal duty of care. If you fail to act with reasonable care, and if someone is injured as a result, you are liable.

Legal duties (common law and statutory) are very common, especially in business. For example, a corporate board's directors have a legal fiduciary duty (duty of trust) to the shareholders. If directors act in their own interests instead of in the interests of the shareholders when conducting corporate business, they will be liable for any harm the shareholders suffer as a result of the breach in their fiduciary duty.

The next sentences in the case can be considered now that the phrase "common-law duty" has some meaning to it.

The Facts of the Case

In order to understand how precedents work, you need to know the case "story" that gave rise to the precedent. Precedents apply to all similar cases, but all similar cases still have differences. To the extent that a case is distinguishable or differentiable from the case that engendered the precedent, there may be other law or other precedents that come into play. In order to fully understand common law, one generally needs to understand the role of the facts in the case in setting the precedent. Here is what the court tells us about this case.

> "Houston Moos consumed alcohol at a party hosted by the Graffs and Hausmons, and allegedly left in his vehicle in an intoxicated condition. En route from the party, Moos collided with a motorcycle, injuring Brett Beard [and killing his wife Dorothy]. Beard sued both Moos and his hosts for his injuries. The trial court ultimately dismissed Beard's claims against the hosts for failure to state a cause of action [prior to which time Beard had settled his claims with Moos]."

Houston Moos, whose name is not in the title of the case, is the one who got drunk at the party, and then went out and drove his car into Brett Beard's motorcycle. One might wonder why Moos is not still a party to this action, but that becomes clear at the end of the quote. Beard had settled with Moos.

A curious person might wonder, if the one who actually caused the accident had already settled with Beard, why is the case still on-going? The answer is a practical one that reflects the financial reality of a serious accident such as the one in this case. Obviously, Mr. Moos' insurance and personal assets were insufficient to cover the full financial cost of Brett Beard's injuries and the loss of his wife, Dorothy. Since Moos' resources were insufficient to cover Beard's damages, Beard needed to look to other culpable parties to get the remainder of his financial compensation for the damage done to him. Beard looked to the Graffs and Hausmons as other culpable parties because they were allegedly the ones who gave Moos the alcohol and then let him drive.

The problem is that up until that point, there was no common-law duty imposed on social hosts. In other words, social hosts had never been found by an appellate court in Texas to have a legal duty to third parties who get hurt by their guests who get drunk. In general, a third party is someone outside of a relationship who makes a claim against someone inside the relationship for reasons that are connected to the relationship. In this case, Moos and the Graffs and Hausmons were the parties who knew each other and were in a relationship with each other. The Graffs and the Hausmons had no relationship with the Beards. Their liability to the Beards (whom they never met or directly hurt) arose from their relationship with Moos. Therefore, the Beards are third parties with respect to the Graffs and Hausmons. In summary, there was, at the time of Beard's claim, no third party right established that would make the Graffs and Hausmons liable for Moos' conduct.

The Grounds for a Lawsuit and the Power to Create Precedents

The last sentence of the aforementioned quote says in part, "The trial court ultimately dismissed Beard's claims against the hosts for failure to state a cause of action.…" This simple statement implies a lot of things. The first implication deals with the trial court's role. Trial courts do not set precedents. They follow precedents. Since there was no existing, established court precedent imposing a duty on social hosts at the time the trial court heard the case, the trial court did not believe it had the power to allow the case to go to trial.

People will often believe that you can sue anyone for anything. Just find the right way to say it, and you will have a lawsuit against someone who has done you wrong. This is simply not the case. In order to have a legal remedy for a wrong that has been done to you, there must be something called a "cause of action." You cannot just make one up. If there is no precedent or statute supporting the legal basis for the claim, the court will throw the case out. More precisely, you can be sued for anything, but the case will be dismissed if the suit is groundless in the law.

That is what the trial court did here—it dismissed the case as groundless in the law. This does not mean that the Graffs and the Hausmons were found innocent of any wrongdoing. It means that the court did not wish to create new precedent that would allow it to even consider the question.

Jurisdiction is another word for power. Courts do not have the power to redress every wrong. They can only compensate victims of acts that are unlawful. Not every act that causes harm is unlawful. That is always difficult for people to understand, especially in today's world where we seem to think that we can be compensated for any harm that is not our own fault, and even some that are.

A trial court is limited to applying the precedents that govern it. If you think about it, a trial court cannot set a new precedent because it only has power over itself. If the judge in the trial court misreads the law, or ventures to new dominions unsupported by law up to that point, it still has not set a precedent because there is no court underneath it that will be bound. A sister court would be able to reach a different outcome without being subject to reversal because the other trial court is an equal—the latter has no power over the former.

Cases become precedents when appellate courts are asked to make a finding about the trial court's interpretation of the law. Appellate courts do not re-examine the facts of the case to see if the judge or jury picked the correct winner. Appellate courts do not rehear evidence or hear new evidence. If evidence was not presented in trial, it is not part of the record, and it will not be permitted to be introduced on appeal.

Appellate courts look at the law that the trial court used when instructing the jury (or applied in reaching its conclusions). If there was error in the trial court's interpretation or application of the law, the appellate court can reverse the trial court. If the trial court was correct, in the appellate court's estimation, the trial court's decision will be affirmed. Either way, in reviewing the legal question, the appellate court sets the precedent. It interprets, expands, applies, leaves as is, or creates

the new law that will bind the trial court next time a similar case arises.

If, after an appellate court has reviewed a case, there is further appeal, the highest court that hears the case creates the precedent in the case. In other words, the highest court on appeal that hears the case is the only one that matters—its opinion virtually obliterates the impact of any preceding appeal. Until a state supreme court hears a case, there can actually be different precedents governing different regions within a state. This happened in California, when the Northern Appellate District set a precedent that mandated trial courts to divide community property one way, and the Southern Appellate District mandated courts in its part of the state to divide community property in a different way. Until the California Supreme Court received a relevant case on appeal and set a new precedent, there were opposing precedents operating in the same state that were theoretically based on the same statutory foundation. Once the California Supreme Court rendered its opinion, any conflicting appellate court precedents were overturned and the state was reunified on the issue. As noted previously, the supreme court of a state binds all the courts within the state.

Dismissals

According to the last sentence quoted above from this case, "The trial court ultimately dismissed Beard's

claims against the hosts for failure to state a cause of action...." The court dismissed this case before it went to trial. There are two ways that can happen in the common law.

The first way is what happened in this case—upon a motion to dismiss, the trial court issued a demurrer. A demurrer is a legal "So what?" Even if everything is true about the party against whom the motion to dismiss is brought, so what? Even if Moos got drunk at the Graff/Hausmon party and they didn't stop him from getting drunk, or from driving once he got drunk, so what? Those facts do not state a cause of action, because there is no law requiring the Graffs or the Hausmons, as social hosts, to either stop Moos from getting drunk, or to stop him from driving once he got drunk.

If a party alleges conduct in a complaint or a cause of action that does not rise to illegal conduct, the complaint will be thrown out of court on a demurrer.

There is one other form of dismissal before trial: the common law "summary judgment" in which a party can get a case thrown out without having to go through a trial. Where a demurrer says, "So what?" about the allegations in a complaint, the summary judgment admits that the allegations state a cause of action, but claims that the allegations cannot be proved. To illuminate this point, consider the following example.

Suppose that a complaint alleges that a bar owner sold liquor to a minor who then was injured as a result of being intoxicated. These allegations would support a cause of action under the Texas Dram Shop Act, will be discussed later. Suppose, however, that the named defendant is not the bar owner at all, and that all sides admit this. The cause of action is valid, but the facts cannot support the case against the named defendant, so the matter is subject to summary judgment. Note that if there were a factual dispute as to whether the named defendant was or was not the bar owner, the matter would not be subject to summary judgment. It is only when the facts, when seen most favorably to the party against whom the motion is made, are insufficient that a summary judgment motion will be granted.

These two forms of dismissals before trial, demurrer and summary judgment, are very similar. In fact, in federal court, they no longer use the term demurrer, and both types of dismissals are called summary judgments.

In looking at the Graff/Hausmon case, the facts are subject to a great deal of debate. It is unknown whether or not Moos consumed additional alcohol after leaving the party of the named defendants. It is unknown whether or not Moos had consumed alcohol before arriving at the Graff/Hausmon party. It is even unknown whether or not Moos was actually intoxicated, since the matter is simply presumed. The disputed facts ultimately do not matter with this type of dismissal, because the complaint itself was insufficient. The allegations did not support the assertion that the Graffs and Hausmons breached a legal duty because the court found they did not have a legal duty, without regard to whether or not any disputed facts could be proven.

An *En Banc* Court of Appeals

The next sentence in the case begins by saying "An *en banc* divided court of appeals reversed the trial court's judgment.…" In order to understand the importance of that phrase, one needs to understand what an "*en banc* court of appeals" is.

The phrase *en banc* translates best to mean "full bench." The assemblage of an *en banc* court of appeals is an interesting, and to some degree unusual, type of proceeding. An interesting part of American jurisprudence history revolves around *en banc* proceedings. In the early days of the U.S. Supreme Court, the justices each would hear appeals in their assigned jurisdictions. They would "ride their circuits" and hear appeals from the federal district courts in their regions. That is how the federal Circuit Courts of Appeal got their name.

When a matter on appeal involved constitutional issues, or when a petition was filed asking for a writ of certiorari (a request that the record of the case be sent up to the U.S. Supreme Court for review), the justice riding the circuit took the matter back to the Supreme Court. The entire court would reconvene (and still reconvenes) on the first Monday in October of each year. When the justices reconvened, they looked at all of the appeals and decided if they were obligated (or simply wished) to hear any of the matters before them as a single unifying court. The U.S. Supreme Court was essentially an *en banc* panel of the nine justices who rode their respective circuits and heard appeals.

We in Arizona are in the Ninth Circuit, and we had our own U.S. Supreme Court judge who rode our circuit, which also included California and Texas. At one time, Mr. Justice Fields was our circuit judge, and the story of his life riding the Ninth Circuit is one which reads stranger than fiction, even for the wild, wild West. More of his story will be told in an appendix this book. Judges today no longer ride circuits, the custom having changed by the time the Tenth, Eleventh and D.C. Circuits were added. The number of U.S. Supreme Court justices did not change after the Tenth and subsequent circuits were added— it remained at nine.

Today, *en banc* hearings have a similar purpose to the one they had in the 1800s. They operate to have a larger group of justices hear matters of importance. Here is how they work.

The usual appellate panel convenes with three justices who hear the appeal, and there are generally several panels that hear appeals in any given jurisdiction. Since the same precedents govern all of the relevant judiciary, this does not create significant problems. However, when especially contentious issues, or issues with strong political undertones are brought up on appeal, a single three-judge panel can reach a decision that might not reflect the general vision of the majority of appellate judges in the district. At such times, a litigant may want a second bite off the appellate apple," and in some circumstances, he or she is given that opportunity. A petition for an *en banc* hearing is requested, asking that nine justices re-hear the matter. Nine judges are presumably more reflective of the entire judicial panel, and represent the majority more closely.

If the petition for an *en banc* hearing is granted, the opinion from the first appellate decision (with the three judges) is essentially erased, and the *en banc* panel reconsiders all the issues on appeal.

In the Graff/Hausmon case, we do not know the decision of the three-judge panel appeal because that decision was functionally erased when the *en banc* court met. It is not even discussed in the case. We do know, however, that the *en banc* court was divided, which means that out of nine justices, there was a split of 5-4. Although this matter may not seem to have enormously compelling moral or social significance, the justices in the Texas appellate system were concerned enough about the outcome to hear the case a second time *en banc*, and that hearing revealed a court that was very divided on the issue.

Remanding a Case and Setting a Precedent

The full sentence from the quote beginning the following section reads as follows:

"An *en banc* divided court of appeals reversed the trial court's judgment and remanded the case, holding for the first time in Texas jurisprudence that social hosts may be liable to third parties for the acts of their intoxicated guests."

When a case is remanded, it is sent back to the trial court for further proceedings. You will remember that this case was thrown out of court without ever having a trial. A demurrer had been granted, because up until that point in time, social hosts had never been subject to claims by third parties for the acts of intoxicated guests. The *en banc* court of appeals' decision remanded (or sent back) the case to the trial court, indicating that Mr. Beard was indeed entitled to a trial and that the Graffs and the Hausmons could (for the first time in Texas jurisprudence) be held accountable for the conduct of Mr. Moos. This would have been a landmark precedent for the State of Texas, but it did not stick. This case did not end at the Court of Appeals level. The caption of the case tells us that the opinion we are reading is from the Texas Supreme Court. We also know that the Graffs and Hausmons are the ones bringing the matter on appeal, since they are the ones whose names come first in the title, and they are the ones who lost in the *en banc* court of appeals.

In other words, although the *en banc* court ordered the matter remanded, the Graffs and Hausmons appealed that order, so instead of the case going back to the trial court, it went to the Texas Supreme Court.

Remember, when reading a case, it is only the opinion in the final appeal that matters. The fact that the judges quote the lower courts for historical reference does not give those earlier rulings any power. Lower court opinions have no effect after a higher court issues an opinion. In summary, the court that is speaking in the final opinion is the only court that matters for purposes of setting common law precedents.

The Statutes and Legislative Histories that Influence this Case's Outcome

After describing the *en banc* decision and its rationale, the Texas Supreme Court begins to reveal the legal reasoning that will determine the outcome of this case. Beginning in the fourth paragraph of this case, the court says:

"The legislatures in most states, including Texas, have enacted dram shop laws that impose a statutory duty to third parties on commercial providers under specified circumstances…. Because the dram shop statute applies only to commercial providers, however, it does not govern the duty asserted in this case.

We think it significant in appraising Beard's request to recognize common-law social host liability that the legislature has considered and declined to cre-

ate such a duty. A version of the bill that eventually became our dram shop statute provided for social host liability. Although that version passed the Senate, the House rejected it. The Senate-House conference committee deleted social host liability from the bill the legislature eventually enacted."

This is perhaps the most theoretically interesting part of the case. It is important to differentiate between common law and statutory law once again, to understand what is going on in this paragraph. The Texas legislature had enacted a dram shop act. (A dram is a unit of weight, but is used colloquially to refer to a small draft or alcoholic drink.) Statutes (or acts, bills, or codes) are passed by the legislative branch of government. Common law is developed in the courts and is set by precedent. When the legislature passes a statute, courts are bound to obey the statute, and when the statute has an ambiguity, the courts have discretion to interpret it.

In the Texas statute, however, there was no ambiguity. The dram shop act clearly stipulated that only commercial providers (taverns, bars, restaurants that serve alcohol, etc.) be liable to third parties for the acts of their intoxicated guests. It clearly did not include social hosts. However, the statute did not specifically indemnify social hosts either, which means it did not specifically say that social hosts could not be held liable. Beard's attorney saw wiggle room in the absence of an indemnity or legal protection for social hosts in the statute, even though the legislature had excluded social hosts from the dram shop act after considering the issue. It should be understood that, even with that legislative history, there was still the possibility that the court could have imposed a common-law duty where the legislature had refused to impose a statutory one.

The court continues its consideration of the issue of statutory versus common-law duty in the next paragraph.

"The highest courts in only four states have done what we are asked to do today: judicially impose a duty to third parties on social hosts who make alcohol available to adult guests. In two of these states, California and Iowa, the legislatures subse-

quently abrogated the judicially created duty. Neither of the two remaining jurisdictions, Massachusetts and New Jersey, had dram shop statutes when their courts acted. Rather, their courts first imposed a common-law duty to third parties on commercial establishments and then extended the duty to social hosts."

Since the court in this case was considering whether to apply a common-law duty to social hosts, it decided to take a look at what other states had done in this regard. They noted only four state supreme courts had imposed such a duty on social hosts. Two states, Massachusetts and New Jersey, the court notes, only had common-law dram shop liability to begin with. In those states, all third party liability to both commercial and social hosts was a construct of the common law, and apparently the legislatures of those states had never felt compelled to augment or intervene to replace court-made law with a statute.

However, the other two states referenced by the court, California and Iowa, did have dram shop acts passed by their legislatures: acts that were almost identical to that passed by Texas. In those states, social hosts were omitted from the dram shop statutes just as they were in Texas. The supreme courts of those states at some point did impose social host liability despite the legislature's excluding social hosts from their dram shop acts, just as Beard was asking the Texas Supreme

Court to do. And in both of those states, the legislature came back and revised their statutes to specifically *abrogate* or nullify the court-imposed duty.

The Texas Court in this case is observing that in California and Iowa, a court-imposed duty on social hosts engendered a battle of the branches with the judicial branch attempting to circumvent legislative intent and the legislature ultimately fighting back.

It was obvious that in California and Iowa, had the legislatures intended social hosts to be liable, they would have included them in their respective dram shop statutes. When the courts engaged the legislatures in battle in those states by imposing the duty under the common law, those legislatures came back and rewrote the law to specifically protect social hosts from liability to third parties. They nullified or cancelled the court imposed duty. It should be noted that despite the wide latitude courts have in wiggling around the law with common law mechanics, ultimately the legislature has the power within constitutional limits

to have the final word. If the legislature overturns a precedent with a new statute, assuming that the new statute is constitutional, the courts are powerless to circumvent that statute with common law. Otherwise, the courts would be the legislators, and we would have no enforceable laws from the elected branch of government.

The Texas Supreme Court observed that their own legislature's clear intent was to distinguish or differentiate social hosts from commercial providers of alcoholic beverages. Although the Texas Supreme Court could have imposed a common-law duty notwithstanding that legislative intent, they observed what had happened in California and Iowa. Although there is frequently friction between the legislative and judicial branches of government, this is one instance where the court saw that it would be unwise from both policy and political perspectives to do battle. (Arizona has a statute which specifically indemnifies or protects social hosts from third party liability under this type of circumstance.)

The Reasoning of the Court

A precedent is not set by merely making a one-line statement of the law. It is set by answering the question of the case with thorough analysis and by putting the decision in context. In this case, the reasoning of the court was as follows:

"Deciding whether to impose a new common-law duty involves complex considerations of public policy. We have said that these considerations include "'social, economic, and political questions,' and their application to the particular facts at hand." Among other factors, we consider the extent of the risk involved, "the foreseeability and likelihood of injury weighed against the social utility of the actor's conduct, the magnitude of the burden of guarding against the injury, and the consequences of placing the burden on the defendant." We have also emphasized other factors. For example, questions of duty have turned on whether one party has superior knowledge of the risk, and whether a right to control the actor whose conduct precipitated the harm exists.

* * *

Ideally, guests will drink responsibly, and hosts will monitor their social functions to reduce the likelihood of intoxication. Once a guest becomes impaired by alcohol to the point at which he becomes a threat to himself and others, we would hope that the host can persuade the guest to take public transportation, stay on the premises, or be transported home by an unimpaired driver. But we know that too often reality conflicts with ideal behavior. And, given the ultimate power of guests to control their own alcohol consumption and the absence of any legal right of the host to control the guest, we find the arguments for shifting legal responsibility from the guest to the host, who merely makes alcohol available at social gatherings, unconvincing. As the common law has long recognized, the imbiber maintains the ultimate power and thus the obligation to control his own behavior: to decide to drink or not to drink, to drive or not to drive. We therefore conclude that the common law's focus should remain on the drinker as the person primarily responsible for his own behavior and best able to avoid the foreseeable risks of that behavior."

Often when the court is imposing liability vicariously, which is to say on someone other than the person who did the harm, there is a policy reason for that imposition.

In this case, the court's reasoning clearly points out that the one who does the drinking and driving is the bad guy—not the social host. The court saw no policy reason to extend liability to social hosts.

You might well ask at this point, "Why, then, are there dram shop acts to begin with? Why make commercial providers liable more than social hosts? If anything, social hosts know their guests better, and are potentially in a better position to determine if someone has had too much to drink."

The reason can best be explained in terms of the concept of market failure discussed elsewhere in this text. Negative externalities are considered market failures because under ordinary free market constructs and absent any governmental regulation, certain costs of business can be unfairly shifted from an enterprise to society. Polluters, for example, can profit from the production of goods and services that create the pollutants, but without regulation, can force society to clean up the mess or live with the pollution. Environmental protection laws operate to correct the negative externality market failure. Dram shop acts serve a similar purpose.

If one lives in the suburbs, most bars are not within walking distance to people's homes. Zoning laws have precluded bars from residential neighborhoods for policy reasons. The residual presumption must then be that if people are going to go to a restaurant that serves alcohol, or to a tavern or bar, they will most likely need to get there in a vehicle.

Absent regulation, it is in the best interests of commercial providers to sell as much liquor as possible to their patrons, without regard to whether or not the patrons drove to the bar. In other words, bar owners profit from getting patrons drunk. Society, however, pays a huge price if a patron leaves drunk and then drives. The tavern owner has profited from getting the patron drunk, but society is paying the bill for the consequences. A dram shop act shifts the cost of the patron's drunkenness back to the party who profited from it.

A social host, on the other hand, has no economic incentive to get his or her guests drunk. Just the opposite is the case, since the more alcohol that is consumed by a guest, the higher the cost of the party is to the host. There is no correlated market failure to the social host's conduct because there is no market or profit function involved. (Workplace parties that serve alcohol pose an entirely different set of legal problems than do ordinary social gatherings such as weddings or graduation parties.)

The Holding of the Court

A precedent is set when the court takes a stand with regard to the specific case before it. In this case, the final conclusion of the court follows:

> "We accordingly reverse the judgment of the court of appeals and render judgment that Beard take nothing."

This is a final and irreversible judgment. The highest court of the state of Texas has spoken, and there are no further appeals from there. You might ask whether or not Mr. Beard could go to the U.S. Supreme Court for relief. It is a good question with a complicated answer. Simply stated, there is no federal or constitutional question involved in the case; therefore, the U.S.

Supreme Court would not have jurisdiction to hear the matter. This is purely a state matter.

Because the case was initially
thrown out of the trial court on a demurrer (that so-what dismissal described earlier), Beard did not ever get
a trial. The court of appeals reversed
the trial court and remanded the case
for trial, but that reversal was appealed
to the Texas Supreme Court which, in
the final analysis, reversed that reversal. Confused? When a reviewing
court affirms (ratifies) or reverses a
case, it is acting upon the immediately
preceding opinion. In this case, the
court of appeals had given Beard the
right to a trial. By reversing the court
of appeals, the Texas Supreme Court
has taken away that right. Therefore
the reversal of the trial court by the appellate court in this case got reversed
by the Texas Supreme Court. Consider
the following analogy: Think of the
courts as people walking. The trial
court begins walking in one direction
when it makes its decision. The appellate court reverses direction when it reverses the case. When the Supreme
Court reverses the appellate court, it
turns around and starts walking in the
same direction as the trial court had
been going.

Once a case has gone to its final appeal, it is over. You might ask whether
or not Beard can bring another lawsuit
in a different court, or in a different
state. The answer is no, there is legal
doctrine that supports the finality of legal judgments after the time for appeal
or the final appeal has been exhausted.

However, there is a final (sometimes confusing) component, which
follows:

"Dissenting   Opinion—Justice
Gammage joined by Justice
Doggett

I respectfully dissent. The majority errs in holding that the
legislature must "create" the
duty for social hosts not to send
intoxicated guests driving in our
streets to maim and kill. Logic,
legal experience and this court's
own earlier decisions dictate a
contrary result.

* * *

All culpable parties should be
liable—the social host who
knowingly intoxicated the guest
and the guest who drunkenly
caused the accident. I am persuaded that both should be liable to the extent of their responsibility   for   the   accident.
"Friends don't let friends drive
drunk." That is sound public
policy. But today the majority
says "Intoxicate your friends
and send them out upon the
public streets and highways to
drive drunk. Don't worry; you
won't be liable." That is, in the
kindest term I can muster, unsound policy."

The above quote is the dissent of
this case. Not every case has a dissent.

Some opinions are unanimous, with all of the justices agreeing. Some cases have concurrences, where one or more of the justices agree with the majority, but not for the reasons that the majority opinion provides.

You might cite the dissent for support of an argument, but this can be a devastating choice, especially on an exam. The dissent is, by definition, the losing argument. It not only does not create precedent, it argues the opposite from the precedent. Its existence does not create a usable alternative legal argument. It merely allows the opposing view to have a forum. An attorney that cites a dissenting opinion as authority can be held in contempt of court. Only the majority opinion is precedent. It is important when you are reading a case to make sure you know where you are in the case—either in the opinion, the concurrence, or the dissent. It literally makes all the difference in the world when trying to understand what the law is in any particular situation.

Court Structures

Looking at the court structure in diagramatic form helps students understand how things move from trial courts up the ladder through the appellate process. In America, things are especially confusing because we actually have two different court systems: federal and state. Within each of those we have lots of subdivisions: crimes, civil law, summary proceedings like bankruptcy, etc. There are times when the federal court system would be the appropriate jurisdiction (meaning where federal court would have power), and time where state courts would be the right venue. And, of course, there are times when there is overlap and both courts might have jurisdiction. When that happens, things can get complicated, and in our early judicial history, things did. (See appendix referenced earlier about Justice Fields, called "A Quagmire.")

In the federal system, a litigant has a right to appeal to the U.S. Circuit Court in the circuit in which the case was decided, however, there is no right to have the U.S. Supreme Court review a case. The U.S. Supreme Court decides whether or not to look at a case by either granting or denying a petition for a "writ of certiorari." The high court takes only a small percentage of the cases it is requested to hear each year. It makes its decision based on several criteria: a) it believes the legal question is of national significance, b) the circuit courts across the country are divided about the issue, c) the case is one of "first impression" and has no law to guide it, d) other compelling reasons which induce the justices to exercise their discretion to review a case.

The diagram below shows how cases move up from the lower courts to the higher ones.

Diagram of the U.S. Court System

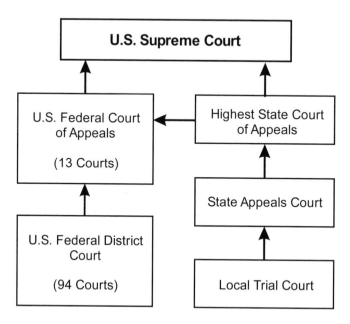

Although the study of which court governs what claim gets beyond the scope of this class, it should be noted that the Graffs/Hausmons case had to end at the Texas Supreme Court because there was no constitutional issue raised in that case, and the U.S. Supreme Court has no authority to rule on the Texas dram shop act or social host liability. That is exclusively a state issue. But sometimes things are not so clear, and jurisdiction between state and federal court can overlap.

In one of the most controversial cases in the business arena the Pennzoil v. Texaco case addresses how important it is to understand the risks of having the wrong forum adjudicate a claim.(3)

The case all started when Pennzoil made an offer to acquire Getty Oil (a company founded by the rather infamous J Paul Getty). Pennzoil wanted the oil reserves and the markets Getty—a relatively small player in the gasoline business—owned. A rather informal meeting led to a handshake agreement, but it is hotly disputed what the agreement actually called for as many items were not yet negotiated, and price was still allegedly soft. Texaco made a higher offer before the shareholders could vote, but Getty was nervous about Pennzoil's aggressive action and their threat of litigation.

Texaco agreed to indemnify Getty if Pennzoil were to win any judgment against them. But they missed a few big issues with respect to Texas law.

First, they missed that Texas had a rather robust "interference with contract" statute. Texaco did not believe that the statute applied, because they did not believe there was a contract at all, and if there was, federal securities law pre-empted its enforcement without proper disclosures, which had not been made.

The other thing that may have been influential is that Texas courts have a reputation of favoring locals almost unabashedly, and they have gotten away with somewhat aggressive behavior in this regard since the Alamo. Although Texaco was founded in Texas, its corporate headquarters were moved to New York years prior to this case. And though Penzoil was founded in the east in the 1970s, it moved its corporate headquarters to Houston. Penzoil was on the "Texas team." In a down-home court, the jury awarded Pennzoil damages for Texaco's interference with their contract in an amount that exceeded the entire purchase price of Getty, and then added $3 billion in punitive damages on top. The total judgment came to over $10 billion dollars, which exceeded Texaco's net worth at that time.

In order to appeal a Texas judgment, however, you need to post a bond in the amount of that judgment. Texaco did not have the money to post that bond, so it went to federal court raising the constitutional issues that attach to a claim that would clearly deny Texaco due process after an outrageous judgment. In Texaco's financial reports, they never reported risk greater than a minimal one for this case, and most legal scholars opined that were Texaco able to go up to an appellate court on the issues of this case, they would have won a complete reversal. But as you might note from the case in this book's appendix "A Quagmire," there is precedent that holds where a case starts is where it will be governed. That among other precedents was influential in this case.

The lower federal court granted Texaco's request for injunctive relief, so that they could proceed on appeal without bond. But the matter went up to the U.S. Supreme Court, and the final judgment was not pretty. Texaco was constrained to fight its battle in the Texas courts, where it had not raised the federal questions in a timely manner. The following gives the U.S. Supreme Court's reasoning.

Pennzoil Co. v. Texaco Inc., 481 U.S. 1 (1987)

481 U.S. 1

Pennzoil Co. v. Texaco Inc.
Appeal from the United States Court of Appeals for the Second Circuit

No. 85-1798.

Argued January 12, 1987
Decided April 6, 1987

Under Texas law, a judgment creditor can secure and execute a lien on a judgment debtor's property unless the debtor files … a bond in at least the amount of the judgment, interest, and costs. Appellant obtained a jury verdict of $10.53 billion in its Texas state-court suit alleging that appellee tortiously [meaning unlawfully in the civil sense] had induced a third oil company to breach a contract to sell its shares to appellant. Because it was clear that appellee would not be able to post a bond in the necessary amount, the verdict had substantial adverse effects on appellee's business and financial situation. Accordingly, even before the trial court entered judgment on the verdict, appellee filed suit in Federal District Court alleging that the Texas proceedings violated its rights under the Federal Constitution and various federal statutes. Appellee did not present these claims to the state court. Appellant argued, inter alia, [meaning among other things] that the Federal District Court should abstain from hearing the case … and, concluding that appellee's constitutional claims had "a very clear probability of success," issued a preliminary injunction barring any action to enforce the state court's judgment, which had now been entered. The Court of Appeals affirmed…

Held:

The lower federal courts should have [not enjoined the Texas Courts].

> (a) …The Texas Constitution contains an "open courts" provision that appears to address appellee's claims more specifically than does the Federal Constitution. Thus, it is

entirely possible that the Texas courts would have re-solved this case on state statutory or constitutional grounds, without reaching appellee's federal constitution-al questions.

* * *

...Appellee has not satisfied its burden of showing that state procedural law barred presentation of its claims. When, as here, a litigant has made no effort in state court to present his claims, a federal court should assume that state procedures will afford an adequate remedy, in the absence of unambiguous authority to the contrary.

784 F.2d 1133, reversed and remanded.

The U.S. Supreme Court's decision found that Texaco did not follow cor-rect procedure because it failed to raise all of its claims in state court, includ-ing the federal and constitutional claims. Texaco erroneously believed those issues could be raised spearately in federal court. Because Texaco never raised the federal issues in the state ac-tion and because the Texas court did not have those issues before it, the Texas court had no requirement or right to rule on them. Therefore, the U.S. Supreme Court found that the Texas court did not make any revers-ible error. Texaco was never allowed to raise the federal or consititutional issues upon which they might likely have prevailed. The Texas lower court denied all of Texaco's claims with respect to allowing the case to proceed on appeal, and Texaco was forced into bankruptcy. Ultimately, Pennzoil was paid $3 billion out of bankruptcy so that Texaco could reorganize and continue doing business.

Notes

1. *Roe v. Wade*, 410 U.S. 113, 1973

2. *Graff and Hausmon v. Beard*, 858 S.W.2d 198

3. *Pennzoil Co. v. Texaco Inc.*, 481 U.S. 1 (1987)

Chapter 4
The Executive, Regulators, and Separation of Powers

It is highly unlikely that had the founders of our great nation attempted to look into the future, they would have anticipated that in two centuries there would be almost three million federal civil employees (excluding the military) working to implement federal programs and regulations.(1) In fact, the first regulatory agency, the Interstate Commerce Commission, did not form until 1887. Our first agency centered around commerce, and virtually every agency that has formed since impacts it. Businesses are impacted by regulation—the rules passed by regulatory or administrative agencies—substantially more than by legislation or court precedent.

We have come to where we are today, with millions of federal workers and tens of thousands of regulations, through a circuitous route that started with the Constitution, and evolved from there. We will look at the strange twists that regulatory law has taken, but we will start with an exploration of how the executive branch came to mean and involve so much more than just the presidency.

Article II of the Constitution provides the foundation of the Executive Branch by describing the powers of the President. On the most basic level, the President:

- serves as Commander-in-Chief of all the Armed Forces,

- swears or affirms to "faithfully execute the office" and "preserve, protect and defend the Constitution of the United States,"

- takes "care that the laws be faithfully executed," and

- commissions all the officers of the United States.

With the advice and consent of the Senate, the President has the power to make treaties and appoint Supreme Court judges, public ministers and ambassadors. Finally, as chief executive, the President has the power to write Executive Orders to direct the operation of government. For example, in 2001, President Bush issued an Executive Order limiting federal funding for embryonic stem cell research, except to projects using specific stem cell lines. The National Institute of Health (NIH) curtailed its funding of stem cell research to comply with President Bush's order. The private sector is unimpeded by this order, but it binds the

NIH and any other related administrative agencies that might give federal grants for noncomplying stem cell research.

It might appear that discussion of the Executive Branch should end now. But if you gazed ahead, you would see (perhaps sadly) that this chapter continues on for many more pages. This is because the Executive Branch is not just the Office of the President. As stated on the government-generated Web site www.USA.gov:(2)

> "The Executive Branch of the government is responsible for enforcing the laws of the land. The president, vice president, department heads (cabinet members), and heads of independent agencies carry out this mission."

The evolution and expansion of the power of federal administrative agencies has complicated the role of the Executive Branch since the time the Constitution was drafted.

Most people are familiar with at least some well-known administrative agencies such as the Food and Drug Administration (FDA) or the Internal Revenue Service (IRS), but there are over 100 agencies at the federal level and over 100,000 federal regulations that have been promulgated (passed) by them.

Many political scientists have questioned the breadth of authority that has been delegated to administrative agencies. Becasue the legislature is mandated to be the branch of government primarily responsible to write legislation, it is not intuitive how the agencies have garnered the power to create such an abundance of regulation, nor is it obvious how they fit under the Executive Branch.

How Administrative Agencies Fit in This Government

Agencies are enabled (given specific power) by Congress, led by political appointees of the President with the consent of the Senate, and subject to review by the Judicial Branch.

Because agencies are a construct of all three branches, they might not appear to fit under any single one. Some scholars have asserted that federal administrative agencies comprise a "fourth branch" of government, but as there is no Constitutional provision for a fourth branch, the operation of ad-

ministrative agencies would be unconstitutional under that definition.

The way that power has been transferred to the administrative agencies is the result of legal twists and turns through both Congress and the courts. Although the Constitution does not permit Congress to delegate away its law-making authority, it can delegate regulatory power for rules that are (at least theoretically) administrative and not legislative. Administration legitimately falls under the Executive Branch. Legislation does not.

Consider the following example:

When Congress decided it needed to legislate the disposal of nuclear waste, it could have been bogged down indefinitely, haggling over specific solutions to the problem. Members of Congress do not have the expertise to understand complicated issues surrounding nuclear waste, and neither do ordinary citizens.

Instead, Congress enabled the Nuclear Regulatory Commission (NRC) to establish rules for safe nuclear waste disposal. Appointees to the NRC are experts in the field and can regulate the relevant issues more effectively than Congress.

Importantly, this example illustrates how practical needs yield practical solutions in government. On a more subtle level, however, it illustrates how Congress has the power to delegate quasi law-making power to nonelective officials. The NRC currently passes rules under its own legislative system through which it can file complaints against violators, impose penalties, and adjudicate disputes. Some would say that within its jurisdictional arena, it is its own mini-government.

Departmental and Independent Agencies

There are two types of federal agencies: those that operate under the general supervision of the White House (departmental agencies), and those that operate independently (independent agencies). Presidents appoint the heads of independent agencies (with the advice and consent of the Senate) when the term of a previous head expires, but beyond that, there is no formal relationship between the independent agency and the president. The NRC in the example above operates independently and does not report to the Office of the President. Despite this, it is part of the Executive Branch. That is not an obvious point, and one that is frequently misunderstood. Independent rule-making agencies are part of the Executive Branch because that is what they have to be in order to be Constitutional.

Most federal agencies are not independent; they are departmental and are directly connected to the President through the Cabinet.

The Cabinet is composed of the most senior appointed officers under the president. According to the White House Web site (3), "The tradition of the Cabinet dates back to the beginnings of the Presidency itself." President George Washington appointed a Cabinet of four people (Secretary of State, Thomas Jefferson; Secretary of the Treasury, Alexander Hamilton; Secretary of War, Henry Knox; and

Attorney General, Edmund Randolph). Today, the president appoints fifteen cabinet secretaries with the advice and consent of the Senate.

Those fifteen secretaries oversee fifteen departments including Commerce, Defense, Health and Human Services, Homeland Security, State, Justice (headed by the Attorney General), Transportation, and the Treasury. Under each department there are multiple agencies.

Consider the Department of Defense. The Defense Secretary serves as the chief executive officer (CEO) and oversees the Secretaries of the Army, Navy and Air Force (although those agencies have a direct link to the president as well). The Secretary of Defense is also the CEO of all of the following agencies:

- Armed Forces Radiobiology Research Institute (AFRRI)

- Ballistic Missile Defense Organization (BMDOLINK)

- Defense Advanced Research Projects Agency (DARPA)

- Defense Commissary Agency (DeCA)

- Defense Contract Audit Agency (DCAA)

- Defense Finance and Accounting Service (DFAS)

- Defense Information Systems Agency (DISA)

- Defense Intelligence Agency (DIA)

- Defense Legal Services Agency

- Defense Logistics Agency (DLA)
  - ∞ Corporate Administration
    - DLA Environmental and Safety Policy Office (CAAE)
    - Defense Automatic Addressing System Center (DAASC)
    - DLA Office of Operations Research and Resource Analysis (DORRA)
  - ∞ Information Operations(formerly: Chief Information Officer)
    - Defense Systems Design Center (DSDC)
  - ∞ Defense Automated Printing Service Center
    - Defense Automation and Production Service
    - Defense Administrative Support Center
  - ∞ Defense Contract Management Command (DCMC)
    - Defense Contract Management District East (DCMDE)
    - Defense Contract Management District International (DCMDI)
    - Defense Contract Management District West (DCMDW)
  - ∞ Defense Logistics Support Command (DLSC)

- Automatic Identification Technology Office
- Inventory Control Points
  - Defense Energy Support Center (DESC)
  - Defense Industrial Supply Center (DISC)
  - Defense Supply Center Columbus (DSCC)
  - Defense Supply Center Richmond (DSCR)
  - Defense Supply Center Philadelphia (DSCP)
- Defense Distribution Center (DDC)
- Service Centers
  - Defense Reutilization and Marketing Service (DRMS)
  - Defense Logistics Information Service (DLIS)
  - Defense National Stockpile Center (DNSC)
  - Defense Distribution Systems Center (DDSC)
- Defense Security Cooperation Agency (DSCA) (formerly Defense Security Assistance Agency)
- Defense Security Service (DSS) (formerly Defense Investigative Service)
- Defense Technical Information Center (DTIC)
- Defense Threat Reduction Agency (DTRA)
  - ∞ On-Site Inspection Operations

- National Imagery and Mapping Agency (NIMA)
- National Security Agency/Central Security Service
- Department of Defense Field Activities
- American Forces Information Service
- Defense Medical Programs Activity
- Defense Prisoner of War/Missing Personnel Office
- Defense Technology Security Administration
- Department of Defense Human Resources Field Activity
  - ∞ Defense Civilian Personnel Management Service (CPMS)
  - ∞ Defense Manpower Data Center (DMDC)
  - ∞ Department of Defense Education Activity
  - ∞ Office of Civilian Health and Medical Program of the Uniformed Services
  - ∞ Office of Economic Adjustment
  - ∞ TRICARE Military Health System
  - ∞ Washington Headquarters Services
  - ∞ Department of Defense Libraries
  - ∞ Unified Commands

- U.S. European Command, Stuttgart-Vaihingen, Germany
- U.S. Pacific Command, Honolulu, HI
- U.S. Atlantic Command, Norfolk, VA
- U.S. Southern Command, Miami, FL
- U.S. Central Command, MacDill Air Force Base, FL
- U.S. Space Command, Peterson Air Force Base, CO
- U.S. Special Operations Command, MacDill Air Force Base, FL
- U.S. Transportation Command, Scott Air Force Base, IL
- U.S. Strategic Command, Offutt Air Force Base, NE (4)

Defense is the largest department in the Executive Branch, as one might expect, but none of the cabinet departments could be considered tiny. The Department of Transportation is mid-size, with 12 agencies under its control and a host of smaller agencies under each of those 12. The Department of Agriculture controls 25 agencies, and the Department of Education has 14. The Department of Veterans Affairs is the smallest, with only three.

There are also at least 60 independent agencies, the most notable of which include the Securities and Exchange Commission (SEC) and the Environmental Protection Agency (EPA). As indicated earlier in this section, the NRC is also an independent agency.

Given the sheer number of departmental and independent agencies, the likelihood for overlapping areas of concern is overwhelming, and the consequences of overlapping can be daunting. This is best illustrated by example:

Assume you run a company that builds roads. You grade, pave with either asphalt or cement, and paint lines on the road when it is ready. It should be simple. Here are the federal and Arizona state regulations (including industry regulations incorporated into state regulations) to which you might be required to comply:

Environmental Protection Agency (EPA), Chemical Federal Registry (CFR), American Association of State Highway and Transportation Officials (AASHTO), Federal Specifications and Standards (FSS), Arizona Radiation Regulatory Agency (ARRA), Arizona Department of Environmental Quality (ADEQ), Arizona Department of Transportation (ADOT), Arizona Rock Products Association (ARPA), and other standards and guidelines including American Concrete Institute (ACI), American Concrete Pipe Association (ACPA),

Asphalt Institute (AI), American National Standards Institute (ANSI), and American Society for Testing Materials (ASTM).(5)

The cost to both businesses and consumers of each of those regulatory impositions is burdensome. One of government's biggest challenges is to control the amount and type of regulation, limit overlapping, and keep both the tax and private sector costs within rational limits.

Creating and Constraining an Agency

Even though regulatory power falls under the Executive Branch of our government, the power must first be granted by the legislature for it to be Constitutional. The President cannot simply wake up one morning and establish a federal agency. Agencies are created by Congress in what is known as enabling legislation. An act or bill is passed by which an agency is either created or altered. The agency is enabled to act under that legislation, and its power theoretically extends only to what the legislation authorizes.

Sometimes agency power is extremely broad with a large mandate to fulfill its purpose, and sometimes it is very detailed, giving little discretionary power. The enabling legislation for the Environmental Protection Agency (EPA) is quite broad in nature, leaving specific implementations within the EPA's discretion. Conversely, the Internal Revenue Service is given very tight statutory guidelines within which it must operate.

Of course, Congress cannot delegate more power than is available to it. Assume that an enabling statute allows an agency to search the interior of people's homes at its own discretion, without a warrant. This would be an *unconstitutional delegation of authority*. It is generally unconstitutional for the government to search a home without a warrant, so it is equally unconstitutional to give an administrative agency that authority.

In addition to Constitutional limitations, agencies are constrained by the Administrative Procedures Act, which limits (among other things) how an agency can promulgate rules and how it must give notice of them. Although agencies have some choices regarding the rules under which they operate, they must follow the rules they have chosen.

In some ways agencies mimic the way that Congress enacts legislation. A proposal for a new rule might come from within the agency, from industry, or from the community. If the proposal is to go forward, the process formally begins with the publication of the proposed rule in a daily periodical called the Federal Register, which gives "notice" when the agency is either:

1) considering imposing a new or changed rule,

2) having public hearings about a proposed new or changed rule, and/or

3) promulgating (passing) the new rule.

Any new rule must be published in the Federal Register. From the time that the rule is published, the public is bound by it, even before it is fully integrated into the Code of Federal Regulations (CFR), which is the book that catalogs regulations in the same way that the United States Code catalogs federal statutes. (The CFR contains over 130,000 pages of regulation.)

How *Chadha* Case Changed Congressional Oversight

Ironically, given the enormous impact of federal regulation, Congress has lost much of its ability to oversee the conduct of the agencies. In order to understand the reasoning of the U.S. Supreme Court in the landmark 1986 *INS v. Chadha* case, it is important to review two principles of relevant Constitutional law and a short set of "factoids" that help to explain the case:

- **Constititutional Principle #1:** Congress is generally required to act in a bicameral manner, where both chambers (House and Senate) must act to pass law. Any exceptions to this requirement are found in the Constitution itself. For example, the President only needs the advice and consent of the Senate when making ministerial appointments; there is no bicameral role.

- **Constititutional Principle #2:** Although we have seen substantial evidence that the lines between the branches are anything but clear, the basic structure of the U.S. government designates Congress to legislate and the President to faithfully execute the law. Any delegation of authority from Congress to the Executive Branch must be ministerial (non-legislative) in order to be Constitutional. The nature of the separation of powers is that if something falls under the power of the Executive Branch, it cannot be under the power of Congress (although Congress can decide to re-legislate an enablement and either limit, expand, or alter its powers).

- **Factoids:** The Department of Justice is headed by the Attorney General, who is a member of the Executive Branch. This is a bit confusing in that usually the title for the head of a Department in the President's cabinet is Secretary. Justice is the lone exception, with the title for its chief being Attorney General instead of Secretary of Justice. At the time of the Chadha case, the Immigration and Naturalization Service had been part of the Justice Department under the authority of the Attorney General. This is why the statute at issue in the Chadha case refers to giving authority to the Attorney General. Today the Immigration and Naturalization Service is under the Department of Homeland Security and falls under the Secretary of Homeland Security's authority.

In the 1952 Immigration and Naturalization Act, Congress gave the Attorney General discretion to suspend deportation of aliens of good moral character who would otherwise suffer undue hardship. It also included a provision for what is known as a legislative veto. Under that portion of the statute, either the House **or** the Senate could overturn the decision of the INS/Attorney General.

According to the U.S. Supreme Court, this portion of the enabling statute was unconstitutional in two ways. First, if overturning the decision of the INS was **legislative**, the enablement allowed a unicameral act (empowering only one chamber of Congress—either the House or the Senate—to act) so it violated the doctrine of bicameralism. If overturning the INS decision was **ministerial** rather than legislative, the enabling statute was unconstitutional because it violated the separation of powers, as the Executive Branch is in charge of administration of the laws, not Congress.

The case follows, in two parts. First, the court summary of the facts gives a very general overview of the case up through the Ninth Circuit Court of Appeals. Then the abridged text of the majority opinion follows, giving the facts again but in greater detail, and then presenting the analysis and decision of the U.S. Supreme Court.

Due to the complexity of the decision, "translations" by this author are interspersed throughout the case to try and make it more readily comprehensible.

Immigration and Naturalization Service v. Chadha (1983)

United States Supreme Court (462 U.S. 919)

Chief Justice Warren E. Burger delivered the opinion of the court.

Summary

Section 244(c)(2) of the Immigration and Nationality Act (Act) authorizes either House of Congress, by resolution, to invalidate the decision of the Executive Branch, pursuant to authority delegated by

Congress to the Attorney General to allow a particular deportable alien to remain in the United States.

[**Translation:** When Congress passed the enabling statute authorizing the INS to let "illegal" aliens stay here, it held back the right to look over the INS's shoulder, and overrule it with the vote of **either** the House or Senate—not both.]

Appellee-respondent Chadha, an alien who had been lawfully admitted to the United States on a nonimmigrant student visa, remained in the United States after his visa had expired and was ordered by the Immigration and Naturalization Service (INS) to show cause why he should not be deported. He then applied for suspension of the deportation, and, after a hearing, an Immigration Judge, acting pursuant to § 244(a)(1) of the Act, which authorizes the Attorney General, in his discretion, to suspend deportation, ordered the suspension, and reported the suspension to Congress as required by § 244(c)(1).

[**Translation:** Mr. Chadha came as a student and then didn't want to leave. So he became a model citizen—worked hard, paid taxes, maybe got married, maybe had some kids, hard to know. Anyway, the INS finally figured out that Mr. Chadha's visa had expired 15 months earlier, so they told him he was going to get deported. He complained, indicating that this would cause him a lot of hardship, and so he asked to have the deportation suspended under the INS enabling statute section 244(c)(1) that gave the Attorney General— who headed up the INS at that time—the power to do that.

The Attorney General (through an administrative law judge) sympathized with Mr. Chadha and agreed he could stay. When a deportation is suspended, the immigrant gets to remain in the U.S. as a permanent resident.]

Thereafter, the House of Representatives passed a resolution pursuant to § 244(c)(2) vetoing the suspension, and the Immigration Judge reopened the deportation proceedings. Chadha moved to terminate the proceedings on the ground that § 244(c)(2) is unconstitutional, but the judge held that he had no authority to rule on its constitutionality, and ordered Chadha deported pursuant to the House Resolution. Chadha's appeal to the Board of Immigration Appeals was dismissed, the Board also holding that it had no power to declare § 244(c)(2) unconstitutional. Chadha then filed a petition for review of the deportation order in the Court of Appeals, and the INS joined him in arguing that § 244(c)(2) is unconstitutional.

[**Translation:** The House found Mr. Chadha's case unpersuasive to say the least. But Mr. Chadha wasn't fighting alone here. In this appeal, the INS and Mr. Chadha argue for the same result, which is to keep Congress out of the INS's back yard. So even though Mr. Chadha is suing the INS, they do not disagree on what the Supreme Court should decide. This was the subject of a great deal of procedural debate in the arguments before the court because Congress's interests were not represented in the case. The court fixes that as you will see later in the case.]

The Court of Appeals held that § 244(c)(2) violates the constitutional doctrine of separation of powers and accordingly directed the Attorney General to cease taking any steps to deport Chadha based upon the House Resolution.

[**Translation:** Chadha won at the Court of Appeals—the U.S. Supreme Court agreed to take a look.]

Abridged Decision

Chadha is an East Indian who was born in Kenya and holds a British passport. He was lawfully admitted to the United States in 1966 on a nonimmigrant student visa. His visa expired on June 30, 1972. On October 11, 1973, the District Director of the Immigration and Naturalization Service ordered Chadha to show cause why he should not be deported for having "remained in the United States for a longer time than permitted." Pursuant to § 242(b) of the Immigration and Nationality Act (Act), a deportation hearing was held before an Immigration Judge on January 11, 1974. Chadha conceded that he was deportable for overstaying his visa, and the hearing was adjourned to enable him to file an application for suspension of deportation under § 244(a)(1) of the Act. Section 244(a)(1), at the time in question, provided:

> As hereinafter prescribed in this section, the Attorney General may, in his discretion, suspend deportation and adjust the status to that of an alien lawfully admitted for permanent residence, in the case of an alien who applies to the Attorney General for suspension of deportation and—

> (1) is deportable under any law of the United States except the provisions specified in paragraph (2) of this subsection; has been physically present in the United States

for a continuous period of not less than seven years immediately preceding the date of such application, and proves that during all of such period he was and is a person of good moral character; and is a person whose deportation would, in the opinion of the Attorney General, result in extreme hardship to the alien or to his spouse, parent, or child, who is a citizen of the United States or an alien lawfully admitted for permanent residence.

[**Translation:** In this section, the U.S. Supreme Court reviewed the first part of the Attorney General's enablement, which said that if an immigrant overstayed his or her visa, they could be allowed to appeal a deportation order if having to leave would be a hardship— This is about what used to be section 244(a)(1) of the Immigration and Nationality Act—now revised since this case.]

After Chadha submitted his application for suspension of deportation, the deportation hearing was resumed on February 7, 1974. On the basis of evidence adduced at the hearing, affidavits submitted with the application, and the results of a character investigation conducted by the INS, the Immigration Judge, on June 25, 1974, ordered that Chadha's deportation be suspended. The Immigration Judge found that Chadha met the requirements of § 244(a)(1): he had resided continuously in the United States for over seven years, was of good moral character, and would suffer "extreme hardship" if deported.

* * *

[**Translation:**The Supreme Court is summarizing that Chadha won his case in front of the Immigration Judge, which we all know by now.]

Once the Attorney General's recommendation for suspension of Chadha's deportation was conveyed to Congress, Congress had the power under § 244(c)(2) of the Act to veto the Attorney General's determination that Chadha should not be deported. Section 244(c)(2) provides:

(2) In the case of an alien specified in paragraph (1) of subsection (a) of this subsection—

if during the session of the Congress at which a case is reported, or prior to the close of the session of the Congress next following the session at which a case is reported, ei-

Immigration and Naturalization Service v. Chadha (1983)

ther the Senate or the House of Representatives passes a resolution stating in substance that it does not favor the suspension of such deportation, the Attorney General shall thereupon deport such alien or authorize the alien's voluntary departure at his own expense under the order of deportation in the manner provided by law. If, within the time above specified, neither the Senate nor the House of Representatives shall pass such a resolution, the Attorney General shall cancel deportation proceedings.

The June 25, 1974, order of the Immigration Judge suspending Chadha's deportation remained outstanding as a valid order for a year and a half. For reasons not disclosed by the record, Congress did not exercise the veto authority reserved to it under § 244(c)(2) until the first session of the 94th Congress. This was the final session in which Congress, pursuant to § 244(c)(2), could act to veto the Attorney General's determination that Chadha should not be deported. The session ended on December 19, 1975. Absent congressional action, Chadha's deportation proceedings would have been canceled after this date and his status adjusted to that of a permanent resident alien.

On December 12, 1975, Representative Eilberg, Chairman of the Judiciary Subcommittee on Immigration, Citizenship, and International Law, introduced a resolution opposing "the granting of permanent residence in the United States to [six] aliens," including Chadha. The resolution was referred to the House Committee on the Judiciary. On December 16, 1975, the resolution was discharged from further consideration by the House Committee on the Judiciary and submitted to the House of Representatives for a vote.

The resolution had not been printed and was not made available to other Members of the House prior to or at the time it was voted on. So far as the record before us shows, the House consideration of the resolution was based on Representative Eilberg's statement from the floor that

> [i]t was the feeling of the committee, after reviewing 340 cases, that the aliens contained in the resolution [Chadhaand five others] did not meet these statutory requirements, particularly as it relates to hardship; and it is the opinion of the committee that their deportation should not be suspended.

The resolution was passed without debate or recorded vote. Since the House action was pursuant to § 244(c)(2), the resolution was not treated as [a] legislative act; it was not submitted to the Senate or presented to the President for his action.

[**Translation:** At the last minute legally possible, the House of Representatives said the legal equivalent of, "You have got to be kidding me," and under section (244)(c)(2) overturned the Attorney General's suspension of Chada's deportation, telling Chadha to go home.]

After the House veto of the Attorney General's decision to allow Chadha to remain in the United States, the Immigration Judge reopened the deportation proceedings to implement the House order deporting Chadha. Chadha moved to terminate the proceedings on the ground that § 244(c)(2) is unconstitutional. The Immigration Judge held that he had no authority to rule on the constitutional validity of § 244(c)(2).

[**Translation:** Chadha appealed to the INS for a reversal of the House's deportation order, but the INS said they couldn't help him because, under their enabling statute, in this case the House was the boss over them.]

On November 8, 1976, Chadha was ordered deported pursuant to the House action. Chadha appealed the deportation order to the Board of Immigration Appeals, again contending that § 244(c)(2) is unconstitutional. The Board held that it had "no power to declare unconstitutional an act of Congress," and Chadha's appeal was dismissed.

Pursuant to § 106(a) of the Act, Chadha filed a petition for review of the deportation order in the United States Court of Appeals for the Ninth Circuit. The Immigration and Naturalization Service agreed with Chadha's position before the Court of Appeals and joined him in arguing that § 244(c)(2) is unconstitutional. In light of the importance of the question, the Court of Appeals invited both the Senate and the House of Representatives to file briefs amici curiae.

[**Translation:** *Amici curiae* means "friends of the court." Because neither the House nor the Senate were parties in the case and the INS and Chadha were on the same side with regard to the Constitutional issue, the court invited both Chambers of Congress—the House and the Senate—to bring their arguments to the table.]

After full briefing and oral argument, the Court of Appeals held that the House was without constitutional authority to order Chadha's de-

Immigration and Naturalization Service v. Chadha (1983)

portation; accordingly it directed the Attorney General "to cease and desist from taking any steps to deport this alien based upon the resolution enacted by the House of Representatives." The essence of its holding was that § 244(c)(2) violates the constitutional doctrine of separation of powers.

We granted certiorari in Nos. 80-2170 and 80-2171, and postponed consideration of our jurisdiction over the appeal...and we now affirm.

[**Translation:** The Court of Appeals said that the enabling statute section 244(c)(2) was unconstitutional based on the problems talked about in this textbook just before this case. The U.S. Supreme Court agreed to take a look, but they ended up agreeing with what the Court of Appeals said.]

* * *

The congressional veto provision in § 244(c)(2) is unconstitutional.

(a) The prescription for legislative action in Art. I, § 1—requiring all legislative powers to be vested in a Congress consisting of a Senate and a House of Representatives—and § 7—requiring every bill passed by the House and Senate, before becoming law, to be presented to the President, and, if he disapproves, to be repassed by two-thirds of the Senate and House—represents the Framers' decision that the legislative power of the Federal Government be exercised in accord with a single, finely wrought and exhaustively considered procedure. This procedure is an integral part of the constitutional design for the separation of powers.

(b) Here, the action taken by the House pursuant to § 244(c)(2) was essentially legislative in purpose and effect, and thus was subject to the procedural requirements of Art. I, § 7, for legislative action: passage by a majority of both Houses and presentation to the President. The one-House veto operated to overrule the Attorney General and mandate Chadha's deportation. The veto's legislative character is confirmed by the character of the congressional action it supplants; that is, absent the veto provision of § 244(c)(2), neither the House nor the Senate, or both acting together, could effectively require the

Attorney General to deport an alien once the Attorney General, in the exercise of legislatively delegated authority, had determined that the alien should remain in the United States. Without the veto provision, this could have been achieved only by legislation requiring deportation. A veto by one House under § 244(c)(2) cannot be justified as an attempt at amending the standards set out in § 244(a)(1), or as a repeal of § 244 as applied to Chadha. The nature of the decision implemented by the one-House veto further manifests its legislative character. Congress must abide by its delegation of authority to the Attorney General until that delegation is legislatively altered or revoked. Finally, the veto's legislative character is confirmed by the fact that, when the Framers intended to authorize either House of Congress to act alone and outside of its prescribed bicameral legislative role, they narrowly and precisely defined the procedure for such action in the Constitution.

[**Translation:** The Supreme Court explains itself, with a lot of words. See an explanation of this constitutional argument in the three or four paragraphs before this case starts in the textbook. Chadha wins once and for all—and 244(c)(2) loses—as in it is unconstitutional. The House of Representatives also loses (even though it was not a party)—as in it cannot overturn Mr. Chadhas deportation.]

Many have questioned the Chadha case and the amount of power that fell into the Executive Branch without Congress fully intending to delegate it there. Nothing stops Congress from enacting legislation to correct a perceived wrong or from drafting legislation that prohibits the exercise of Executive discretion. On the other hand, Congress can no longer retain oversight once authority has been delegated, and this further distances the regulators from the voters.

Separation of Powers

Separation of powers remains a controversial area, and the Judiciary, Congress, and the President frequently battle each other for control. A recent case involving American citizen Jose Padilla illustrates where conflicts can arise in a dramatic way.

Jose Padilla is an American citizen who was born in Brooklyn, New York. In 2002, while the country was still reeling from the attacks of September 11, 2001, Padilla was arrested at Chicago O'Hare airport after returning from a trip through the Middle East. Padilla had traveled to Egypt, Saudi Arabia, Afghanistan, Pakistan, and Iraq, where the government alleges that he collaborated and conspired with Al Qaeda and plotted terrorist acts.

President Bush issued an order to detain Padilla as an "enemy combatant," claiming authority under the powers given to him by Congress under the Authorization for Use of Military Force (AUMF).

In a highly contentious ruling, the Fourth Circuit Court of Appeals upheld the President's power, but the matter was destined for the Supreme Court. Prior to a Supreme Court ruling on the issue, the President ordered that Padilla be transferred to a civilian prison where he was formally charged with various counts of conspiracy and provided the due process ordinarily afforded American citizens charged with criminal acts. (He was convicted in August 2007 after a day and a half of deliberation following a three-month criminal trial.)

The issue of whether Congress really delegated the authority to the President to hold Padilla as an enemy combatant (which involves the complete withholding of all civil rights), or if it did, whether it was Constitutional for Congress to do so, is still sharply debated.

Obviously, the manner in which the executive branch characterized Padilla influenced the rights afforded (or in this case not afforded) to him, but the courts ultimately would have been able to put that characterization to a Constitutional test. However, there are certain instances where the courts have no say in the policy of law enforcement. That is where the Executive Branch declines to prosecute.

That refusal to prosecute can create substantial controversy, the issue of medical marijuana is an example of that.

Concurrent State and Federal Power

The most interesting political controversies in recent years have been where there is potentially concurrent state and federal power. The federal government can wholly occupy an area and preempt states from legislating in that realm under the Supremacy Clause of the Constitution. However there are many instances where states can co-regulate along with the federal government, and those areas can generate legal battles. The governor of Arizona, Jan Brewer, and President Obama have engaged in conflict over what is properly state as opposed to federal power—and their somewhat dramatic confrontations have made headlines. Examples follow:

Marijuana is an illegal drug under federal law. Over half the states, however, have passed medical marijuana laws that allow the use of marijuana for medical reasons. Theoretically, federal law should preempt states from allowing the use of marijuana for medical purposes but from a practical perspective, nothing can compel states to enforce the federal prohibition against marijuana. The U.S. Supreme Court has upheld federal authority to prohibit states from legalizing marijuana, but even the Supreme Court cannot compel the states to prosecute what the states have decided to allow. In those states that have legalized medical marijuana, only the FBI can come in and prosecute charges in this realm. The threat of federal prosecution was significant until President Obama changed the game.

The executive branch can decide which laws to enforce on the federal level, and which laws to ignore. President Obama issued an executive order declaring that the FBI would no longer enforce federal marijuana laws where the user complies with state mandates. This theoretically means that although marijuana remains illegal under federal statutes, nobody will be charged with a federal crime if they are acting in compliance with state medical marijuana laws. There is no federal statute or court precedent that mandates this, just an executive decision on the use of federal resources. Executive orders can change with administrations, but they generally have staying power through administrations until they are codified, in order to maintain stability. They can, as is obvious here, have significant policy impact on the nation.

For Arizona, the story does not end with this truce between the federal and state governments. The governor of Arizona did not want this truce. After Arizona voters passed a medical marijuana initiative permitting its use under narrow circumstances and regulating its distribution through state licensure, the state began its own battle between its executive and legislative branches of government (in this case the legislative function was served by the voters themselves who passed the medical marijuana proposition). Governor Brewer was virulently opposed to the medical marijuana legislation, and came up with a strategy to stall the statute from taking effect. She instructed the state employees not to license marijuana dispensaries until she could obtain a declaratory judgment from the federal courts saying that licensing the distribution of marijuana was legal under federal law. The basis of the governor's claim was that state employees who violated federal rules could be subject to federal prosecution.

In January 2012, the court dismissed Governor Brewer's claim, indicating that there is no genuine threat of federal prosecution of state employees who issue dispensary licenses under Arizona's law, in part because of President Obama's executive order. No appeal was taken from that dismissal, but Arizona's executive branch is moving very slowly to issue permits. Currently, Arizona's Department of Health Services is undertaking a lottery system to determine who, among those who apply, can have licenses, given that the medical marijuana statute significantly limits the number of dispensaries in each area. In addition, local zoning ordinances have preempted many locations from eligibility for dis-

pensary licenses based on security and community concerns.(6) It is expected that it will take some time before dispensaries become accessible across the state.

With both the President's executive order, and the Governor's response, the state and federal executive branches trumped the judicial and legislature branches, at least temporarily.

More Power Struggles

The marijuana games pale by comparison to the recently waged battle over immigration enforcement issues between the state of Arizona and the federal government. In frustration related to the burden created by the influx of undocumented aliens, Arizona passed a bill known as Senate Bill (SB) 1070, which, among other things,

purported to make being an unregistered alien a misdemeanor under Arizona state law. The U.S. Supreme Court decided the constitutionality of SB 1070 in June 2012.

Below is a summary of the conclusions of the court with regard to the constitutionality of SB 1070.(7)

Arizona et al. v. United States (2012)

United States Supreme Court

No. 11–182. Argued April 25, 2012—Decided June 25, 2012

Syllabus

An Arizona statute known as S. B. 1070 was enacted in 2010 to address pressing issues related to the large number of unlawful aliens in the State. The United States sought to enjoin the law as preempted. The District Court issued a preliminary injunction preventing four of its provisions from taking effect. Section 3 makes failure to comply with federal alien-registration requirements a state misdemeanor; §5(C) makes it a misdemeanor for an unauthorized alien to seek or engage in work in the State; §6 authorizes state and local officers to arrest without a warrant a person "the officer has probable cause to believe…has committed any public offense that makes the person removable from the United States"; and §2(B) requires officers conducting a stop, detention, or arrest to make efforts, in some circumstances, to verify the person's immigration status with the Federal Government. The Ninth Circuit affirmed, agreeing that the United States had established a likelihood of success on its preemption claims.

Held:

1. The Federal Government's broad, undoubted power over immigration and alien status rests, in part, on its constitutional power to "establish an uniform Rule of Naturalization," Federal governance is extensive and complex. Among other things, federal law specifies categories of aliens who are ineligible to be admitted to the United States,…requires aliens to register with the Federal Government and to carry proof of status, imposes sanctions on employers who hire unauthorized workers, and specifies which aliens may be removed and the procedures for doing so. Removal is a civil matter, and one of its principal features is the broad discretion exercised by immigration officials, who must decide whether to pursue removal at all. Immigration and Customs Enforcement (ICE), an agency within the Department of Homeland Security, is responsible for identifying, apprehending, and removing illegal aliens. It also operates the Law Enforcement Support Center, which provides immigration status information to federal, state, and local officials around the clock.

The Supremacy Clause gives Congress the power to preempt state law.… States are precluded from regulating conduct in a field that Congress has determined must be regulated by its exclusive governance.…

Sections 3, 5(C), and 6 of S. B. 1070 are preempted by federal law. Pp. 8–19.

* * *

[However, Section 2(B) of SB 1070, the part of the statute that requires an Arizona arresting officer to inquire into the immigration status of a detainee, is constitutional if used properly.]

(b) This Court finds unpersuasive the argument that…§2(B) must be held preempted at this stage.

Arizona et al. v. United States (2012)

(1) The mandatory nature of the status checks does not interfere with the federal immigration scheme. Consultation between federal and state officials is an important feature of the immigration system. In fact, Congress has encouraged the sharing of information about possible immigration violations. The federal scheme thus leaves room for a policy requiring state officials to contact ICE as a routine matter.

(2) It is not clear at this stage and on this record that §2(B), in practice, will require state officers to delay the release of detainees for no reason other than to verify their immigration status. **This would raise constitutional concerns.** [emphasis added]

[End of summary of Court's conclusions.]

Still, the battle between the Arizona governor and the president goes on....

While review of SB 1070 was pending in the U.S. Supreme Court in August 2011, Secretary of Homeland Security Janet Napolitano (a former governor of Arizona) set forth an executive policy to prioritize deportation proceedings and give work permits to individuals waiting for a hearing as long as those individuals have not been involved in criminal activity. According to a news report on August 18, 2011 (formerly published online at www.bnd.com/2011/08/19/1827014/us-undertaking-case-by-case-review.html#ixzz1VVjosNWE):

"The Obama administration said Thursday it will allow many undocumented immigrants facing deportation the chance to stay in this country and apply for a work permit, while focusing on removing from the U.S. convicted criminals and those who might be a national security or public safety threat.

That will mean a case-by-case review of approximately 300,000 undocumented immigrants facing possible deportation in federal immigration courts, Homeland Security Secretary Janet Napolitano said in announcing the policy change.

Advocates for an immigration overhaul have said that the administration, by placing all undocumented immigrants in the same category for deportation, has failed to live up to its promise to only deport the 'worst of the worst,' as President Barack Obama has said.

...[The] chairman of the Latino Roundtable of Southwestern Illinois, said the decision will help law enforcement focus on issues like human trafficking and drug-running instead of arresting farm workers.

'We're spending money trying to deport people that are trying to feed their families, go to school, and want to be contributing taxpayers,' Avendano said. 'I think it is a good move for the president to try to get law enforcement and Homeland Security to look where the problems are and where the priorities should be, not to blame everything on people who are undocumented.... We all agree we have to prosecute the people who are making our community unsafe, regardless of their race or immigration status or socioeconomic status.'"

Secretary Napolitano (who serves under the President) has created a barrier for Arizona police officers who now must investigate immigration status under the constitutional remains of SB 1070. Should those officers discover that a detainee is indeed an undocumented alien, the officers must release that alien unless he or she has committed a crime (other than being here illegally). ICE (Immigration and Customs Enforcement) cannot use its resources to detain and deport undocumented aliens who are not felons under Napolitano's orders.

Judicial Function and Judicial Review

Most agencies have a judicial function as well as an executive and legislative role. When a dispute arises (such as a rule being challenged or the imposition of a sanction being opposed), the complainant must avail itself of all of the judicial functions within the agency before it can pursue any relief from an outside court. This is called "exhausting administrative remedies." Hearings and appeals in front of a commissioner or an administrative law judge (such as the hearing Mr. Chadha had to suspend his deportation) are part of the judicial function of an agency.

The process of taking an agency to court is called judicial review. It is important to distinguish between the judicial function *within* an agency and judicial review by an outside court. While there are a variety of claims that can be brought within an agency under its own judicial function, the grounds for judicial review by a court are extremely narrow.

Neither dissatisfaction with a decision nor disagreement with interpretation of the facts are grounds to ask a court to review an agency's conduct. The separation of powers would require allowing the Executive Branch to administer the congressional mandate without undo interference from the Judicial Branch (the third branch of our government). But separation of powers co-exists with the notion of checks and balances. Neither the Executive nor the Legislative Branch can run roughshod over the Constitution or its inherent notions of due process. In a tenuous balance, the narrow grounds for judicial review must be based on one of the following allegations:

1) that the enabling legislation unconstitutionally delegated power (power that it had no right to give) to the agency;

2) that the agency acted outside of its enabling legislation, thereby exerting power that it did not have; or

3) that there was *no* evidentiary support for the agency's conclusions. (It is not enough to prove that there was better evidence in support of the opposite conclusion.)

If one of these three conditions can be proven, the agency's decision will be reversed. If the validity of a rule is successfully challenged, the rule will be struck down. This is true whether the court agrees or disagrees with the substance of the rule.

On the other hand, if none of the conditions for judicial review are met, the agency will be upheld even when its decisions are only marginally rational. The power rests with the agency to effectuate the will of Congress, and though legal protests against agency decisions are many, victories are few.

Obviously, agencies cannot run amuck without reaction by Congress

and the voters. At one point, the Internal Revenue Service had been used by the dominant political party as a tool against its opponents. When an agency's implementations begin to appear irrational or abusive, Congress will generally step in and amend the agency's power. This is what happened when the IRS abuses were brought to light.

The courts, however, have less ability than Congress to interfere with agency conduct. In the Chadha case, the court completely supported the agency and overturned the statute section that constrained its power. Probably the most famous case regarding the power of an administrative agency is the *FCC v. Pacifica Foundation* case, where the agency's exertion of power was questioned in terms of whether it was ever given the authority to act as it did. After a careful review of the enabling legislation, agency power was pitted directly against the First Amendment.

Because the First Amendment has not been discussed in this book, the following information is important for understanding the FCC case.

- In this case, the word obscenity is used analogously to the word pornography. Obscenity does not mean a dirty word.

- Pornography is not protected by the First Amendment. While the courts may not have clearly defined exactly what pornography is, that does not pose a problem in the FCC case. By stipulation of the litigants and in the Court's own perception, the speech in this case falls within the First Amendment.

Because the *FCC v. Pacifica Foundation* case is extraordinarily complicated, and because the FCC's power has been further clarified by the Supreme Court since, this case is presented *only* in paraphrase and/or summary here.

Author's translation of the FCC v. Pacifica Foundation (1978)

A satiric humorist named George Carlin recorded a 12-minute monologue entitled "Filthy Words" that was filled with (you guessed it) filthy words. The recording was played by Pacifica Foundation's New York radio station at about 2 o'clock in the afternoon on Tuesday, October 30, 1973. A few weeks later, a man wrote a letter to the FCC saying that he had heard the broadcast while driving with his young son and he was less than happy about it.

Pacifica admitted that it had aired the monologue as the complaining letter said, but argued it had the right to do so. The FCC disagreed and claimed it had the right to impose penalties (although this time it just issued a warning.)

The FCC relied on two different enabling statutes for its decision. First was section 1464 of the Communications Act, which forbids the use of "any obscene, indecent, or profane language by means of radio communications." The second is section 303 of the Communications Act, which requires the Commission to "encourage the larger and more effective use of radio in the public interest." The FCC opined that fewer people would listen to the radio if they believed they might be blasted with the filthy words in Carlin's monologue.

Pacifica had an enabling (or more accurately a disabling) statute, too—arguing that section 326 of the Communications Act specifically prohibits the FCC from engaging in censorship of broadcast material. Pacifica also waived the First Amendment flag arguing that the Constitution is not too fond of censorship either.

The Supreme Court found no conflict between sections 326 and 1464 even though section 326 means, "FCC, thou shalt not censor broadcasts," and section 1464 means "FCC, thou shalt definitely keep potty talk off the air." The Court found that because Congress enacted both sections 326 and 1464 simultaneously, it must have meant that the censorship restraint on the FCC was not intended to apply to potty talk.

The Court gave a lot of consideration to the First Amendment issue, but found for Pacifica in spite of its also finding the monologue to fall within the First Amendment's protection. The Court reasoned that communication containing patently offensive sexual and excretory language need not be protected in every context.

This case emphasizes that different forms of expression present different First Amendment problems and different levels of protection. This is especially true of context: A spontaneous demonstration down a busy street at rush hour will likely be stopped. Small numbers of individuals holding political signs while standing on public sidewalks is likely to be protected. But in this case, it is content that is an issue along with context. In that regard, the Court noted that of all forms of communication, it is broadcasting that has received the *least* First Amendment protection.

The Court noted, "broadcasting is uniquely accessible to children, even those too young to read.... Pacifica's broadcast could have enlarged a child's vocabulary in an instant." (The Court adopted the reasoning that most parents quickly learn: kids repeat exactly what we do not want them to have heard in the first place.)

The Court emphasized the narrowness of its holding. It supported the FCC's decision based on a "nuisance rationale under which context is all-important." The time of day that this broadcast aired was emphasized by the Commission.

More law has followed in the recent decade.

Among other things, the above case illustrates the enormous power that has been delegated to the FCC, which is representative of the power of many administrative agencies. In this case, the FCC virtually has the power to keep satirical political content off the air if it contains dirty words.

The broadcast media continues to struggle with testing the balance between the freedom of expression promised by the First Amendment and regulatory constraints imposed by the FCC. CBS television was engaged in a four-year-long dispute with the FCC over a $550,000 fine that the Commissioner levied against it after an alleged

Author's translation of the FCC v. Pacifica Foundation (1978)

"wardrobe malfunction" during the Super Bowl 2004 half-time show. The fine was levied because, during that show, Janet Jackson (she claims unintentionally) revealed her breast on national network television for a fraction of a second. After losing all available appeals within the FCC, CBS asked for judicial review and won a reversal of the fine in the Third Circuit Court of Appeals. The Third Circuit determined that the FCC rules in place at the time of that Super Bowl would not have permitted a fine for "fleeting profanity" such as that which occurred in this case. The matter was remanded back to the FCC to give it the opportunity to articulate a rule that would apply in the future to this type of occurrence, which the FCC did, but the FCC was not allowed to change its rules retroactively to apply to CBS.

In 2009, the U.S. Supreme Court reversed a Second Circuit Court decision that supported the Fox network's position that the FCC's indecency rule was arbitrary and capricious. (ABC was a codefendant with respect to fines levied against it for a shower scene that showed a buttocks for seven seconds in an "NYPD Blue" episode.) (8) The Second Circuit didn't address the First Amendment issue of whether or not the FCC rule itself, banning all fleeting profanity, was unconstitutional for overly restricting speech under the First Amendment. The U.S. Supreme Court also did not address the First Amendment issue (since it was not something from which the appeal was taken), but disagreed with and re-

versed the Second Circuit Court, finding for the FCC in asserting that the new rule itself was not arbitrary or capricious on its face. The matter was remanded back to the Second Circuit for reconsideration of the Constitutional issues.

Then, in 2012, the U.S. Supreme Court heard the same Fox case again, after the Second Circuit Court considered the constitutional issues and determined that the FCC rules as applied to both Fox and ABC were unconstitutional due to vagueness. This time the Supreme Court found for both Fox and ABC, indicating that the FCC fleeting profanity rule was not enacted until after the shows had broadcast, and any previous rule was unconstitutionally vague as applied to these particular programs.(9)

Again the Supreme Court did not decide on the constitutionality of the new fleeting profanity ban in terms of whether the rule imposed undue restraints of free speech under the First Amendment. However, there was a cautionary tone to the Court's final conclusion, which reads as follows:

"It is necessary to make three observations about this decision's scope. First, because the Court resolves these cases on fair notice grounds under the Due Process Clause, it need not address the First Amendment implications of the Commission's indecency policy or reconsider *Pacifica* at this time. Second, because the Court rules that Fox and ABC lacked notice at the time of their broadcasts that their material could be found actionably indecent under then-existing policies, the Court need not address the constitutionality of the current indecency policy as expressed in the *Golden Globes* Order and subsequent adjudications. Third,

this opinion leaves the Commission free to modify its current indecency policy in light of its determination of the public interest and applicable legal requirements and leaves courts free to review the current, or any modified, policy in light of its content and application."

Commentary

We are, as a nation, conflicted with regard to administrative agencies. On the one hand, we appreciate their efficiency as compared to the political process; they are generally staffed with knowledgeable experts, and they have a degree of separation from the political whims of the short term. On the other hand, although they may be efficient compared to Congress, by most other standards they are laborious bureaucracies. They have significant power, no direct link to the voter, and sometimes they act like bullies.

The Fox case demonstrates that an agency (the FCC) can tighten its regulatory authority over time, changing acceptable conduct to unacceptable even if that is not the best policy—just a permissible one under the enabling statute, so long as the agency does not act in a manner that offends the Constitution.

Most people would agree that in market failure areas, we need regulatory agencies to keep the market from harming itself or being grossly inefficient. Arguments around regulation tend to focus on insuring reasonableness on the part of the regulators, and on how to craft regulation that is the least onerous and the most beneficial.

Notes

1. Bureau of Labor Statistics: http://www.bls.gov/opub/mlr/1985/10/art1full.pdf

2. U.S. Government Web site of independent executive agencies:
   http://www.usa.gov/Agencies/Federal/Independent.shtml

3. http://www.whitehouse.gov/administration/cabinet

4. http://www.defense.gov/orgchart/

5. City of Mesa Web site:
   http://citydoc.cityofmesa.org/citydoc1/groups/public/documents/
   jobdescriptions/c5_004747.pdf

6. http://www.azcentral.com/news/articles/2011/05/01/20110501marijuana-dis-
   pensaries-zoning-rules.html

7. *Arizona v. United States*, U.S. Supreme Court, June 2012

8. *Federal Communications Commission et al. v. Fox Television Stations, Inc. et
   al.*, June 2009

9. *Federal Communications Commission et al. v. Fox Television Stations, Inc. et
   al.*, June 2012

Chapter 5
Interstate Commerce

From the beginning, and as was touched upon in Chapter 4, our country has struggled with the tension between states' rights and federal power. The evolution of law moving the dividing line between state and federal power is directly correlated to the greatest moral and ethical conflict this country ever faced—slavery and its vestiges.

Issues surrounding slavery, racism, the Civil War, and the consequent shift to greater federal power will be discussed at length in this chapter. First, though, it is important to introduce some constitutional concepts that have not yet been presented or only superficially referenced so far in this book.

Full Faith and Credit

Article IV of the Constitution says, "Full faith and credit shall be given in each state to the public acts, records, and judicial proceedings of every other state." Referred to as the "Full Faith and Credit" clause, this part of the Constitution allows the United States to function in most respects as a seamless national entity.

The clause is intended to be practical. It mandates that a birth certificate from one state is proof of birth for every state. With rare exceptions, the prevailing party of a lawsuit involving one state (New Jersey for example) can enforce its judgment in any other state (California for example). A marriage that takes place in a state that allows 18-year-olds to marry without parental consent is a valid marriage in every other state, even in those states that have different rules about the age people can marry without parental consent. Again with rare exceptions, whether or not states have differing laws, each has to credit the actions, judgments, and records of every other state.

Over the years, Full Faith and Credit has become controversial. In areas of significant moral concern, some states have passed laws denying credit to certain actions or judgments of other states. These laws have generally been held to be constitutional. For example, in the 19th century, several states allowed polygamy. Those states that rigorously disagreed with the notion of multiple marriages were permitted to disregard those marriages, not giving Full Faith and Credit to their validity even though the marriages were valid in the states where they were performed.

However, as a general rule, the courts have been reluctant to allow states to interfere with the notion of Full Faith and Credit. For example, as noted in an earlier chapter, prior to *Roe v. Wade*, California had legalized medical abortions performed for the emotional health of the mother. Some anti-choice states considered legislation to make it illegal for anyone, including a parent, to take a minor to California for the purpose of allowing that minor to get an abortion. The courts would most likely have found any such statute unconstitutional for (among other things) violating Full Faith and Credit. That clause generally prevents a state from punishing a person for conduct that occurred in a state where the conduct was lawful. The matter became irrelevant after *Roe v. Wade*.

More recent controversies surrounding the Full Faith and Credit clause involve what constitutes a marriage. The Massachusetts Supreme Judicial Court's case finding in 2004 that same-sex marriage could not be discriminated against under that state's constitution has created fear from other states that they may be compelled to recognize those marriages.

The question of whether those marriages must be given Full Faith and Credit in other states is the subject of much debate. Many states have passed laws that prohibit gay marriage, and the federal government has passed the Defense of Marriage Act (DOMA) specifically protecting states from having to acknowledge same-sex marriages even if they were lawfully formed in other states. On the other hand, in 2012, four states passed ballot measures specifically legalizing same-sex marriage. While the constitutionality of DOMA has been challenged, as of the end of 2012, the outcome is not known.

It is interesting that the characterization of marriage has been the subject of such considerable controversy in our history. Utah was not allowed to become a state until it banned polygamy. And Congress, in 1870, passed a law prohibiting anyone who believed in polygamy from holding public office. It is unlikely that if one state legalizes polygamy, other states would be required to give those marriages full faith and credit, but it is an argument that may happen as tolerances and perceptions change.

The Supreme Law of the Land

Article VI of the Constitution says that federal law is the "supreme law of the land; and the judges in every state shall be bound thereby...." Known as the Supremacy Clause or the Pre-emption Doctrine, this part of the Constitution says that where there is a federal law, a conflicting state law is invalid.

State law is pre-empted by federal law in the same area.

At other times, state and federal law can operate supportively with each other. For example, federal law controls the national minimum wage. State law can increase the minimum within its own borders, however a state statute that attempts to set a state minimum wage that is lower than the federally set level is unconstitutional; it violates the Supremacy Clause.

In our early history, there were certain areas left entirely within state control. Most criminal statutes were state-based. States controlled education and "police power." Each state mandated its own rules for licensing businesses and medical doctors and for determining safety rules in the workplace, etc.

States still control those areas, but in certain subsets they no longer have exclusive power. Federal power has expanded widely into these domains, allowing concurrent jurisdiction in many areas. Physicians must be licensed in the state in which they practice, but the Drug Enforcement Administration (DEA) and the Food and Drug Administration (FDA) federally control the availability of drugs and how doctors are allowed to prescribe them. Workplace safety is regulated at both the state and federal levels.

This complicated evolution can be summarized as follows: The Constitution provided for very limited federal power when the nation was first formed, but things changed after the Civil War.

The Freedoms Guaranteed by the Constitution

The freedoms that we are guaranteed in both the Constitution and the Bill of Rights protect us from interference by the *government* in our private lives. It is critically important to keep in mind that *nothing* in the Constitution protects us from the business world or its prerogatives. Who gets hired, fired, included, or excluded by private sector entities is not addressed in the Constitution.

In part this is because there is theoretically no benefit from governmental tampering with the operation of free enterprise. Business decisions are presumably guided by the free market's "invisible hand" which, if functioning properly, propels commerce where there is profitability and restrains it where there is not, letting natural laws of supply and demand democratically control the production and distribution of goods and services.

However, the world as an imperfect place creates an imperfect free market. Our history of racism and gender bias in both the public and private sectors of the United States ultimately distorted both the social fabric of the country and the optimal functioning of our free market. This distortion compelled governmental intervention, but that intervention was not easily accomplished.

The Tenth Amendment

As noted previously, the framers of the Constitution implemented safeguards to control federal power once it was established. The states did not want to "reinvent" a King George III by developing a domestic federal government that had the potential to become a tyrant. State power was protected against the "tyranny of the majority" by the creation of the Senate. In that co-equal chamber of the legislative branch, each state has equal representation irrespective of size, and no law can pass without the Senate's consent. However, the existence of the Senate alone was insufficient to insure that the federal government would not take or usurp power from the states.

It was in this spirit that the framers included the Tenth Amendment in the Bill of Rights. Known as the States' Rights amendment, the Tenth Amendment says, "The powers not delegated to the United States by the Constitution, nor prohibited by it to the States, are reserved to the States respectively, or to the people." By limiting Congress to governing areas specifically enumerated in Article I, Section 8 of the Constitution, federal power was limited to the necessary minimum for which it was created.

Emancipation

In the Constitutional Convention of 1787, slavery was a contentious issue, left on the table for lack of the ability to form any consensus. Slavery was a moral anathema for the North but an economic foundation for the South. It persisted for almost 80 years after the Constitution was signed, until the conflict actually split the nation. The South, facing the forced emancipation of the slaves by federal law, attempted to secede from the union. The Civil War forced the South to remain unified with the northern states, and two critical Constitutional amendments followed.

In 1865, the Thirteenth Amendment, abolishing all forms of slavery and involuntary servitude, was ratified. Congress understood that this amendment alone would not end slavery, should any given state seriously attempt to circumvent its intent. And so, in 1868, Congress enacted the Fourteenth Amendment to insure that former slaves would be given the opportunity to live as free people. In this Amendment, the federal government for the first time dictated how states were to treat their citizens. The Fourteenth Amendment reads in relevant part:

> "No State shall make or enforce any law which shall abridge the privileges or immunities of citizens of the United States, nor shall any State deprive any person of life, liberty, or property, without *due process* of law; nor deny to any person within its ju-

risdiction *the equal protection of the laws.*" [Emphasis added.]

Particularly in its Due Process and Equal Protection clauses emphasized above, this amendment precluded any state from enforcing any law that would treat its minority citizens in a manner different than its majority under either federal law or under its own laws. (The Fifteenth Amendment, passed in 1870, provided similar assurances in terms of voting rights.) It also mandated that states give every citizen due process.

This change, though appearing to relate to issues connected to slavery, changed the way the United States functioned in general. The Bill of Rights had started out as a limitation on federal power. After the Civil War, the Fourteenth Amendment opened the gates of federal power and gave the United States control over how individual states treated their own citizens. It was the consummate role reversal.

Any student of American history knows that though the Civil War ended slavery, it did not attempt to remedy racism or discriminatory treatment. Neither the North nor the South were willing to absorb the notion of equality into their respective cultures—cultures that had always separated people by color, gender, and religion. The South was especially unwilling to change a culture that had partly rationalized slavery based on a self-aggrandizing perspective of white superiority. The North would be more liberal in tone, but its neighborhoods would still draw

racial boundaries, its schools would remain segregated, and its populations would remain isolated from each other. The "equal protection" guaranteed by the Fourteenth Amendment was severely limited by segregation and bias.

In 1896, 28 years after the passing of the Fourteenth Amendment, the case of *Plessy v. Ferguson* (1) was argued in the U.S. Supreme Court, challenging the South's rights to segregate public transportation within its own state boundaries. Lisa Cozzens, in her Web-published article entitled "Plessy v. Ferguson," summarizes the case as follows:

"On June 7, 1892, a 30-year-old colored shoe-maker named Homer Plessy was jailed for sitting in the 'White' car of the East Louisiana Railroad. Plessy was only one-eighths [sic] black and seven-eighths white, but under Louisiana law, he was considered black and therefore required to sit in the 'Colored' car. Plessy went to court and argued, in *Homer Adolph Plessy v. The State of Louisiana*, that the Separate Car Act violated the Thirteenth and Fourteenth Amendments to the Constitution. The judge at the trial was John Howard Ferguson, a lawyer from Massachusetts who had previously declared the Separate Car Act 'unconstitutional on trains that traveled through several states.' In Plessy's case, however, he decided that the state could choose to regulate railroad companies that operated only within Louisiana. He found Plessy guilty of refusing to leave the white car. Plessy appealed to the Supreme Court of Louisiana, which upheld Ferguson's decision. In 1896, the Supreme Court of the United States heard Plessy's case and found him guilty once again. Speaking for a seven-person majority, Justice Henry Brown wrote:

'That [the Separate Car Act] does not conflict with the Thirteenth Amendment, which abolished slavery…is too clear for argument…. A statute which implies merely a legal distinction between the white and colored races—a distinction which is founded in the color of the two races, and which must always exist so long as white men are distinguished from the other race by color—has no tendency to destroy the legal equality of the two races…. The object of the [Fourteenth Amendment] was undoubtedly to enforce the absolute equality of the two races before the law, but in the nature of things it could not have been intended to abolish distinctions based upon color, or to enforce social, as distinguished from political, equality or a commingling of the two races

upon terms unsatisfactory to either.'

The lone dissenter, Justice John Harlan, showed incredible foresight when he wrote:

'Our Constitution is color-blind, and neither knows nor tolerates classes among citizens. In respect of civil rights, all citizens are equal before the law…. In my opinion, the judgment this day rendered will, in time, prove to be quite as pernicious as the decision made by this tribunal in the Dred Scott case. The present decision, it may well be apprehended, will not only stimulate aggressions, more or less brutal and irritating, upon the admitted rights of colored citizens, but will encourage the belief that it is possible, by means of state enactments, to defeat the beneficent purposes which the people of the United States had in view when they adopted the recent amendments of the Constitution.'"(2)

The precedent set in *Plessy* remained law for 58 years. For 91 years after the emancipation of the slaves, and 86 years after the Constitution was amended to provide for equal protection of all citizens under the Fourteenth Amendment, forced segregation was considered to be constitutional.

Civil Rights

In early 1950, an embryonic civil rights movement awaited the opportunity to challenge the "separate but equal" doctrine. Schools across America, in the South and in the North, were segregated by law, custom, or both, and the impact on minority populations was measurable. The National Association for the Advancement of Colored People (NAACP) found the vehicle to test the "separate but equal" doctrine when the father of black third-grader Linda Brown complained about his daughter being prohibited from going to the neighborhood school only a few blocks from their home. Linda Brown had been required to walk an unsafe path for an unreasonable distance to go to the "colored" school. The Browns sued the school system of Topeka, Kansas, alleging that it violated Linda's rights under the Fourteenth Amendment's equal protection provisions. Others joined the suit, and it progressed through the lower courts to the U.S. Supreme Court. On May 17, 1954, more than three years after the case was tried in District Court, Chief Justice Earl Warren delivered the decision of a unanimous court in the case of *Brown v. Board of Education*:

> "We come then to the question presented: Does segregation of children in public schools solely on the basis of race, even though the physical facilities and other 'tangible' factors may be equal, deprive the children of the minority group of equal educational opportunities? We believe that it does…. We conclude that in the field of public education the doctrine of 'separate but equal' has no place. Separate educational facilities are inherently unequal. Therefore, we hold that the plaintiffs and others similarly situated for whom the actions have been brought are, by reason of the segregation complained of, deprived of the equal protection of the laws guaranteed by the Fourteenth Amendment."

The Private Sector

The public school system was transformed after the *Brown v. Board of Education* decision. Mandatory busing was instituted in cities across the country so that neighborhoods that were divided by color would not be functional barriers to desegregating the schools. There were small rebellions—hostilities were acted out on playgrounds and in town halls alike.

Public employment, education, transportation, and service were all desegregated as a matter of law, but not in a harmonious way. One reason for the continuing racial tension was obvious. Although the public schools and the colleges were forcibly desegregated, the private system of enterprise that fueled the country's wealth was still segregated, not by law, but by racial bias. The Fourteenth Amendment now protected every citizen against political inequity, but the private sector was unaffected. To the extent that it absorbed prejudice and bias, the private sector was the mechanism through which inequality still flourished.

During the early 1960s, major companies still openly enforced segregated, discriminatory work environments. One sobering example was recited in the U.S. Supreme Court case of *Griggs v. Duke Power Co.* Prior to the Civil Rights Act, the highest paid black employee at Duke Power Co. was paid less than the lowest paid white employee. Irrespective of the quality and effort of an employee of color, he or she could never earn as much as the lowest paid white person working at Duke Power. For the most part, employment possibilities offered no genuine opportunity for African Americans, and opportunities for black entrepreneurship were stymied by both bias in the education system and a banking system enmeshed in the same racism that plagued the rest of American society.

The Equal Protection clause could not be invoked to solve this enormous social problem. That portion of the Constitution only applies to governmental conduct. To the extent that racial discrimination was the result of

personal prejudice, the government could not interfere on constitutional grounds.

In addition, there were political reasons for the government to be reticent to pass laws to resolve this problem. Private enterprise had always been perceived to be the same as other forms of private property. The notion that a person would not be the master of his or her own home was unthinkable. The distinction between a private home and a private business had not yet been explored by most Americans, despite the fact that big business with dispersed corporate ownership had even then become the most significant form of enterprise in the U.S. free market.

By the 1960s, federal legislators were inclined to move toward remediating the clear societal inequities being suffered by minorities in the United States, but the Constitution itself was an obstacle.

The Tenth Amendment (discussed earlier in this chapter), which was enacted so that states would maintain their right to self-determination, now constrained the federal government from attempting to exert power in an area not specifically delegated to it in Article I, Section 8 of the Constitution. Although states had the right to pass laws individually and independently to protect people of color in the private sector, there could be no uniform national policy if the Tenth Amendment precluded federal action.

In 1963, President John F. Kennedy had been assassinated, the American civil rights movement had captured the conscience of the nation, and Chief Justice Earl Warren sat at the head of the court. He had shown a willingness to expand federal power in cases where fundamental justice would be served. Cases had been adjudicated under his influence where congressional powers under the Commerce Clause had been expanded beyond previously imagined boundaries. The Warren Court proved willing to affirm the constitutional authority of Congress to act if justice demanded it. Some people were appalled at the activism of the Warren Court, and some still consider that period of time in American jurisprudence to be an affront to the Constitution.

However, if there was going to be an end to discrimination in the private sector in America, this was the time for Congress to make its move, while the Warren Court was in place. Under President Lyndon Baines Johnson, in the wake of continued national mourning for a beloved President Kennedy, Congress passed the Civil Rights Act of 1964. Its effective date was deferred until July 2, 1965, in anticipation that constitutional challenges would be forthcoming. It would be up to the U.S. Supreme Court to determine whether or not Congress had the authority to regulate the private sector and enact the Civil Rights Act, or whether it had gone beyond its delegated power into the Tenth Amendment–protected territory of states' rights.

The *Heart of Atlanta Motel v. United States* was the "test case" brought before the U.S. Supreme Court. The Heart of Atlanta Motel was a segregated facility that did not wish to serve black patrons. It would be required to do so under the section of the Civil Rights Act that regulated private enterprises engaging in the business of public accommodation: hotels, motels, restaurants, and gas stations.

The Heart of Atlanta and its co-plaintiffs argued that Congress had exceeded its authority under the Commerce Clause by trying to regulate patronage of their businesses. (The Commerce Clause of the Constitution, found in Article I, Section 8, Clause 3, simply states that Congress shall have the power to "regulate Commerce with foreign Nations, and among the several States, and with the Indian Tribes.")

The relevant portions of the *Heart of Atlanta* case appear below. Although the Tenth Amendment is never mentioned, its presence is clear in the arguments made about the limitations the Constitution imposes on federal power.(3)

Heart of Atlanta Motel v. United States (1964)

United States Supreme Court (379 U.S. 241)

Justice Tom C. Clark delivered the opinion of the court.

[Summary]

Appellant, the owner of a large motel in Atlanta, Georgia, which restricts its clientele to white persons, three-fourths of whom are transient interstate travelers, sued for declaratory relief and to enjoin enforcement of the Civil Rights Act of 1964, contending that the prohibition of racial discrimination in places of public accommodation affecting commerce exceeded Congress' powers under the Commerce Clause and violated [the Tenth Amendment] and other parts of the Constitution.

* * *

[Opinion]

This is a declaratory judgment action attacking the constitutionality of Title II of the Civil Rights Act of 1964. In addition to declaratory relief the complaint sought an injunction restraining the enforcement of the Act and damages against appellees based on allegedly resulting injury in the event compliance was required.

* * *

1. The Factual Background and Contentions of the Parties.

The case comes here on admissions and stipulated facts. Appellant owns and operates the Heart of Atlanta Motel which has 216 rooms available to transient guests. The motel is located on Courtland Street, two blocks from downtown Peachtree Street. It is readily accessible to interstate highways 75 and 85 and state highways 23 and 41. Appellant solicits patronage from outside the State of Georgia through various national advertising media, including magazines of national circulation; it maintains over 50 billboards and highway signs within the State, soliciting patronage for the motel; it accepts convention trade from outside Georgia and approximately 75% of its registered guests are from out of State. Prior to passage of the Act the motel had followed a practice of refusing to rent rooms to Negroes, and it alleged that it intended to continue to do so. In an effort to perpetuate that policy this suit was filed.

The appellant contends that Congress in passing this Act exceeded its power to regulate commerce under Art. I, 8, cl. 3, of the Constitution of the United States....

The appellees counter that the unavailability to Negroes of adequate accommodations interferes significantly with interstate travel, and that Congress, under the Commerce Clause, has power to remove such obstructions and restraints....

2. The History of the Act.

Congress first evidenced its interest in civil rights legislation in the Civil Rights or Enforcement Act of April 9, 1866.... [Those early attempts failed.] [O]n June 19, 1963, the late President Kennedy called for civil rights legislation in a message to Congress to which he attached a proposed bill. Its stated purpose was

> "to promote the general welfare by eliminating discrimination based on race, color, religion, or national origin in...public accommodations through the exercise by Congress of the powers conferred upon it...to enforce the provisions of the fourteenth and fifteenth amendments, to regulate commerce among the several States, and to make laws necessary and proper to execute the powers conferred upon it by the Constitution."

...The Act as finally adopted was most comprehensive, undertaking to prevent through peaceful and voluntary settlement discrimination in voting, as well as in places of accommodation and public facilities, federally secured programs and in employment. Since Title II is the only portion under attack here, we confine our consideration to those public accommodation provisions. [379 U.S. 241, 247]

3. Title II of the Act.

This Title is divided into seven sections beginning with 201 (a) which provides that:

> "All persons shall be entitled to the full and equal enjoyment of the goods, services, facilities, privileges, advantages, and accommodations of any place of public accommodation, as defined in this section, without

Heart of Atlanta Motel v. United States (1964)

discrimination or segregation on the ground of race, color, religion, or national origin."

There are listed in 201 (b) four classes of business establishments, each of which "serves the public" and "is a place of public accommodation" within the meaning of 201 (a) "if its operations affect commerce, or if discrimination or segregation by it is supported by State action." The covered establishments are

> "(1) any inn, hotel, motel, or other establishment which provides lodging to transient guests, other than an establishment located within a building which contains not more than five rooms for rent or hire and which is actually occupied by the proprietor of such establishment as his residence;
>
> (2) any restaurant, cafeteria....
>
> (3) any motion picture house...."

* * *

4. Application of Title II to Heart of Atlanta Motel.

It is admitted that the operation of the motel brings it within the provisions of 201 (a) of the Act and that appellant refused to provide lodging for transient Negroes because of their race or color and that it intends to continue that policy unless restrained.

The sole question posed is, therefore, the constitutionality of the Civil Rights Act of 1964 as applied to these facts. The legislative history of the Act indicates that Congress based the Act on…its power to regulate interstate commerce under Art. I, 8, cl. 3, of the Constitution.

The Senate Commerce Committee made it quite clear that the fundamental object of Title II was to vindicate "the deprivation of personal dignity that surely accompanies denials of equal access to public establishments." At the same time, however, it noted that such an objective has been and could be readily achieved "by congressional action based on the commerce power of the Constitution."

* * *

6. The Basis of Congressional Action.

While the Act as adopted carried no congressional findings, the record of its passage through each house is replete with evidence of

Heart of Atlanta Motel v. United States (1964)

the burdens that discrimination by race or color places upon interstate commerce.... This testimony included the fact that our people have become increasingly mobile with millions of people of all races traveling from State to State; that Negroes in particular have been the subject of discrimination in transient accommodations, having to travel great distances to secure the same; that often they have been unable to obtain accommodations and have had to call upon friends to put them up overnight...; and that these conditions had become so acute as to require the listing of available lodging for Negroes in a special guidebook which was itself "dramatic testimony to the difficulties" Negroes encounter in travel.... These exclusionary practices were found to be nationwide, the Under Secretary of Commerce testifying that there is "no question that this discrimination in the North still exists to a large degree" and in the West and Midwest as well.

* * *

7. The Power of Congress over Interstate Travel.

* * *

[T]he determinative test of the exercise of power by the Congress under the Commerce Clause is simply whether the activity sought to be regulated is "commerce which concerns more States than one" and has a real and substantial relation to the national interest.

* * *

That Congress was legislating against moral wrongs...render[s] its enactments no less valid. In framing Title II of this Act Congress was...dealing with what it considered a moral problem. But that fact does not detract from the overwhelming evidence of the disruptive effect that racial discrimination has had on commercial intercourse. It was this burden which empowered Congress to enact appropriate legislation, and, given this basis for the exercise of its power, Congress was not restricted by the fact that the particular obstruction to interstate commerce with which it was dealing was also deemed a moral and social wrong.

It is said that the operation of the motel here is of a purely local character. But, assuming this to be true, "[i]f it is interstate commerce that feels the pinch, it does not matter how local the operation which applies the squeeze." United States v. Women's Sportswear Mfrs. Assn., 336 U.S. 460, 464 (1949).

* * *

We, therefore, conclude that the action of the Congress in the adoption of the Act as applied here to a motel…is within the power granted it by the Commerce Clause of the Constitution….

Affirmed.

At first, it may appear that this case hinges on the Heart of Atlanta's interstate market. Heart of Atlanta Motel was a locally owned and operated concern, but it was primarily frequented by out-of-state patrons. The interstate component of its business turned out not to be a critical factual point, however. As the court quoted from its prior precedent: "[i]f it is interstate commerce that feels the pinch, it does not matter how local the operation which applies the squeeze." Consequently, even local businesses with no interstate character are bound under the Civil Rights Act in the wake of this case.

Without some constitutional power on which to "hang its hat," Congress would have been powerless to enact the Civil Rights Act of 1964. The Tenth Amendment compels Congress to limit its activity to powers specifically enumerated in the Constitution, leaving all other powers to the states and the people, respectively. It is no small irony that the Tenth Amendment, enacted to protect democracy against federal "tyranny," was the single biggest obstacle to desegregation in the private sector. It is no small victory that the Civil Rights Act of 1964 was declared constitutional in spite of that obstacle.

Federal Regulation of the Private Sector since 1964

The *Heart of Atlanta* case affirmed the reach of the Commerce Clause to allow Congress to use it to effectuate social change. Since then, as you might have suspected, federal power has grown enormously in virtually every other social arena. For example, the Drug Enforcement Administration (DEA), which prosecutes drug traffickers, was enabled by Congress under its Commerce Clause power.

In recent years, the U.S. Supreme Court has rebuffed some congressional attempts to place social issues under federal power by using the Commerce Clause. In this respect, the court appears to be as politically driven in its reticence as it was in its activism. It has ruled unconstitutional a federal rape law (Women Against Rape) and a federal school gun control act, both of which attempted to enable federal power by arguing the negative effects on commerce that, respectively, rape and guns in schools imposed. The court declined to allow the stretch.

States rights arguments can come from both sides. Though Democrats were more likely than Republicans to have supported federal interventions in the past century, it was Republican President George W. Bush who federalized a "No Child Left Behind" policy supporting federal standardized tests for public schools. This was an unusual foray into the quality and delivery of education, which has historically been considered to be under the providence of the states.

In 2012, the PPACA (Patient Protection and Affordable Care Act referenced by its critics as "Obamacare") was challenged on the grounds that compelling individuals to buy health insurance or face financial penalty is an unconstitutional exertion of federal power. Lower courts were split on that issue, and in June 2012, the United States Supreme Court issued its controversial decision. Although it did not find power for the federal government to pass the PPACA under the Commerce Clause, it found that the law was constitutional under the clause that allows the federal government to tax for the general welfare.

The case was complex in many ways. The court drew a distinction between a tax scheme where taxpayers are forced to pay tax for a service they may or may not want (i.e., Medicare or Social Security), and one where they are compelled to buy a product from the private sector (health insurance).

The financial penalty was ultimately determined to be a tax for constitutional purposes.(4)

Double Jeopardy

Though federal power is not unlimited, the growth of federal legislation and regulation in the last century shows a significantly expanded role of the federal government in American society. Of course states have also increased their own laws and rules, and an abundance of local city and county regulations add to the mix. The United States is definitely a nation of laws.

With so much overlap between the local, state, and federal systems, there might appear to be a problem with double jeopardy or multiple trials for one course of conduct. The term double jeopardy relates to the Fifth Amendment right that no person can be tried twice for the same crime. Ordinarily that means that any action or series of actions in the commission of a crime can result in only one trial. This is meant to prevent the government from retrying old criminal cases by simply restating them with different charges.

However, the U.S. Supreme Court decided more than half a century ago that it is not double jeopardy when someone criminally charged in a state action is also charged in federal court with a separate federal crime based on the same facts.

For example, states generally have laws against police brutality. An officer who assaults a suspect can be charged with a host of state crimes related to that conduct. In the 1992 Rodney King case, officers were caught on tape beating King with clubs and kicking him while he was on the ground. The officers were acquitted or left with hung juries in state court. The U.S. Attorney brought charges in federal court, based on the same facts, for the criminal violation of Mr. King's civil rights. In the federal proceedings, the two officers who behaved most egregiously were convicted.

Knowing that there can be criminal charges in both state and federal court on the same conduct, one might ask why, after the controversial 1994 acquittal of O.J. Simpson for the murder of his former wife and Ron Goldman, federal charges were not filed. There was no federal crime involved in that case. Murder still remains a state crime except under rare factual circumstances. The Tenth Amendment would make it very difficult for the federal government to legislate against violent crimes that occur within a state.

The next question that might logically be raised is whether or not double jeopardy applies in civil actions, as most business-related legal issues are civil and not criminal. Double jeopardy as it appears in the Constitution does not apply to civil actions, but under other law, civil cases cannot be tried more than once on the same facts. This is true even if there is concurrent jurisdiction in both federal and state courts. When filing a lawsuit, the plaintiff has to pick a forum and bring its case on the facts (and the relevant state and federal law) to that single forum. The defendant might try to take legal steps to change the forum, but ultimately once the forum is finalized, the case is tried, and the appeals are exhausted, the case on those facts is over. It cannot be brought again in any other jurisdiction.

State Legislation Is Still Significant in Interstate Commerce

Though from the previous segments of this chapter it would appear that the role of states in interstate commerce is probably disintegrated, that is not at all the case. The first chapter of this book dealt with the nature of the corporate entity, but did not get specific regarding how corporations form. Furthermore, the term corporation was used, but today there are a large number of fictitious entities that can be formed that provide the same insulation as the corporate entity, with a wide ranging choice of taxation options and management structure. There also remain non-corporate forms of businesses where individuals retain liability for the actions of their enterprises.

It will surprise some people that all of business formations are regulated by state (not federal) law. As a consequence, most publicly traded companies incorporate in Delaware so that there can be a uniform perception of the rules under which they operate. But it is not always the case that publicly traded firms incorporate in Delaware, and before diving into publicly traded companies, it would be appropriate to consider the smaller scale. So first, the types of business formations available to entrepreneurs at the onset of their ventures should be addressed.

The Traditional Forms of Business

Sole Proprietorship

If a person were to wake up one morning with an idea for a business and start working on the development and execution of that idea, that person has started a business. The business and the individual, however, are indistinguishable. The individual is liable for all of the business debts, and the business is liable for the individual's debts. The taxation on the business is directly applied to the individual. This, in a nutshell, is the "sole proprietorship" form of business. Sole proprietorships are governed by state and local licensure requirements, although for formational purposes, the sole proprietorship actually has no formal construct—it manifests at the will of its creator.

Other than for taxation, there is no federal law governing formation of sole proprietorships.

General Partnerships

Similarly, if two people were to collaborate on an idea for a business, and if they were to start working on the development and execution of that idea together, those individuals have started a business in the form of a partnership. The taxation on that partnership is directly applied to the partners, and liabilities of the partnership apply directly to each partner.

Although partnerships were historically most often the result of a formal agreement between the business originators, today they primarily occur somewhat accidentally without any formal legal contract. For example, suppose two students decide they will try to go into business together after graduation. One student uses her credit cards to fund the venture, with the other agreeing to pay half the bills. One of the students incurs some additional debt to help the business along, but the venture does not succeed in the manner the two had hoped, and the pair agree to part ways. Even absent any formal agreement, the pair had operated as a general partnership. When that happens, both partners are liable for the debts of the business. This means that legally either partner can be held accountable for the *full* debt owed to creditors—if one partner does not have the money to pay his or her share, the other partner can get stuck with the bill. In other words, like the sole proprietorship, partnerships manifest at the will of their creators, even if their creators do not consciously know that they are forming this type of business.

Partnerships are consequently a significantly higher risk than sole proprietorships. Absent agreement to the contrary (although this can vary by state), the partnership is not bankrupt until each partner is bankrupt. Even though one partner may only own 25% of the business, he or she may be held liable for 100% of the debts of the business if the other partner(s) cannot pay the creditors.

With the other more owner-friendly business forms available today, general partnerships are not usually formed anymore, and when they do form, it is most often the result of accident or ignorance.

The historical appeal of the partnership was both its ease of formation, and the fact that the entity is not separately taxed from the individual owners. The individual owners can deduct losses on their personal income tax as they occur.

Although the states have enacted a set of uniform rules that guide the governance of partnership operation and liability, just as the case with sole proprietorships, there is no federal law with respect to formation of a partnership entity. All states have adopted (in whole or in part) the Uniform Partnership Act to give some consistency between the states with respect to partnership operation and liability. However no federal law compels the states to adopt the Act, and each state can re-

ject certain provisions, or impose its own "spin" on certain sections.

Corporations

As noted in Chapter 1, the corporate form of business was created to build a liability wall between the business and its owners. Entrepreneurs form a corporation by filing articles of incorporation or with a Secretary of State under whom there is generally some form of Corporations Commission. The incorporators may or may not file in the state where they have their principle place of business. Some states are friendlier to incorporators than others, and specifically some are cheaper. Incorporators get to choose.

The Secretary of the state of incorporation then certifies the articles or charter, which causes the corporate entity to be "born."

Although large corporations generally conduct business in every state of the Union, the legal construct of the formation is actually governed by the laws of the state in which it is incorporated. So, for example, state laws determine by what date shareholders must own shares in order to vote in the next election. This is called the shareholder record date, and it varies from state to state. Boards of Directors may be required to be elected in a staggered manner instead of all at the same time, depending upon what state laws provide, and what choices the incorporators are given under statute.

After the Secretary of State certifies or issues a certificate of incorporation for the entity, the corporation is its own legal "person." Its owners may or may not be the incorporators. Ownership in the corporation is represented by shares of stock that are owned by one or more people or entities such as other corporations, mutual funds, or pension funds.

In theory, shareholders do not run the corporation. In practice, in small companies, officers, directors, and shareholders are often the same people who wear different hats as they shift from role to role. The next chapter will cover how this operates in a publicly traded company, but in theory, even in a small company, the shareholder's governance rights are limited to the election of the board of directors. The board then picks the officers and sets their compensation. It is the officers who actually run the company.

Consequently, the owners of a corporation (the shareholders) are two degrees of separation away from the running of the business (at least to the extent they are wearing the shareholder hat). The directors form a bridge between owners and officers, representing the shareholders' interests through their selection, compensation, oversight, and advising of the officers of the corporation.

In theory, shareholders can sell their interest in the corporation by simply selling their shares to someone else. The operation of the business is independent of who owns shares. In reality, in small closely held corporations (where stock is not publicly traded), shareholders are often contractually restricted from selling their stock, and comport themselves more like partners than distant owners, as they generally are officers and directors as well as shareholders.

Tax Breaks and Easy Governance for Small Businesses

Large corporations pay (or don't pay) income tax based on their income, and then shareholders pay tax based on the dividends that are distributed to them, or on the capital gains they receive upon the sale of their stock. This means that there are two times that corporate income is taxed: upon its own realization of gain, and upon the receipt of gain by the shareholder.

Today, however, there are forms of corporate legal entities that permit in-

dividuals to take gains or losses directly onto their personal income tax, avoiding the double dip. State legislatures (with limited blessings from the Internal Revenue Service) have created a series of "hybrid" business forms, where the investor has the liability shield provided by the corporate form and the tax advantages of the sole proprietorship or partnership. The road to good policy in this area has been rocky.

In fact, there are many forms of business today that (until they reach a certain size) allow for this simultaneous liability shield with the tax benefits of a sole proprietorship or general partnership. Some of these operate with the same ease (although not the same formational simplicity) as those traditional forms of business.

All these forms are constructed under state (not federal) laws. States have all adopted a range of business formations for smaller enterprises to make ease of formation, operation, and taxation more appealing to would-be entrepreneurs. The most common formation is the LLC or Limited Liability Company, which removes the formality of having to have a board of directors and instead allows for "member" voting and more direct owner/leadership. There are several other common structures. The Limited Liability Partnership (LLP) or Limited Liability Limited Partnership (LLLP), depending upon the state nomenclature, allows enterprises to function and do bookkeeping in the same manner as traditional partnerships, with the liability immunities of a traditional corporation. A Subchapter S corporation is a form of closely held corporation (C-Corp) that provides the tax benefit of the sole proprietorship with the liability shield and formal structure of a corporation.(5) Subchapter S is a tax status under federal law, but the company must form as a C-Corp and be governed in that respect by state law.

Formalizing the structure of a small business today is a user-friendly operation. States want business entities to form within their borders, and they compete for that business just as any enterprise competes for market share. In Arizona, there is a single Web page that lists the forms required for incorporation, and these forms can be downloaded and printed in a minute or two. The process is clearly outlined in online support materials, and most people do not find it necessary to hire counsel to become incorporated in Arizona. Maintaining the formalities of a corporate structure can be tricky, so many small businesses choose the LLC form for a more intuitive operating structure without having formal meetings or clear delineation of tasks between shareholders, directors, and officers. The same forms can be used for LLCs, LLPs or C-Corps.

It should be noted that in the one area where federal rules do govern, which is federal income taxation of businesses, there are limits imposed on the size and dollar income that these entities can have. Subchapter S Corporations cannot have more than 75 shareholders (as of this writing), and there are limitations to the maximum dollar amount a company or its individual shareholders, members, and partners can earn while maintaining Subchapter S status. Although states form LLCs and LLPs with larger numbers of owners, the IRS does not give the tax benefit when those entities reach a certain size. It has been a slow evolution for the IRS and the states to come to accord on how LLCs and LLPs fit under the Internal Revenue Code.

On the other hand, creating the relevant income statements to allow for individual taxation for 75 owners with varying degrees of ownership can be extraordinarily complex and expensive. If a company is profitable, it may choose to hold its money and pay the corporate tax rate before it even gets to the IRS limitations. In other words, with the corporate tax rate lower than the individual tax rate, there is a certain point where there is an economic advantage to facing the double dip.

The next chapter will show that as a corporation grows into publicly traded status, the role of the federal side of the regulation grows exponentially, and the influence of state law on corporate governance recedes.

Notes

1. *Plessy v. Ferguson* 163 U.S. 537 (1896)

2. Cozzens, Lisa, "Plessy v. Ferguson,"
   http://www.watson.org/~lisa/blackhistory/post-civilwar/plessy.html

3. *Heart of Atlanta Motel v. United States* (1964), U.S. Supreme Court (379 U.S. 241)

4. *National Federation of Independent Business et al. v. Sebelius, Secretary of Health and Human Services, et al., U.S. Supreme Court*, June 2012 (PPACA case)

5. When you want a Subchapter S Corp
   http://definitions.uslegal.com/s/s-corporation/

Chapter 6
Publicly Traded Corporations

From Closely Held to Publicly Traded: The 1933 Securities Act

A closely held corporation is often owned by just one or two shareholders. If the closely held corporation were to be sold, usually the buyer would purchase the shares from the existing shareholders. If one or more shareholders representing a minority of the issued shares refused to sell, they could be forced out by the majority owner, as long as they were dealt with fairly. Frequently, closely held corporations are family-owned businesses, and they are sold or dissolved when the family ceases to operate the business.

When a company grows sufficiently large, however, its shareholders may want to "go public." The legal structures of a publicly held corporation and a closely held corporation are similar, but the former is very different in substance.

It is important to understand that public (government) ownership and publicly held ownership are very different things. When the government owns or runs something, that thing is publicly owned and part of the public sector. For example, the National Park Service and the federal parks it oversees are public sector entities and properties. However, publicly traded companies are part of the private sector, owned by people who have purchased interests in them. When a company is publicly traded, anyone can buy a piece of that company by buying a share of its stock from one of the stock exchanges. The New York Stock Exchange (NYSE), American Stock Exchange (Amex), and NASDAQ are the three large exchanges in the United States, and though they are heavily regulated, they are private (not government) companies. Each exchange has a different construct, for example technically the NYSE can be characterized as a not-for-profit company.

When a company goes public, the issuance and initial sale of its stock is heavily regulated under the Securities Act of 1933. After getting on an exchange, the stock continues to be heavily regulated by the Securities Exchange Act of 1934.

Considering what was going on in 1933 will provide some sense of the purpose of this first grand legislative scheme to regulate the sale of securities. The 1929 Great Depression, in full swing by 1933, was precipitated by a market that had run out of investor confidence. Investors had been poorly informed, readily manipulated, and heavily leveraged. The market collapsed. Some would argue that what happened in 1929 is not significantly different from what happened in the mid-1990s when the bubble burst in the dot com industry, or in 2008 when mortgaged-backed securities collapsed.

Since the imperfect information received by investors was presumed to be a significant factor in the market's collapse in the early 1930s, the government attacked that market failure with a legislative plan that would impose disclosure requirements that carried both civil and criminal penalties if violated. No longer would market information be tainted with either rose-colored glasses or avaricious manipulation. The truth about a security was going to be told, or the 1933 Act would impose penalties that were severe and non-negotiable.

History Lesson on Market Shenanigans

From the early stock sellers who successfully sold stock in companies that allegedly turned sheep into gold, to the robber barons of the mid-19th century who manipulated the market without conscience, the sale of stock has been cloaked in disreputability.

Jay Gould is perhaps the most famous market manipulator (although Leland Stanford and his cronies were close on Gould's heels). Gould invented what is known today as the "short sale," but not in a nice way. Today, a short sale is a heavily regulated transaction, where you count on the market going down, so you sell stock before you actually own it (technically "borrowing" the stock from the broker until you buy shares and pay the broker back). Gould made a significant part of his fortune by borrowing the stock of corporate shareholders. He would pay those shareholders interest on the loan of their stock and promise to return an equal number of shares at some point in the future. He would then sell the borrowed stock and immediately start rumors or take action to force the price of the stock dramatically down. After his manipulation of the corporate rumors, he would buy up the stock at a rock bottom price, returning it to the original owners from whom he borrowed it. The original stock owner was now in possession of worthless stock—or stock worth significantly less than it was at the time Gould borrowed it. Gould made his money on the sale before he orchestrated the price plummet.

Nothing prohibited this type of conduct before the government began to regulate the securities markets. The New York Stock Exchange, owned by the brokers who started it, assumed a self-regulatory role to penalize this type of conduct, but those self-imposed constraints proved insufficient to stave off the Great Depression of 1929.

In 1933, in the midst of a collapsed market, high unemployment, and abject poverty, the United States government decided to try to regulate the market. It attacked new issues of stock first, then went on to the brokerage and exchange side of the industry in 1934.

As we have already discussed, one way in which the free market falters is in the area of disclosure. The market failure concept of imperfect information rests on the hypothesis that little compels a willing seller to give a willing buyer negative information. Absent regulatory intervention, information that is not reasonably available to a purchaser will not be given by a seller if it is detrimental to the seller to provide that information. On the other hand, for a free market to function properly, supply and demand must set output and price, not government. Free market proponents assert that the laws of supply and demand provide the only

real economic freedom in society, because the goods and services that get produced are those that the people want to buy—not those that the government thinks people should have. To remain a free market society, any regulatory schemes enacted by Congress would have to balance leaving market forces to reflect free choice, while compelling disclosures that ensure that free choices are informed ones.

Once Congress had addressed issues surrounding the disclosure of information regarding new issues of securities, it still had the daunting task of regulating the continuation of disclosures once a corporation was publicly traded. The 1934 Act was passed to provide a legislative mandate requiring publicly traded companies to advise new and existing shareholders about corporate performance on a continuous basis after the stock was in play.

The IPO and Subsequent New Issues

As mentioned in the "history lesson" above, the first set of legislative enactments under the Securities Act of 1933 set out to govern all new issues of stock, which means more than it might imply. It not only sets the rules for the Initial Public Offering (IPO) for the first time a stock of a company is offered to the public, but it also sets the rules for any subsequent security offerings that the company might issue over time. Although this is obvious to some, to others it might come as some-

thing of a surprise that the IPO is not the only time companies issue new stock. Companies issue and sell various kinds of equity at various times for various purposes, long after they become publicly traded. Typical reasons to issue new stock are to retire debt, expand existing business capacity, and acquire other properties. Each time there is a new issue (be it the IPO, secondary, or otherwise), the 1933 Act's rigorous requirements must be met.

Interesting Side Note

Textbooks on securities regulation consistently note that the Securities and Exchange Commission (SEC) was not established until Congress passed the Securities Exchange Act of 1934. People have asked, "How did the 1933 Act operate if the SEC didn't even exist until a year after the 1933 Act passed?" Here is the answer.

Originally, "the Commission" referenced in the Securities Act of 1933 referred to the Federal Trade Commission (FTC). As the textbooks note, it was not until the 1934 Act that Congress established the SEC, which now oversees both new issues and the exchange of stock. Statutes under the 1933 Act were amended with the 1934 Act, to reflect that the word "commission" would thereafter reference the SEC and not the FTC.

Registration of Stock under the 1933 Act

Before a company can take its stock public (whether in the IPO, secondary, or subsequent offering), it must register its stock with the SEC through the filing of a registration statement. There are various types of registrations available depending on the size and stability of the issuer. (The issuer is the corporation whose stock is being put on the market.) Most of the time a corporation has only a short time between the time it files its registration statement and when the new issue must begin trading. A very established issuer, however, may file a shelf registration statement, following which it can leave its stock on a figurative shelf for up to two years (filing updates periodically with the SEC), before it must list the stock. No matter the type of registration statement, the disclosure requirements are exhaustive. Although the SEC does not independently check the accuracy of the information in a registration statement,

they aggressively prosecute both criminally and civilly if misstatements are discovered by shareholders, analysts, or creditors.

In the past, people have asked how misstatements in a registration statement are discovered if nobody checks statements for accuracy, and only the insiders know the real truth. Almost always the misstatements are discovered when the company starts to fail. Had Enron been truly profitable, any shenanigans by the officers may have never been discovered. However, when a company becomes insolvent, creditors, investors, and even employees begin to comb through the rubble to find ways to place blame. Ultimately, nobody can hide a bottom line when a company cannot pay its bills.

Most people have never seen a document that is called a registration statement. This is because by the time the final document is ready for circulation, it is gussied up for the public and called a prospectus.

Since the SEC does *not* ever approve a registration statement, nor does it endorse the issue or its value, the SEC's role is to accept or reject a registration. The Commission looks at the information given in the registration statement to see if there are discrepancies or unexplained anomalies. It makes comments and asks questions if it sees a problem. For example, suppose there are significant shifts from year to year in the financial statements representing historical performance (which would be statements from the period during which the company was closely held in the case of an IPO). Example questions that have been raised by the SEC include, "Why is your depreciation expense so much greater this year than in the previous reporting years?"; "Given your debt security agreement with the bank, it does not appear that you will be allowed to take on additional debt without bank approval. How do you know you will be able to get the bank to subordinate its interest?"; and "How did you manage to decrease your receivables so dramatically in 2002?"

After 20 days, the SEC either accepts the registration statement or it asks questions or makes comments as suggested in the previous paragraph. Although the issuer cannot sell stock until the registration statement has been accepted, the underwriters will want to start measuring interest among investment groups before the offering

is made. Therefore, during the period after the registration statement has been submitted but before it has been accepted, the issuer and underwriter can go to the investment community with something known as a red herring.

The red herring gets its name from the fact that it bears a giant red banner across the top to alert potential investors that the registration statement's acceptance has not been granted yet.

The red herring is simply a preliminary prospectus or solicitation instrument that is used by the issuing company to figure out market demand, an opening price, and the overall viability of the offering. In other words, the red herring is the document that goes on the road (in what the investment community refers to as a road show) to promote an issue before the stock is actually offered for sale. During the road show, the underwriter and corporate principals travel together to Europe, to California, and across the country to New York, trying to get investors (mutual funds, investment banks, private capital) interested. The underwriter is generally an investment bank that guarantees the issuer that it will buy all the stock of an offering at a price that is determined just before the stock goes public. The underwritten price for the issue is generally established with information and informal offers acquired during the road show.

During this road show/solicitation period that precedes the SEC's acceptance of the registration statement, stock cannot actually be sold. However, the investment community can and does submit revocable orders indicating how much stock they would hypothetically buy and at what price. Although investors are not bound to purchase stock in accordance with these orders, nor is the issuer bound to sell at the price offered, there is an expectation that stated interest on the part of investors is genuine, based on habit and the reliability of the invitees to the road show. This is the value that the underwriting investment banker brings to the table (for which they charge a gigantic amount, by the way). They get the right people to come see the road show.

On the other hand, the investment bankers try to price the stock low in order to benefit their best customers who buy into the IPO with the expectation that there will be a jump in stock price within minutes after trading starts. The wealth related to the jump goes into the hands of those who get in on the IPO (and to the underwriters who have rights to buy shares at the opening price) as opposed to the issuing company itself.

Google by-passed much of the underwriting/road show part of their IPO and opened their stock with something called a Dutch Auction when they went public. Thirty different investment banks were allowed to register so that their customers could directly bid for shares. There was a great deal of interest in the company, so shares sold quickly even though the price remained stable, and there was no big jump for the early acquirers. Google believed this to be a more fair and democratic way to offer their stock in an IPO, but very few other companies have followed suit.

After the Registration Statement Is Accepted

Once the registration statement is accepted by the SEC, the issuer can proceed with the offering. The date for the IPO (or any new issue) is usually set long before the road show, but there is some fluidity depending upon SEC questions and comments that delay registration acceptance. Once the date is finally determined, however, the process moves predictably and quickly.

The opening price is set by the issuer (with strong pressure from the un-

derwriter to keep the price low and attractive). That price is not firmly decided until sometime around midnight the night before opening day— the day that the stock is first listed on the exchange. It is that opening day on the exchange that the stock first actually sells. Depending upon which exchange the stock is traded, it may take several hours to show a trade price— there is a lot of suspense and excitement in the process.

In the case of an IPO on the New York Stock Exchange, the Chief Executive Officer (CEO) of the issuing company generally gets to ring the closing bell on the opening day. Images of Martha Stewart serving brioches and juice and ringing the closing bell on the day her Omnimedia company went public were broadcast in sharp contrast to her being taken to jail for charges relating to being tipped on a stock sale. NASDAQ is completely computer driven, and its new issues are a bit less dramatic.

Each person who participates in the registration of the IPO and signs the statement (which all principals, officers, and directors must do) can be held personally liable for its accuracy. Only if the signor was diligent in trying to uncover misstatements is he or she off the hook under the 1933 Act. In the 1968 *Escott v. BarChris Construction* case, even the newly appointed banker/director was liable, and he had only signed a blank page with a small amendment (after the registration statement had been submitted).(1)

Originally, 1934 Act filings were less onerous than those of the 1933 Act; but since the Sarbanes/Oxley bill was passed in 2002, the rigor with which post-registration filings are scrutinized has increased significantly. The culpability for misstatements on quarterly and annual reports has grown to nearly match the liabilities for signors of registration statements under the 1933 Act; this will be discussed in the next section of this chapter.

Given both the initial and continuing risks involved, it is difficult to understand why anybody with any personal assets would serve as a director for a publicly traded corporation today. In response to the risks, a variety of different protective devices have evolved. Today, virtually all large companies have Director and Officer Liability Insurance (known as D&O insurance) to attract qualified directors to serve on their boards. Wise directors watch closely to make sure the premiums are paid properly. State corporation statutes have been changed to allow corporations to indemnify officers and directors where there is no personal gain or malice on the part of the director or officer who signed the misstatement. These fail-safes have the potential to disappear, however, if the company becomes insolvent. If the D&O insurance has not been paid, there is no insurance to protect the director. If the corporation has no money with which to pay any judgments, the indemnity provisions are worthless, because the creditor is not bound by such provisions. Risks for directors in today's post-Enron corporate world can be mitigated, but they cannot be eliminated. An ironic result is that in a world where excessive payments to top-of-the-ladder officers and directors is publicly criticized, knowledgeable directors are being paid more and more to accept the risks and stick with their boards through difficult times.

The Securities Exchange Act of 1934

The 1934 Act governs securities and the people who sell them once the securities are traded. Quarterly and annual reports (forms 10-Q and 10-K), intermittent events of importance (form 8-K) and shareholder solicitations (proxy statements) are all required and regulated by the 1934 Act.

As noted previously, the original standards for reporting under the 1934 Act were not as rigorous as those for registering stock under the 1933 Act. For example, a registration statement must be written in "plain English," so that ordinary investors do not get duped by double-talk. No such requirement was present in the 1934 Act until after Sarbanes-Oxley was passed. A misrepresentation under the 1933 Act could be punishable even if unintentional. This was not true under the 1934 Act.

With Sarbanes-Oxley, officers and directors have higher accountability standards and must certify the accuracy of the financial reporting documents under penalty of perjury. Disclosures now have a "plain English" requirement similar to that under the 1933 Act. No longer can important revelations be postponed, potentially giving insiders a chance to jump in front of ordinary investors. Important information must be disclosed immediately to the public and to the SEC (on form 8-K), in plain English. Conflicts of interest between consultants and auditors have been identified and prohibited. It is a tough time to be an officer or director of a publicly traded corporation.

The SEC and its prosecutorial arm have been unrelenting in prosecuting high-profile corporate wrongdoers, ostensibly because the SEC believes that investors will only play in a market where everyone plays fair. However, it is important to remember that the SEC is a regulatory agency, not the legislature. Its employees are hired, not elected. Like most bureaucratic institutions, it has the potential to try to justify its own existence with zealousness. Although respectful of the SEC as an important institution in our market system, Ben Lytle, former Chairman and CEO of WellPoint, once quipped, "Those guys have no sense of humor."

Insider Trading

In addition to regulating ongoing disclosures of publicly traded corporations, the 1934 Act also regulates the conduct of brokers, exchanges, dealers, and traders. Inside information and other forms of market manipulation are made unlawful under Section 10(b) of the 1934 Act. SEC regulations regarding insider trading and illegal market manipulation are found under Rule 10b-5 in the Code of Federal Regulations. A preventative measure called the short-swing profit rule can be found under Rule 16.

The short-swing profit rule is designed to pre-empt the opportunity for certain types of insider trading. Although often mistaken for an insider-trading prohibition, it really deals more with the appearance of impropriety than any actual malfeasance.

Under the short-swing profit rule, a statutory insider cannot profit from a trade that is made any time within a six month period. That sounds really simple, but it is not. First of all, it is necessary to distinguish a statutory insider from other insiders. Anyone can be an insider in general, if their position gives them information not otherwise available to the public. A janitor who cleans the waste baskets can be an insider. So can a photocopy clerk, or a Web master.

The enabling statute for Rule 16 sets out a particular group of people, and names them as insiders for purposes of short-swing profits only. These statutory insiders are officers, directors, and 10% or greater shareholders. Those are the *only* people who can be held accountable under the short-swing profit rule.

Not all trades make a profit. If one of those statutory insiders loses money on a trade within a six-month period, there is no problem with the short-swing profit rule because there is no profit. Even if the statutory insider trades at less of a loss than would have been suffered had the trader held the stock for six months, there is generally no Rule 16 problem because there is no profit.

However, the definition of profit for Rule 16 purposes is very odd. Any sale for more money than any buy within any six-month period creates a profit in the short swing. Assume that a statutory insider sells stock on January 15 for $50 per share. Assume further than the same person buys back the stock on March 15 for $40 per share. There was a buy and a sell within the same six-month period, the sell was for more than the buy, so there was a short-swing profit. Even if that same person sells the shares he or she purchased in March a few weeks later for $30 per share, there was still a short-swing profit between the January and March transactions.

However, the penalty for a short-swing profit is the profit itself. There are no fines and no criminal culpability. The trader simply has to give the profit (or imputed profit as described in the previous paragraph) back to the issuer. This is because Rule 16 is not a punitive measure. Most of the time, if a statutory insider sells stock within the short-swing period, it is because he or she either needs the money or is leaving the company under unhappy circumstances and wants to divest. There is no evil afoot.

The rule was put in place to give investors assurance that insiders who trade in the short swing will not be able to profit from it. Investors then know that the insiders are not able to "jump" the market ahead of them and get all the big gains for themselves. The rule removes incentives to statutory insiders to try and make money quickly off of their own company.

If there *is* culpable conduct on the part of an insider (statutory or otherwise), Rule 16 is not the key player. It is Rule 10b-5 that makes insider trading unlawful where the trade is based on material, nonpublic information. There is no statutory limitation on who is an insider for purposes of prosecution under Rule 10b-5. The legislative weapons with which insiders can be prosecuted under this rule are extensive. An astute observer will note that statutory insiders can be forced to disgorge their profit under Rule 16 *and* be prosecuted under Rule 10b-5. There is definitely the possibility for this "double whammy" under securities law.

It is important to note that if an individual is *not* a statutory insider, he or she can swing profits lawfully in the short term. Day traders swing profits within the hour if they can. However, a day trader who is not a *statutory* insider can be an insider for purposes of Rule 10b-5 and be prosecuted if his or her trading was based on material, nonpublic information. This concept of insider trading can be very slippery in practice. A great investor finds out things about a company that other people do not know but could find out if they did the same things that the great investor did. That great investor is not an insider trader under those facts.

The precedents on insider trading differentiate who knew things based on their position in or relationship to the company, versus those who find things out by doing a lot of homework. The law has struggled with trying to differentiate innocent versus more venal types of stock tips, but predictability in this area of the law is less than perfect.

The single *caveat* one can readily infer is that trying to take advantage of the stock market based on information that comes from places to which the investing public has no access is a risky business. Although never formally charged with insider trading, Martha Stewart's conduct was such that the SEC clearly believed that her friend, then ImClone President Sam Waksal, had tipped her to sell her stock before making a public disclosure that caused the price of the stock to plummet. Stewart was charged and convicted for obstruction of justice. It is noteworthy that the U.S. Attorney's office did not give up just because her specific conduct was not actionable under the securities laws. They did not like what they saw, and they found a way to prosecute the conduct.

The following U.S. Supreme Court case examines the notion of "misappropriation theory," where a trader gets information on a security for one lawful reason, and then uses that information to trade on the security. The court affirms the illegality of misappropriation in this case, thereby extending the law on what constitutes unlawful insider trading.(2)

United States v. O'Hagan (1997)

Supreme Court of the United States (5221 U.S. 642)

Justice Ruth Bader Ginsburg delivered the opinion of the court.

This case concerns the interpretation and enforcement of §10(b) and §14(e) of the Securities Exchange Act of 1934, and rules made by the Securities and Exchange Commission pursuant to these provisions, Rule 10b-5 and Rule 14e-3(a). …In particular, we address and resolve…:

(1) Is a person who trades in securities for personal profit, using confidential information misappropriated in breach of a fiduciary duty to the source of the information, guilty of violating §10(b) and Rule 10b-5?

* * *

Respondent James Herman O'Hagan was a partner in the law firm of Dorsey & Whitney in Minneapolis, Minnesota. In July 1988, Grand Metropolitan PLC (Grand Met), a company based in London, England, retained Dorsey & Whitney as local counsel to represent Grand Met regarding a potential tender offer for the common stock of the Pillsbury Company, headquartered in Minneapolis. Both Grand Met and Dorsey & Whitney took precautions to protect the confidentiality of Grand Met's tender offer plans. O'Hagan did no work on the Grand Met representation. Dorsey & Whitney withdrew from representing Grand Met on September 9, 1988. Less than a month later, on October 4, 1988, Grand Met publicly announced its tender offer for Pillsbury stock.

On August 18, 1988, while Dorsey & Whitney was still representing Grand Met, O'Hagan began purchasing call options for Pillsbury stock. Each option gave him the right to purchase 100 shares of Pillsbury stock by a specified date in September 1988. Later in August and in September, O'Hagan made additional purchases of Pillsbury call options. By the end of September, he owned 2,500 unexpired Pillsbury options, apparently more than any other individual investor. See App. 85, 148. O'Hagan also purchased, in September 1988, some 5,000 shares of Pillsbury common stock, at a price just under $39 per share. When Grand Met announced its tender offer in October, the price of Pillsbury stock rose to nearly $60 per share. O'Hagan then sold his Pillsbury call options and common stock, making a profit of more than $4.3 million.

The Securities and Exchange Commission (SEC or Commission) initiated an investigation into O'Hagan's transactions, culminating in a 57 count indictment. The indictment alleged that O'Hagan defrauded his law firm and its client, Grand Met, by using for his own trading purposes material, nonpublic information regarding Grand Met's planned tender offer. According to the indictment, O'Hagan used the profits he gained through this trading to conceal his previous embezzlement and conversion of unrelated client trust funds. O'Hagan was charged with 20 counts of mail fraud...; 17 counts of securities fraud...; 17 counts of fraudulent trading in connection with a tender offer..., and 3 counts of violating federal money laundering statutes. A jury convicted O'Hagan on all 57 counts, and he was sentenced to a 41 month term of imprisonment.

A divided panel of the Court of Appeals for the Eighth Circuit reversed all of O'Hagan's convictions. Liability under §10(b) and Rule 10b-5, the Eighth Circuit held, may not be grounded on the "misappropriation theory" of securities fraud on which the prosecution relied.

* * *

We address first the Court of Appeals' reversal of O'Hagan's convictions under §10(b) and Rule 10b-5. [T]he Eighth Circuit rejected the misappropriation theory as a basis for §10(b) liability. We hold, in accord with several other Courts of Appeals, that criminal liability under §10(b) may be predicated on the misappropriation theory.

In pertinent part, §10(b) of the Exchange Act provides:

> "It shall be unlawful for any person, directly or indirectly, by the use of any means or instrumentality of interstate commerce or of the mails, or of any facility of any national securities exchange,
>
> ...
>
> (b) To use or employ, in connection with the purchase or sale of any security registered on a national securities exchange or any security not so registered, any manipulative or deceptive device or contrivance in contravention of such rules and regulations as the [Securities and Ex-

United States v. O'Hagan (1997)

change] Commission may prescribe as necessary or appropriate in the public interest or for the protection of investors."

The statute thus proscribes (1) using any deceptive device (2) in connection with the purchase or sale of securities, in contravention of rules prescribed by the Commission. The provision, as written, does not confine its coverage to deception of a purchaser or seller of securities.... Rather, the statute reaches any deceptive device used "in connection with the purchase or sale of any security."

Pursuant to its §10(b) rulemaking authority, the Commission has adopted Rule 10b-5, which, as relevant here, provides:

> "It shall be unlawful for any person, directly or indirectly, by the use of any means or instrumentality of interstate commerce, or of the mails or of any facility of any national securities exchange,
>
> (a) To employ any device, scheme, or artifice to defraud, [or]
>
> ...
>
> (c) To engage in any act, practice, or course of business which operates or would operate as a fraud or deceit upon any person, in connection with the purchase or sale of any security."

* * *

Under the "traditional" or "classical theory" of insider trading liability, §10(b) and Rule 10b-5 are violated when a corporate insider trades in the securities of his corporation on the basis of material, nonpublic information. Trading on such information qualifies as a "deceptive device" under §10(b), we have affirmed, because "a relationship of trust and confidence [exists] between the shareholders of a corporation and those insiders who have obtained confidential information by reason of their position with that corporation." That relationship, we recognized, "gives rise to a duty to disclose [or to abstain from trading] because of the 'necessity of preventing a corporate insider from...tak[ing] unfair advantage of...uninformed...stockholders.' The classical theory applies not only to officers, directors, and other permanent insiders of a corporation, but also to attorneys, accountants, consultants, and others who temporarily become fiduciaries of a corporation.

The "misappropriation theory" holds that a person commits fraud "in connection with" a securities transaction, and thereby violates §10(b) and Rule 10b-5, when he misappropriates confidential information for securities trading purposes, in breach of a duty owed to the source of the information.... Under this theory, a fiduciary's undisclosed, self serving use of a principal's information to purchase or sell securities, in breach of a duty of loyalty and confidentiality, defrauds the principal of the exclusive use of that information. In lieu of premising liability on a fiduciary relationship between company insider and purchaser or seller of the company's stock, the misappropriation theory premises liability on a fiduciary turned trader's deception of those who entrusted him with access to confidential information.

The two theories are complementary, each addressing efforts to capitalize on nonpublic information through the purchase or sale of securities. The classical theory targets a corporate insider's breach of duty to shareholders with whom the insider transacts; the misappropriation theory outlaws trading on the basis of nonpublic information by a corporate "outsider" in breach of a duty owed not to a trading party, but to the source of the information. The misappropriation theory is thus designed to "protec[t] the integrity of the securities markets against abuses by 'outsiders' to a corporation who have access to confidential information that will affect th[e] corporation's security price when revealed, but who owe no fiduciary or other duty to that corporation's shareholders."

In this case, the indictment alleged that O'Hagan, in breach of a duty of trust and confidence he owed to his law firm, Dorsey & Whitney, and to its client, Grand Met, traded on the basis of nonpublic information regarding Grand Met's planned tender offer for Pillsbury common stock. App. 16. This conduct, the Government charged, constituted a fraudulent device in connection with the purchase and sale of securities.

We agree with the Government that misappropriation, as just defined, satisfies §10(b)'s requirement that chargeable conduct involve a "deceptive device or contrivance" used "in connection with" the purchase or sale of securities. We observe, first, that misappropriators, as the Government describes them, deal in deception. A fiduciary who "[pretends] loyalty to the principal while secretly converting the principal's information for personal gain," "dupes" or defrauds the principal....

___

It is important to note that O'Hagan had no relationship at all with the issuer (Pillsbury) and none of his confidential information was from Pillsbury. It was all from the would-be acquirer. So the theory of misappropriation is detached from the "insider" part of the insider trading rule – even an outsider who has confidential information from someone and uses that information in a manner that changes stock prices is theoretically liable under this theory.

Securities Are a Many-Splendored Thing

Up until now, we have been speaking about a specific type of security, stock. There are, however, many other types of investment vehicles that constitute securities. As a law school professor once quipped, "A security is a place where an investor puts his or her money, expecting to get something for nothing." This professor was not a communist. He was trying, in a somewhat inaccurate but humorous way, to differentiate investment from labor. When you run a company, for example, some of your return comes from your effort—this would be remunerated in terms of wages. But some of the money comes from the labor of others and from the return on the capital (human or otherwise) that has been invested in the firm. If the firm has tradable shares that the owner can sell to separate out the instrument that carries financial return without the effort of its owner, that share is a security.

Securities represent intangible as opposed to tangible interests in property. Real estate might be a profitable investment, but it is tangible, and it is not a security. Interest in a Real Estate Investment Trust (REIT), however, would be a security. The 1933 Act defines security as:

"any note, stock, treasury stock, bond, debenture, evidence of indebtedness, certificate of interest or participation in any profit-sharing agreement, collateral-trust certificate, pre-organizational certificate or subscription, transferable share, investment contract, voting-trust certificate, certificate of deposit for a security, fractional undivided interest in oil, gas, or other mineral rights, or, in general, any interest or instrument commonly known as a 'security,' or any certificate of interest or participation in, temporary or interim certificate for, receipt for, guarantee of, or warrant or right to subscribe to or purchase, any of the foregoing."

Each type of security is susceptible to different regulatory controls both under the 1933 and 1934 Acts, and under other legislative enactments. For example, back in the days of Limited Partnership real estate deals, many partnership interests were only sold within a given state, exempting them from federal regulation. However, they did fall within the Blue Sky laws of the state in which the instruments were offered for sale. Blue Sky laws are laws that were enacted to protect investors from being tricked into buying shares in the blue sky—nothing but air. Many promoters were charged with Blue Sky violations during the days following the fall of the Limited Partnership tax loopholes.

In one case, investors were sold an inaccessible piece of an actual orange grove, which the sellers irrevocably contracted to "tend" for the investor at the time of the sale. The contract at the time of the sale provided that the orange yield from the investor's lot would be combined with the yield from other grove owners and then sold. The proceeds of the sale of oranges would be distributed to all grove owners in a pro rata share based on ownership (irrespective of any lot's actual production). No disclosures were made regarding long-term historical data or risks with regard to the orange grove or any piece thereof. Investors lost lots of money, and sued for securities violations. The sellers of the grove lots asserted that they were selling real estate and not securities—that this was tangible property and outside the reach of the 1933 Act. The court sided with the investors, that, taken as a whole, this was never really a sale of real estate. It was the sale of an interest in an investment contract based on a scheme to return money without direct effort of the buyer, and without being tied to the specific property to which the buyer held the nominal title (the investor's lot's oranges were not segregated in any way from all the other oranges). The sellers were charged with securities violations and appropriately held liable for what was seen as a scam on investors.

Officers and Directors Do Not Need Crystal Balls

If Enron's officers had not personally benefited from their bad acts, and had the decisions they made been the result of lawful but bad judgment, they might not have been either criminally or civilly liable. Although firms are scrutinized for unlawful conduct if they lose money, if that scrutiny does not yield fruit, the fact that those in charge were (for lack of a better word) stupid about their choices does not give shareholders a right of recovery. Stupid is not criminal, even if sometimes we wish it were. Stupid in itself is not a basis for executive financial liability. This is partly because all decisions can look stupid when hindsight is available to illuminate the errors of managements ways. It is also because the law leaves business judgment to business leaders, and the courts try to stay out of it.

In fact, with director and officer liability skyrocketing as a result of the disclosure issues under the 1933 Act, the 1934 Act, and Sarbanes/Oxley, the courts have become very cautious about ascribing liability against directors for negligence as well. According to law cited by McAdams in *Law, Business and Society*, 6th edition, "some states have changed their duty of care standard such that proof of *intentional misconduct or gross negligence* would be required to establish a breach."

Almost every state has a rule of law known as the "Business Judgment Rule." This rule says that absent fraud, illegality, or conflict of interest, the judgment of an officer or director shall not be questioned by the court. The conflict of interest referenced in the rule is a financial one. If the executive makes money personally by harming the corporation, that is a conflict of interest which allows the court subject matter jurisdiction over the executive's decision-making. Likewise, if the executive engages in fraud or unlawful conduct, the court has the power to take a look. However, if the executive is merely narrow minded, too aggressive, or (again) just plain stupid, the problem belongs to the shareholders, and the courts literally do not have the power (subject matter jurisdiction) to make the executive pay up.

Consider the following Illinois case involving chewing gum giant Philip Wrigley, then majority shareholder of the Chicago Cubs, and minority shareholder Mr. Shlensky, who asserted that Wrigley was mismanaging the Cubs. Although the court opined about some possible business justifications for Wrigley's refusal to install night lights at Wrigley field, ultimately it admitted that it was not trying to say that Wrigley was correct in his decision (or incorrect for that matter). Watch for the all important sentence that says, "This is beyond our jurisdiction and ability." This sentence represents the Business Judgment Rule applied and in living black and white print.(3)

Here is the case.

Shlensky v. Wrigley (1968)

Illinois Court of Appeal (237 N.E.2nd 776)

Justice Sullivan delivered the opinion of the court.

Facts

Plaintiff Shlensky, a minority stockholder in the Chicago Cubs major league baseball team, sued the corporation's directors on the grounds of mismanagement and negligence because of their refusal to install lights at Wrigley Field, then the only major league stadium without lights. One of the defendant directors, Philip K. Wrigley, owner of 80% of the stock, allegedly objected to lights because of his personal opinion that, "Baseball is a 'daytime sport' and that the installation of lights and night baseball games will have a deteriorating effect upon the surrounding neighborhood." Allegedly, Wrigley also said that he was not interested in whether the Cubs would benefit financially from lights. Allegedly, the other members of the board of directors deferred to Wrigley on this matter and allowed him to dominate the board.

Shlensky claimed that lights would maximize attendance and revenue. The Cubs, in the years 1961-65, lost money from direct baseball operations. Shlensky attributed those losses to poor attendance and argued that without lights the losses would continue. Shlensky's evidence indicated that the Cubs drew greater attendance on the road than at home and that Chicago White Sox night games during the week drew better than the Cubs' daytime games. Shlensky sought damages and an order requiring the installation of lights and the scheduling of night games. He lost at the trial level and appealed to the Illinois Appellate Court.

The question on appeal is whether plaintiff's amended complaint states a cause of action. It is plaintiff's position that fraud, illegality, and conflict of interest are not the only bases for a stockholder's derivative action against the directors. Contrarywise, defendants argue that the courts will not step in and interfere with honest business judgment of the directors unless there is a showing of fraud, illegality, or conflict of interest.

The cases in this area are numerous…. However, the courts have pronounced certain ground rules…. [The Court has said,]

> It is…fundamental in the law of corporations that the majority of its stockholders shall control the policy of the corporation, and regulate and govern the lawful exercise of its franchise and business…. Everyone purchasing or subscribing for stock in a corporation impliedly agrees that he will be bound by the acts and proceedings done or sanctioned by a majority of the stockholders, or by the agents of the corporation duly chosen by such majority, within the scope of the powers conferred by the charter, and courts of equity will not undertake the control [of] the policy or business methods of a corporation, although it may be seen that a wiser policy might be adopted and the business more successful if other methods were pursued. The majority of shares of its stocks, or the agents by the holders thereof lawfully chosen, must be permitted to control the business of the corporation in their discretion, when not in violation of its charter or some public law, or corruptly and fraudulently subversive of the rights and interests of the corporation or of a shareholder.

* * *

Plaintiff in the instant case argues that the directors are acting for reasons unrelated to the financial interest and welfare of the Cubs. However, we are not satisfied that the motives assigned to Philip K. Wrigley, and through him to the other directors, are contrary to the best interest of the corporation and the stockholders. For example, it appears to us that the effect on the surrounding neighborhood might well be considered by a director who was considering the patrons who would or would not attend the game if the park were in a poor neighborhood. Furthermore, the long-run interest of the corporation in its property value at Wrigley Field might demand all efforts to keep the neighborhood from deteriorating. By these thoughts we do not mean to say that we have decided that the decision of the directors was a correct one. That is beyond our jurisdiction and ability. We are merely saying that the decision is one properly before directors and the motives alleged in the amended complaint showed no fraud, illegality, or conflict of interest in their making of that decision.

Shlensky v. Wrigley (1968)

While all the courts do not insist that one or more of the three elements must be present for a stockholder's derivative action to lie, nevertheless we feel that unless the conduct of the defendants at least borders on one of the elements, the court should not interfere. The trial court in the instant case acted properly in dismissing plaintiff's amended complaint.

* * *

Finally, we do not agree with plaintiff's contention that failure to follow the example of the other major league clubs in scheduling night games constituted negligence. Plaintiff made no allegation that these team's [sic] night schedules were profitable or that the purpose for which night baseball had been undertaken was fulfilled. Furthermore, it cannot be said that directors, even those of corporations that are losing money, must follow the lead of other corporations in the field. Directors are elected for their business capabilities and judgment and the courts cannot require them to forgo their judgment because of the decisions of directors of other companies. Courts may not decide these questions in the absence of a clear showing of dereliction of duty on the part of the specific directors and mere failure to "follow the crowd" is not such a dereliction.

Affirmed.

Although a bit difficult to extract from the case, the Business Judgment Rule as articulated in this case is that absent fraud, illegality, or financial conflict of interest (or something really close to that), the courts do not have—or at least will use their discretion not to take—jurisdiction (power) to evaluate the business judgment of the directors of a corporation.

Merging Public Corporations

Mergers of publicly traded companies are complicated, heavily regulated, and sometimes bitterly fought.

Mergers may be friendly or hostile, although those terms are very misleading. Friendly mergers often involve combining companies that have historically competed against each other in cut-throat fashion. Hostile mergers, to be successful, are welcomed by the majority of the shareholders—they are only hostile to the entrenched board of directors in place prior to the merger.

In order to understand mergers in general, and their friendly or hostile character in particular, it is important to consider how mergers generally occur. Although the word merger implies two companies coming together for the purpose of living happily ever after, that is not generally what happens.

In a merger or takeover, one company is generally trying (usually for synergistic reasons, but not always) to buy another. The buying company is referred to as the acquirer, and the company it is trying to buy is referred to as the target. If the directors of the target company agree that the offer price is a good deal for their shareholders (almost invariably the offer is for a price significantly higher than the market price immediately preceding the tender offer), then theoretically the board recommends the sale of the company, and the takeover is considered friendly.

If the target board is disinclined to accept the offer, and the acquirer still attempts to garner a majority interest in the stock of the company by buying shares in the open market (or in some other way), then the takeover is hostile. In a hostile takeover attempt, the acquirer must file a complete disclosure with the SEC to reveal its intentions before it has acquired 5% of the target's stock. The price of the target stock generally accelerates quickly, sometimes taking the hostile acquirer out of commission before it has gotten a significant stronghold in the stock. Sometimes, would-be hostile acquirers are bought off in what is referred to as "green mail" so that the entrenched board can keep its position. In any

case, what differentiates a friendly takeover from a hostile one is the willingness of the board of directors to support the merger. In today's diffusively held companies, shareholders are generally very happy whenever they get a very inflated price for their stock, irrespective of what happens to the board of directors or the company itself after the merger is complete.

In a friendly takeover, after all the price negotiations are complete and the shareholders have approved the deal, the board of directors of the target company suspends trading of its stock. At that point in time, the stock of the target company goes off the exchange. The shareholders receive the actual friendly tender offer, which is the offer for shareholders to tender shares for the specific price the majority agreed to when the merger was voted upon. Most of the time, the majority of shareholders then tender or redeem their shares for the acquisition price. Tenders are for either cash or stock in the acquiring company. Neither shareholder approval nor the tendering of a majority of the outstanding shares is inevitable. Friendly takeover attempts can fail if shareholders believe that the tender offer is not good enough or that the company would eventually do better going a different route. However, if management is competent and the offer is good, the friendly takeover is accomplished without much angst.

If the takeover is hostile, the acquirer generally buys stock from the marketplace. If the hostile acquirer is able to get enough shares to vote in a new board of directors, it takes over the board by voting in its own directors. (This can be really interesting to watch.) A special election is called, the timing of which is mandated by state law. Each state has a shareholder record date that governs how much time must elapse before a shareholder can vote his or her share. Sometimes a White Knight steps up and tries to get the company away from the hostile acquirer, and sometimes some crazy counter-takeover attempts are made. If the special election goes according to plan, however, the old board is ousted, the new board is in, and the hostile acquirer is in control.

In either case, hostile or friendly, once an acquirer has its directors in place, these new directors vote to merge the target into the acquirer. The target disappears as a legal entity. This is a bit over-simplified, since there are clever business forms through which this process evolves, but that is still basically how it works. At the end of the day, only one company, the acquirer, exists, for it has swallowed up the target like PacMan in action. (In law school, the hypothetical merger examples use the names "Swallow-up Inc." and "Target Inc.")

Many shareholders fail to tender their shares after a merger has been approved. Whether the takeover was hostile or friendly, this is somewhat inevitable. People frequently ask whether the merger still goes forward if there are outstanding shares in the target.

The answer is that absent legal intervention, which is extremely rare, and for which there are narrow grounds, the merger is readily completed even with shares outstanding. However, those shareholders who have not tendered their shares *do not* own a portion of the merged company. Upon completion of the merger, the target company ceased to exist. The shares of stock of the former target became *rights*, empowering former shareholders to be paid the proceeds of the tender. In other words, the former target's shares must be tendered eventually for the shareholder to ever get their money or, in the case of a stock swap, new shares.

Often with computerized brokerage houses, this is done electronically and, to some degree, invisibly. Brokers tender shares under their control because they understand that the acquired company will cease its existence after the merger. Before computerization, however, there were many who held onto stock certificates representing interests in companies that ceased to exist.

Assume that an old-fashioned stockholder has his or her shares in a desk drawer and does not have a broker taking care of these issues. All is not lost to that shareholder for failing to tender at the time of the merger. Generally, the acquirer must hold in trust the money or stock owed to the shareholders who have not tendered their stock. After a certain period of time (which varies from state to state), the residual money or stock escheats (transfers) to the state, which holds it on behalf of the shareholder of the now-deceased company, often for significantly long periods of time. In summary, the shares of stock in a company that is subsequently merged into another company may be redeemed even years after the company ceased to exist.

At one time or another, a television show or newspaper advertisements will claim that certain people are beneficiaries of an inheritance about which they are unaware. To be given the information about that inheritance, the beneficiary must agree to share the proceeds with the television producers or advertisers. Usually this happens when the beneficiary of a shareholder of a previously merged company does not know that the old stock was never redeemcd, and that it still has value that is held by the state on behalf of the beneficiary of the original owner of the unredeemed stock.

Finally, it is often the case that even though a target is merged, the trademarks and trade names survive, so that it appears that the company still "lives" long after it has been dissolved. For example, The Banana Republic began as a small retail chain with two stores and a safari motif. The store name and brand survive, although the founding company was merged into The Gap, Inc., in 1983.

Tying Things Together

The following case has a bit of everything: a hostile takeover attempt (Occidental trying to acquire Old Kern), a White Knight that saved Old Kern from the takeover (Tenneco), a claim for damages under rule 16(b)'s prohibition against short-swing profits taken by 10% shareholders in a sale within six months of a buy (Old Kern trying to get Occidental to give back the money it made after its failed takeover attempt), a bit of green mail (Tenneco happy to pay to get rid of Occidental as a strong minority shareholder), and the finding that underneath 16(b) is the notion that despite its "no-fault" character, the court will use a very limited application of rule 16(b) when it can, if there are no shenanigans involved.(4)

Kern County Land Co. v. Occidental Petroleum Corp., **411 U.S. 582 (1973)**

U.S. Supreme Court

Certiorari to the United States Court of Appeals for the Second Circuit

No. 71-1059. Argued December 5-6, 1972, Decided May 7, 1973.

During a tender-offer campaign, respondent bought more than 10% of the outstanding stock of petitioner's predecessor (Old Kern). Respondent (Occidental) was blocked in its takeover efforts by a defensive merger between Old Kern and Tenneco, in which Old Kern stockholders were to receive new Tenneco stock on a share-for-share basis. Less than a month after its initial tender offer, [Occidental] thereupon negotiated a binding option to sell to Tenneco at a date over six months after the tender offer expired all the new Tenneco stock to which [Occidental] would be entitled when the merger took place. Sale of the post-merger stock yielded respondent a profit of some $19 million, which petitioner sought to recover by a suit under 16 (b) of the Securities Exchange Act of 1934, prohibiting profitable short-swing speculation by statutory insiders. The District Court's summary judgment for petitioner was reversed by the Court of Appeals. Held: The transactions, which were not based on a statutory insider's information and were not susceptible of the speculative abuse that 16 (b) was designed to prevent, did not constitute "sales" within the meaning of that provision. Pp. 591-604.

> (a) There was nothing in connection with respondent's tender-offer acquisition of Old Kern stock or the exchange thereof for the Tenneco stock that gave respondent "inside information," and once the merger, which respondent did not engineer, was approved the Old Kern-Tenneco stock exchange was involuntary. Pp. 596-600.
>
> (b) The option agreement was not of itself a "sale," the option was grounded on the mutual advantages to respondent as a minority stockholder that wanted to terminate an investment it had not chosen to make and Tenneco

whose management did not want a potentially trouble-
some minority stockholder; and the option was not a
source of potential speculative abuse, since respondent
had no inside information about Tenneco or its new
stock. Pp. 601-604.

Affirmed.

Justice White delivered the opinion of the Court.

Section 16 (b) of the Securities Exchange Act of 1934, 48 Stat. 896,
15 U.S.C. 78p (b), provides that officers, directors, and holders of
more than 10% of the listed stock of any company shall be liable to
the company for any profits realized from any purchase and sale or
sale and purchase of such stock occurring within a period of six
months. Unquestionably, one or more statutory purchases occur
when one company, seeking to gain control of another, acquires
more than 10% of the stock of the latter through a tender offer made
to its shareholders. But is it a 16 (b) "sale" when the target of the tender offer defends itself by merging into a third company and the tender offeror then exchanges his stock for the stock of the surviving
company and also grants an option to purchase the latter stock that is
not exercisable within the statutory six-month period? This is the
question before us in this case.

I

On May 8, 1967, after unsuccessfully seeking to merge with Kern
County Land Co. (Old Kern), Occidental Petroleum Corp. (Occidental) announced an offer, to expire on June 8, 1967, to purchase on a
first-come, first-served basis 500,000 shares of Old Kern common
stock at a price of $83.50 per share plus a brokerage commission of
$1.50 per share. By May 10, 1967, 500,000 shares, more than 10%
of the outstanding shares of Old Kern, had been tendered. On May
11, Occidental extended its offer to encompass an additional 500,000
shares. At the close of the tender offer, on June 8, 1967, Occidental
owned 887,549 shares of Old Kern.

Immediately upon the announcement of Occidental's tender offer,
the Old Kern management undertook to frustrate Occidental's takeover attempt. Λ management letter to all stockholders cautioned
against tender and indicated that Occidental's offer might not be the
best available, since the management was engaged in merger discus-

sions with several companies. When Occidental extended its tender offer, the president of Old Kern sent a telegram to all stockholders again advising against tender. In addition, Old Kern undertook merger discussions with Tenneco, Inc. (Tenneco), and, on May 19, 1967, the Board of Directors of Old Kern announced that it had approved a merger proposal advanced by Tenneco. Under the terms of the merger, Tenneco would acquire the assets, property, and goodwill of Old Kern, subject to its liabilities, through "Kern County Land Co." (New Kern), a new corporation to be formed by Tenneco to receive the assets and carry on the business of Old Kern. The shareholders of Old Kern would receive a share of Tenneco cumulative convertible preference stock in exchange for each share of Old Kern common stock which they owned. On the same day, May 19, Occidental, in a quarterly report to stockholders, appraised the value of the new Tenneco stock at $105 per share.

Occidental, seeing its tender offer and takeover attempt being blocked by the Old Kern-Tenneco "defensive" merger, countered on May 25 and 31 with two mandamus actions in the California courts seeking to obtain extensive inspection of Old Kern books and records. Realizing that, if the Old Kern-Tenneco merger were approved and successfully closed, Occidental would have to exchange its Old Kern shares for Tenneco stock and would be locked into a minority position in Tenneco, Occidental took other steps to protect itself. Between May 30 and June 2, it negotiated an arrangement with Tenneco whereby Occidental granted Tenneco Corp., a subsidiary of Tenneco, an option to purchase at $105 per share all of the Tenneco preference stock to which Occidental would be entitled in exchange for its Old Kern stock when and if the Old Kern-Tenneco merger was closed. The premium to secure the option, at $10 per share, totaled $8,866,230 and was to be paid immediately upon the signing of the option agreement. If the option were exercised, the premium was to be applied to the purchase price. By the terms of the option agreement, the option could not be exercised prior to December 9, 1967, a date six months and one day after expiration of Occidental's tender offer. On June 2, 1967, within six months of the acquisition by Occidental of more than 10% ownership of Old Kern, Occidental and Tenneco Corp. executed the option. Soon thereafter, Occidental announced that it would not oppose the Old Kern-Tenneco merger and dismissed its state court suits against Old Kern.

The Old Kern-Tenneco merger plan was presented to and approved by Old Kern shareholders at their meeting on July 17, 1967. Occidental refrained from voting its Old Kern shares, but in a letter read at the meeting Occidental stated that it had determined prior to June 2 not to oppose the merger and that it did not consider the plan unfair or inequitable. Indeed, Occidental indicated that, had it been voting, it would have voted in favor of the merger.

Meanwhile, the Securitics and Exchange Commission had refused Occidental's request to exempt from possible 16 (b) liability Occidental's exchange of its Old Kern stock for the Tenneco preference shares that would take place when and if the merger transaction were closed. Various Old Kern stockholders, with Occidental's interests in mind, thereupon sought to delay consummation of the merger by instituting various lawsuits in the state and federal courts. These attempts were unsuccessful, however, and preparations for the merger neared completion with an Internal Revenue Service ruling that consummation of the plan would result in a tax-free exchange with no taxable gain or loss to Old Kern shareholders, and with the issuance of the necessary approval of the merger closing by the California Commissioner of Corporations.

The Old Kern-Tenneco merger transaction was closed on August 30. Old Kern shareholders thereupon became irrevocably entitled to receive Tenneco preference stock, share for share in exchange for their Old Kern stock. Old Kern was dissolved and all of its assets, including "all claims, demands, rights and chooses in action accrued or to accrue under and by virtue of the Securities Exchange Act of 1934…," were transferred to New Kern.

The option granted by Occidental on June 2, 1967, was exercised on December 11, 1967. Occidental, not having previously availed itself of its right, exchanged certificates representing 887,549 shares of Old Kern stock for a certificate representing a like number of shares of Tenneco preference stock. The certificate was then endorsed over to the optionee-purchaser, and in return $84,229,185 was credited to Occidental's accounts at various banks. Adding to this amount the $8,886,230 premium paid in June, Occidental received $93,905,415 for its Old Kern stock (including the 1,900 shares acquired prior to issuance of its tender offer). In addition, Occidental received dividends totaling $1,793,439.22. Occidental's total profit was $19,506,419.22 on the shares obtained through its tender offer.

On October 17, 1967, New Kern instituted a suit under 16 (b) against Occidental to recover the profits which Occidental had realized as a result of its dealings in Old Kern stock. The complaint alleged that the execution of the Occidental-Tenneco option on June 2, 1967, and the exchange of Old Kern shares for shares of Tenneco to which Occidental became entitled pursuant to the merger closed on August 30, 1967, were both "sales" within the coverage of 16 (b). Since both acts took place within six months of the date on which Occidental became the owner of more than 10% of the stock of Old Kern, New Kern asserted that 16 (b) required surrender of the profits realized by Occidental. New Kern eventually moved for summary judgment, and, on December 27, 1970, the District Court granted summary judgment in favor of New Kern. The District Court held that the execution of the option on June 2, 1967, and the exchange of Old Kern shares for shares of Tenneco on August 30, 1967, were "sales" under 16 (b). The Court ordered Occidental to disgorge its profits plus interest. In a supplemental opinion, Occidental was also ordered to refund the dividends which it had received plus interest.

However, on appeal, the Court of Appeals reversed and ordered summary judgment entered in favor of Occidental. …The Court held that neither the option nor the exchange constituted a "sale" within the purview of 16 (b). We granted certiorari. We affirm.

…Although traditional cash-for-stock transactions that result in a purchase and sale or a sale and purchase within the six-month, statutory period are clearly within the purview of 16 (b), the courts have wrestled with the question of inclusion or exclusion of certain "unorthodox" transactions.

…In the present case, it is undisputed that Occidental became a "beneficial owner" within the terms of 16 (b) when, pursuant to its tender offer, it "purchased" more than 10% of the outstanding shares of Old Kern. We must decide, however, whether a "sale" within the ambit of the statute took place either when Occidental became irrevocably bound to exchange its shares of Old Kern for shares of Tenneco pursuant to the terms of the merger agreement between Old Kern and Tenneco or when Occidental gave an option to Tenneco to purchase from Occidental the Tenneco shares so acquired.

We see no satisfactory basis or reason for disagreeing with the judgment of the Court of Appeals in this respect.

The judgment of the Court of Appeals is affirmed. [Occidental is entitled to keep its profits from the exercise of the option it negotiated.]

So ordered.

_____

Notes

1. Escott v. BarChris Construction, 283 F.Supp. 643 (1968)

2. United States v. O'Hagan, U.S. Supreme Court, 5221 US 642, (1997)

3. Shlensky v. Wrigley, Illinois Court of Appeal (237 N.E.2nd 776) 1968.

4. Kern County Land Co. v. Occidental Corp., United States Supreme Court, 411 U.S. 582 (1973)

Chapter 7
The Monopoly Game

A simplistic or pure definition of a monopoly is a market condition where there is only one seller in the market.(1) However, that definition is not very useful for understanding how courts see monopolies today. In modern case law, monopolies are reframed as firms that can price with monopoly power, and those are defined as firms or organizations that control enough of the supply in a given market to have the ability to price without competitive stress.(2)

You may remember that monopoly is one of the market failure areas that, absent regulation, can interfere with a properly functioning free market. Businesses have a strong interest in maximizing profits and eliminating competition, and they will monopolize if they are able. In this regard, there is a direct conflict between the interests of a single enterprise and the interests of a free market society. Individual businesses benefit from monopoly and monopoly-level pricing, but society does not.

The history of our antitrust laws (and why they are not called antimonopoly laws) is discussed in the next chapter, but at this point it is necessary to understand that antitrust laws do not protect competitors, they protect competition itself. A properly functioning market produces the most goods at the highest quality for the least money, and a market where monopoly flourishes cannot do that. However, a market where one competitor destroys other competitors through lower prices and better products is one that is functioning as it should, even though it too may eliminate competition for a time.

Market Concentration

The term "market concentration" relates to the number of competitors in a given market. The more competitors, the less concentrated or more diffuse the market. The fewer competitors, the more concentrated the market. Although the number of competitors in a given market does not absolutely determine the existence or absence of monopoly power, a very concentrated market (where there are few competitors) is the first clue of a problem. The fewer competitors there are in a market, the greater the likelihood of monopoly pricing.

It is clear that when two or more companies merge or combine, the result (at least in the short term) is a reduction in the number of competitors in the market place. If mergers occur with an intent to monopolize, they are unlawful, and sometimes even criminal. The Sherman Act, in section 2, says in relevant part:

> "Every person who shall monopolize, or attempt to monopolize, or combine or conspire with any other person or persons, to monopolize any part of the trade or commerce among the several States, or with foreign nations, shall be deemed guilty of a felony, and, on conviction thereof, shall be punished by fine not exceeding $10,000,000 if a corporation, or, if any other person, $350,000, or by imprisonment not exceeding three years, or by both said punishments, in the discretion of the court."

The previous chapter spoke briefly about hostile and friendly mergers but did not explore why mergers might be in the best interests of the companies involved.

There are a host of good reasons why companies try to join together. For example, companies can be motivated to combine their resources to take advantage of economies of scale or greater efficiency. In a world of "cut-throat" competition, one competitor may legitimately sell itself to another rather than bleeding out entirely.

However, even with the best of legitimate reasons to combine, mergers can have anticompetitive effects.

Statutes passed subsequent to the Sherman Act have been enacted to empower the Federal Trade Commission (FTC) and the U.S. Department of Justice to control mergers. The job of the Department of Justice is to determine when mergers are likely to harm competition and increase prices. A concentrated market is the first thing that the Department of Justice examines to determine whether or not there is a problem.

The Department of Justice measures market concentration with an index known as the Herfindahl-Herschman Index (HHI). This is a simple measurement, ranging from zero to 10,000, that is calculated by taking the market share of each participant in a given market, squaring it, and then adding those squares together. Consider the following example: Assume there are seven competitors in a given market. Three have 20% of the market each, and four have 10% each. Square each of the 10% and 20% shares.

Share	Square
10	100
10	100
10	100
10	100
20	400
20	400
20	400
100	1600

The sum of the market shares before they are squared will always add up to 100%. The sum of the squares will increase as the market becomes more concentrated. In this case the sum of the squares is 1600, and that is the HHI.

The maximum possible IIHI, 10,000, occurs when there is a single competitor who has 100% of the market. Any HHI over 1,000 is considered concentrated, and a merger in a market with an HHI of over 1800 is presumed to be anticompetitive, although that presumption is rebuttable.

Keep in mind that market share alone is not sufficient to determine if there is a problem with competition. If there are no barriers keeping new entrants out of the market, there may be absolutely no monopoly problem, even in a very concentrated market. Antitrust laws are less concerned with market concentration at a specific moment in time, and more concerned with the ability of a given competitor to price without fear of either existing or future competition.

The *Syufy* (3) case that follows illustrates the difference between protecting competition and protecting competitors. It limits the significance of market concentration and ties anticompetitive conduct to the presence or absence of barriers to entry to new competitors. The case applauds aggressive and efficient competition, making the argument that when strong competitors eliminate weaker ones, they can serve the free market in a positive and productive way.

United States of America v. Syufy Enterprises; Raymond J. Syufy (1990)

United States Court of Appeals for the Ninth Circuit (903 F.2d 659)

Circuit Judge Alex Kozinski delivered the opinion of the court.

OPINION

Suspect [Suspicious] that giant film distributors like Columbia, Paramount and Twentieth Century-Fox had fallen prey to Raymond Syufy, the canny operator of a chain of Las Vegas, Nevada, movie theatres, the United States Department of Justice brought this civil antitrust action to force Syufy to disgorge the theatres he had purchased in 1982–84 from his former competitors. The case is unusual in a number of respects: The Department of Justice concedes that moviegoers in Las Vegas suffered no direct injury as a result of the allegedly illegal transactions; nor does the record reflect complaints from Syufy's bought-out competitors, as the sales were made at fair prices and not precipitated by any monkey business; and the supposedly oppressed movie companies have weighed in on Syufy's side. The Justice Department nevertheless remains intent on rescuing this platoon of Goliaths from a single David.

After extensive discovery and an 8 1/2 day trial, the learned district judge entered comprehensive findings of fact and conclusions of law, holding for Syufy. He found, *inter alia* [meaning "among other things"], that Syufy's actions did not injure competition because there are no barriers to entry—others could and did enter the market—and that Syufy therefore did not have the power to control prices or exclude the competition. While Justice raises a multitude of issues in its appeal, these key findings of the district court present the greatest hurdle it must overcome.

FACTS

Gone are the days when a movie ticket cost a dime, popcorn a nickel and theatres had a single screen: This is the age of the multiplex. With more than 300 new films released every year—each potentially the next Batman or E.T.—many successful theatres today run a different film on each of their six, twelve or eighteen screens. The multiplex offers something for everyone: Moviegoers can choose from a wider selection of films; theatre operators are able to balance profits and losses from blockbusters and flops, and to reduce manpower by consolidating concession islands; the producers, of course, like having the extra screens on which to display their wares.

Raymond Syufy understood the formula well. In 1981, he entered the Las Vegas market with a splash by opening a six-screen theatre. Newly constructed and luxuriously furnished, it put existing facilities to shame. Syufy's entry into the Las Vegas market caused a stir, precipitating a titanic bidding war. Soon, theatres in Las Vegas were paying some of the highest license fees in the nation, while distributors sat back and watched the easy money roll in.

It is the nature of free enterprise that fierce, no holds barred competition will drive out the least effective participants in the market, providing the most efficient allocation of productive resources. And so it was in the Las Vegas movie market in 1982. After a hard fought battle among several contenders, Syufy gained the upper hand. Two of his rivals, Mann Theatres and Plitt Theatres, saw their future as rocky and decided to sell out to Syufy. While Mann and Plitt are major exhibitors nationwide, neither had a large presence in Las Vegas. Mann operated two indoor theatres with a total of three screens; Plitt operated a single theatre with three screens. Things were relatively quiet until September 1984; in September, Syufy entered into earnest negotiations with Cragin Industries, his largest remaining competitor. Cragin sold out to Syufy midway through October, leaving Roberts Company, a small exhibitor of mostly second-run films, as Syufy's only competitor for first-run films in Las Vegas.

It is these three transactions—Syufy's purchases of the Mann, Plitt and Cragin theatres—that the Justice Department claims amount to antitrust violations. As government counsel explained at oral argument, the thrust of its case is that "you may not get monopoly power by buying out your competitors."

DISCUSSION

Competition is the driving force behind our free enterprise system. Unlike centrally planned economies, where decisions about production and allocation are made by government bureaucrats who ostensibly see the big picture and know to do the right thing, capitalism relies on decentralized planning—millions of producers and consumers making hundreds of millions of individual decisions each year—to determine what and how much will be produced. Competition plays *the key* role in this process: It imposes an essential discipline on producers and sellers of goods to provide the consumer with a better product at a lower cost; it drives out inefficient and marginal producers, releasing resources to higher-valued uses; it promotes diversity, giving consumers *choices* to fit a wide array of personal preferences; it avoids permanent concentrations of economic power, as even the largest firm can lose market share to a feistier and hungrier rival. If, as the metaphor goes, a market economy is governed by an invisible hand, competition is surely the brass knuckles by which it enforces its decisions.

When competition is impaired, producers may be able to reap monopoly profits, denying consumers many of the benefits of a free market. It is a simple but important truth, therefore, that our antitrust laws are designed to protect the integrity of the market system by assuring that competition reigns freely. While much has been said and

United States of America v. Syufy Enterprises; Raymond J. Syufy (1990)

written about the antitrust laws during the last century of their existence, ultimately the court must resolve a practical question in every
monopolization case: Is this the type of situation where market forces are likely to cure the perceived problem within a reasonable period of time? Or, have barriers been erected to constrain the normal
operation of the market, so that the problem is not likely to be self-
correcting? In the latter situation, it might well be necessary for a
court to correct the market imbalance; in the former, a court ought to
exercise extreme caution because judicial intervention in a competitive situation can itself upset the balance of market forces, bringing
about the very ills the antitrust laws were meant to prevent.

It is with these observations in mind that we turn to the case before
us. Perhaps the most remarkable aspect of this case is that the accused monopolist is a relatively tiny regional entrepreneur while the
alleged victims are humongous national corporations with considerable market power of their own. While this is not dispositive —it is
conceivable that a little big man may be able to exercise monopoly
power locally against large national entities—chances are it is not
without significance. Common sense suggests, and experience teaches, that monopoly power is far more easily exercised by larger, economically more powerful entities against smaller, economically pu-
nier ones, than vice versa.

Also of significance is the government's concession that Syufy was
only a monopsonist, not a monopolist. Thus, the government argues
that Syufy had market power, but that it exercised this power only
against its suppliers (film distributors), not against its consumers
(moviegoers). This is consistent with the record, which demonstrates
that Syufy always treated moviegoers fairly: The movie tickets, popcorn, nuts and the Seven-Ups cost about the same in Las Vegas as in
other, comparable markets. While it is theoretically possible to have
a middleman who is a monopolist upstream but not downstream, this
is a somewhat counterintuitive scenario. Why, if he truly had significant market power, would Raymond Syufy have chosen to take advantage of the big movie distributors while giving a fair shake to ordinary people? And why do the distributors, the alleged victims of
the monopolization scheme, think that Raymond Syufy is the best
thing that ever happened to the Las Vegas movie market?

The answers to these questions are significant because, like all antitrust cases, this one must make economic sense. Keeping in mind
that competition, not government intervention, is the touchstone of a

healthy, vigorous economy, we proceed to examine whether the district court erred in concluding that Syufy does not, in fact, hold monopoly power. There is universal agreement that monopoly power is the power to exclude competition or control prices. The district court determined that Syufy possessed neither power. As the government's case stands or falls with these propositions, the parties have devoted much of their analysis to these findings. So do we.

1. Power to Exclude Competition

It is true, of course, that when Syufy acquired Mann's, Plitt's and Cragin's theatres he temporarily diminished the number of competitors in the Las Vegas first-run film market. But this does not necessarily indicate foul play; many legitimate market arrangements diminish the number of competitors. It would be odd if they did not, as the nature of competition is to make winners and losers. If there are no significant barriers to entry, however, eliminating competitors will not enable the survivors to reap a monopoly profit; any attempt to raise prices above the competitive level will lure into the market new competitors able and willing to offer their commercial goods or personal services for less.

Time after time, we have recognized this basic fact of economic life:

A high market share, though it may ordinarily raise an inference of monopoly power, will not do so in a market with low entry barriers or other evidence of a defendant's inability to control prices or exclude competitors.

There is nothing magic about this proposition; it is simple common sense, embodied in the Antitrust Division's own Merger Guidelines:

> If entry into a market is so easy that existing competitors could not succeed in raising price for any significant period of time, the Department is unlikely to challenge mergers in that market.

The district court, after taking testimony from a dozen and a half witnesses and examining innumerable graphs, charts, statistics and other exhibits, found that there were no barriers to entry in the Las Vegas movie market. Our function is narrow: we must determine whether that finding is clearly erroneous. Our review of the record discloses that the district court's finding is amply supported by the record.

United States of America v. Syufy Enterprises; Raymond J. Syufy (1990)

We bypass as surplusage the hundreds of pages of expert and lay testimony that support the district court's finding, and focus instead only on a single—to our minds conclusive—item. Immediately after Syufy bought out the last of his three competitors in October 1984, he was riding high, having captured 100% of the first-run film market in Las Vegas. But this utopia proved to be only a mirage. That same month, a major movie distributor, Orion, stopped doing business with Syufy, sending all of its first-run films to Roberts Company, a dark horse competitor previously relegated to the second-run market. Roberts Company took this as an invitation to step into the major league and, against all odds, began giving Syufy serious competition in the first-run market. Fighting fire with fire, Roberts opened three multiplexes within a 13-month period, each having six or more screens. By December 1986, Roberts was operating 28 screens, trading places with Syufy, who had only 23. At the same time, Roberts was displaying a healthy portion of all first-run films. In fact, Roberts got exclusive exhibition rights to many of its films, meaning that Syufy could not show them at all.

By the end of 1987, Roberts was showing a larger percentage of first-run films than was the Redrock multiplex at the time Syufy bought it. Roberts then sold its theatres to United Artists, the largest theatre chain in the country, and Syufy continued losing ground. It all boils down to this: Syufy's acquisitions did not short circuit the operation of the natural market forces; Las Vegas' first-run film market was more competitive when this case came to trial than before Syufy bought out Mann, Plitt and Cragin.

The Justice Department correctly points out that Syufy still has a large market share, but attributes far too much importance to this fact. In evaluating monopoly power, it is not market share that counts, but the ability to *maintain* market share. Syufy seems unable to do this. In 1985, Syufy managed to lock up exclusive exhibition rights to 91% of all the first-run films in Las Vegas. By the first quarter of 1988, that percentage had fallen to 39%; United Artists had exclusive rights to another 25%, with the remaining 36% being played on both Syufy and UA screens.

Syufy's share of box office receipts also dropped off, albeit less precipitously. In 1985, Syufy raked in 93% of the gross box office from first-run films in Las Vegas. By the first quarter of 1988, that figure had fallen to 75%. The government insists that 75% is still a large number, and we are hard-pressed to disagree; but that's not the point.

The antitrust laws do not require that rivals compete in a dead heat, only that neither is unfairly kept from doing his personal best. Accordingly, the government would do better to plot these points on a graph and observe the pattern they form than to focus narrowly on Syufy's market share at a particular time. The numbers reveal that Roberts/UA has steadily been eating away at Syufy's market share: In two and a half years, Syufy's percentage of exclusive exhibition rights dropped 52% and its percentage of box office receipts dropped 18%. During the same period, Roberts/UA's newly opened theatres evolved from absolute beginners, barely staying alive, into a big business.

The government concedes that there are no structural barriers to entry into the market: Syufy does not operate a bank or similar enterprise where entry is limited by government regulation or licensing requirements. Nor is this the type of industry, like heavy manufacturing or mining, which requires onerous front-end investments that might deter competition from all but the hardiest and most financially secure investors. Nor do we have here a business dependent on a scarce commodity, control over which might give the incumbent a substantial structural advantage. Nor is there a network of exclusive contracts or distribution arrangements designed to lock out potential competitors. To the contrary, the record discloses a rough-and-tumble industry, marked by easy market access, fluid relationships with distributors, an ample and continuous supply of product, and a healthy and growing demand. It would be difficult to design a market less susceptible to monopolization.

Confronted with this record and the district court's clear findings, the government trots out a shopworn argument we had thought long abandoned: that efficient, aggressive competition is itself a structural barrier to entry. According to the government, competitors will be deterred from entering the market because they could not hope to turn a profit competing against Syufy.

The notion that the supplier of a good or service can monopolize the market simply by being efficient reached high tide in the law 44 years ago in Judge Learned Hand's opinion in *United States v. Aluminum Co. of Am.*, 148 F.2d 416 (2d Cir. 1945) In the intervening decades the wisdom of this notion has been questioned by just about everyone who has taken a close look at it.

United States of America v. Syufy Enterprises; Raymond J. Syufy (1990)

The argument government counsel presses here is a close variant of *Alcoa*: The government is not claiming that Syufy monopolized the market by being too efficient, but that Syufy's effectiveness as a competitor creates a structural barrier to entry, rendering illicit Syufy's acquisition of its competitors' screens. We hasten to sever this new branch that the government has caused to sprout from the moribund *Alcoa* trunk.

It can't be said often enough that the antitrust laws protect competition, *not* competitors. As we noted earlier, competition is essential to the effective operation of the free market because it encourages efficiency, promotes consumer satisfaction and prevents the accumulation of monopoly profits. When a producer is shielded from competition, he is likely to provide lesser service at a higher price; the victim is the consumer who gets a raw deal. This is the evil the antitrust laws are meant to avert. But when a producer deters competitors by supplying a better product at a lower price, when he eschews monopoly profits, when he operates his business so as to meet consumer demand and increase consumer satisfaction, the goals of competition are served, even if no actual competitors see fit to enter the market at a particular time. While the successful competitor should not be raised above the law, neither should he be held down by law.

The Supreme Court has accordingly distanced itself from the *Alcoa* legacy, taking care to distinguish unlawful monopoly power from "growth or development as a consequence of a superior product, business acumen, or historic accident…." We make it clear today, if it was not before, that an efficient, vigorous, aggressive competitor is not the villain antitrust laws are aimed at eliminating. Fostering an environment where businesses fight it out using the weapon of efficiency and consumer goodwill is what the antitrust laws are meant to champion.

But we need not rely on theory alone in rejecting the government's argument. The record here conclusively demonstrates that neither acquiring the screens of his competitors nor working hard at better serving the public gave Syufy deliverance from competition. Immediately following the disappearance of Mann, Plitt and Cragin, Roberts took up the challenge, aggressively competing with Syufy for first-run films—and with considerable success. United Artists, with substantial resources at its disposal and nationwide experience in running movie theatres, considered the market sufficiently open that it bought out Roberts in 1987. We see no indication that competition suffered in the Las Vegas movie market as a result of Syufy's challenged acquisitions. The district court certainly had ample basis in the record for its finding that Syufy lacked the power to exclude competitors. Indeed, on this voluminous record we are hard-pressed to see how the district court could have come to the other conclusion.

2. Power to Control Prices

The crux of the Justice Department's case is that Syufy, top gun in the Las Vegas movie market, had the power to push around Hollywood's biggest players, dictating to them what prices they could charge for their movies. The district court found otherwise. This finding too has substantial support in the record.

Perhaps the most telling evidence of Syufy's inability to set prices came from movie distributors, Syufy's supposed victims. At the trial, distributors uniformly proclaimed their satisfaction with the way the Las Vegas first-run film market operates; none complained about the license fees paid by Syufy. Columbia's President of Domestic Distribution testified that "Syufy paid a fair amount of film rental" that compared favorably with other markets. A representative of Buena Vista, a division of Disney, testified that Syufy had never refused to accept its standard terms. Particularly damaging to the government's case was the testimony of the former head of distribution for MGM/UA that his company "never had any difficulty…in acquiring the terms that we thought were reasonable," explaining that the license fees Syufy paid "were comparable or better than any place in the United States. And in most cases better." Indeed, few if any of the distributors were willing to say anything to support the government's claim.

The documentary evidence bears out this testimony. Syufy has at all times paid license fees far in excess of the national average, even higher than those paid by exhibitors in Los Angeles, the Mecca of Moviedom. In fact, Syufy paid a higher percentage of his gross receipts to distributors in 1987 and 1988 than he did during the intensely competitive period just before he acquired Cragin's Redrock.

While successful, Syufy is in no position to put the squeeze on distributors. The one time he tried there was an immediate backlash. In 1984, about seven days after allegedly acquiring its monopoly, Syufy informed Orion Releasing Group that he had cold feet about The Cotton Club and would not honor the large guarantees he had contracted for, only to see his gambit backfire. Orion sued Syufy for breach of contract, see *Orion Pictures Distrib. Corp. v. Syufy Enters.*, 829 F.2d 946 (9th Cir. 1987), licensed the film to Roberts and cut Syufy off cold turkey. To this day, Orion refuses to play its films in any Syufy theatre, in Las Vegas or elsewhere. Accordingly, Syufy lost the opportunity to exhibit top moneymakers like Robocop, Platoon, Hannah and Her Sisters and No Way Out. The district court found no evidence that Orion considered Roberts/UA's theatres a less than adequate substitute for Syufy's.

Because he needs plenty of first-run films to fill his many screens (22 at the time of trial; 34 now), Syufy is vulnerable. Distributors like Orion have substantial leverage over Syufy and they know it.

* * *

More fundamentally, in a free economy the market itself imposes a tough enough discipline on all market actors, large and small. Every supplier of goods and services is integrated into an endless chain of supply and demand relationships, making it dependent on the efficiency and goodwill of upstream suppliers, as well as the patronage of customers. Absent structural constraints that keep competition from performing its leveling function, few businesses can dictate terms to customers or suppliers with impunity. It's risky business even to try. As Syufy learned in dealing with Orion and his other suppliers, a larger company often is more vulnerable to a squeeze play than a smaller one. It is for that reason that neither size nor market share alone suffice to establish a monopoly. Without the power to exclude competition, large companies that try to throw their weight around may find themselves sitting ducks for leaner, hungrier competitors. Or, as Syufy saw, the tactic may boomerang, causing big trouble with suppliers.

On this record, we have no basis for overturning the district court's finding that Syufy lacked the power to set the prices he paid his suppliers. As with the district court's finding as to Syufy's power to exclude competition, we believe the record here lent itself to only one sensible conclusion.

* * *

It is a tribute to the state of competition in America that the Antitrust Division of the Department of Justice has found no worthier target than this paper tiger on which to expend limited taxpayer resources.

Yet we cannot help but wonder whether bringing a lawsuit like this, and pursuing it doggedly through 27 months of pretrial proceedings, about two weeks of trial and now the full distance on appeal, really serves the interests of free competition.

* * *

CONCLUSION

The judgment of the district court is affirmed.

The *Syufy* case integrates fundamental free market economic philosophy as it analyzes the law. The case itself is not very complicated, but Judge Kozinski uses very colorful imagery and alludes to concepts that may be difficult to understand. As a result, it is appropriate to spend some time going over the language and meaning of the case.

This case is about a merger, where Syufy acquired virtually all of his previous competitors in the Las Vegas movie theatre market, leaving only a second-run, small movie house to survive on the fringes. The remedy the Department of Justice sought was to force Syufy to "disgorge" or sell off the Cragin, Mann, and Plitt movie theatres that he had purchased in the early 1980s. The reasons for the Department of Justice's concern are largely theoretical, and probably center on Syufy's dealings with Orion, one of the younger successful production companies in Hollywood at that time.

The "government" in this case is represented by the U.S. attorney general under the Department of Justice's antitrust division. It is important to not confuse the government with the court—they are not the same in a lawsuit. The government in this case is a party to the action, and the court is the arbiter of the outcome. They deal at arms length, as you will see clearly in this case.

The government is concerned both with Syufy's substantial market share in the Las Vegas movie market and its fear that the end result would harm competition. However, the facts in this case did not support the argument that Syufy harmed consumers, which makes the case very unusual. Most of the time, an antitrust case is brought when there is at least the argument that consumers have been harmed. In this case, the only incidence where the Department of Justice could demonstrate ostensible harm was in the manner in which Syufy treated Orion, one of the movie producers. The court was less than impressed with the need for the government to protect the movie production industry. When describing the relative sizes of the movie producers versus Raymond Syufy, the court notes, "The Justice Department never-theless remains intent on rescuing this platoon of Goliaths from a single David." If this sounds sarcastic, it is. A judge's tone and choice of words is as instructive as his reasoning. In this case the tone gives us a clear message that antitrust laws are extremely political when applied, and that there is going to be little tolerance by a conservative judge for governmental interference where none may (as a practical matter) be warranted.

The court focused on the government's argument that Syufy's monopoly position harmed suppliers. The court said that the government's argument centered around Syufy being "a monopsonist, not a monopolist." A monopsonist is a monopolist of sorts, but one that exercises market power against its suppliers rather than against its consumers.

At this point it is important to *not rely on a dictionary* for comprehension of this case. The dictionary may say a monopsonist controls all of the demand of a certain type of product. That is no truer than that monopoly occurs only when a monopolist controls all of the supply of a given product. Monopsony or monopoly power can come with significantly less than 100% of the market on the demand or supply side, and conversely, (as you can see from the *Syufy* case) it may not occur even where there is 100% control of a given market.

Those unsophisticated definitions become downright misleading in context. When looking for whether a firm does or does not have monopoly or monopsony power, one must first examine if the firm has pricing power, which means the power to price above normal profit levels without fear of competitive stress. Pricing power can be had with any significant market share, if there are other conditions present to keep competition at bay. If demand is significantly higher than supply, and if there are barriers to entry that keep out new competitors, then there is monopoly pricing power. If, on the other hand, competition can enter the market without fear of what Judge Kozinski refers to as "monkey business," then the threat of competition will generally keep a wise entrepreneur within competitive pricing levels, rather than inviting new competition in. Pricing power may sometimes be obtained lawfully, but when it is obtained unlawfully, there does not need to be a 100% market share for there to be a valid prosecution against the monopolist or monopsonist.

It is also important to note that the way a court defines a market will often determine the outcome of a case. Had the market definition been "movie theatres in America" in the *Syufy* case, there would have been no case at all. The courts agreed that the proper market definition for that case was the "Las Vegas movie market," which is why the case ever came to court.

The *Alcoa* Case

The *Syufy* case is a Ninth Circuit case decided in 1990. It takes a very conservative view of the role of the government in regulating business, especially in the context of antitrust regulation. A very different view was taken by Second Circuit appellate court Judge Learned Hand in the *Aluminum Company of America (Alcoa)* case in 1945. In that case, the court held Alcoa liable for being so aggressive competitively that it pre-empted others from entering in the market and thereby violated the Sherman Act. Paraphrasing Judge Hand:

> It was not inevitable that Alcoa should always anticipate increases in the demand for aluminum and be prepared to supply it. Nothing compelled Alcoa to keep doubling and redoubling its capacity before others entered the field. Alcoa insists that it never excluded competitors, but we can think of no more effective exclusion than to embrace each new opportunity as it occurs, and to face every newcomer with new capacity already geared into a great organization.

Judge Kozinski, in the *Syufy* case, says that this argument by Judge Hand has been "long since abandoned" and virtually insults the Department of Justice for even asserting the argument that "efficient, aggressive competition is itself a…barrier to entry…." In fact, Alcoa remains a valid precedent that has never been formally overturned. It certainly has been criticized by the other circuits and narrowed by the U.S. Supreme Court, but it remains a precedent.

The U.S. Supreme Court has not simply overlooked the fact that a great Ninth Circuit judge (Kozinski) has acted as if a great Second Circuit judge (Hand) is completely wrong about what constitutes monopolistic behavior; it has intentionally ignored it. Antitrust law is based on a host of variables including the political climate, corporate restraint or excess, fundamental market economics, the economy at any given point in time, the personality of those in charge of antitrust in the Department of Justice, and the biases of the judiciary itself. The legal precedents are as wide-ranging as they are inconsistent, because any one of those precedents may be appropriate at some point in time. The Supreme Court is reticent to set down hard and fast rules in this domain because conditions and context can be so variable.

Predicting the precise outcome of an antitrust case is about as easy as winning the Lotto. One does not study the law on competitive behavior in order to know how a case will come out if it is filed, but rather to know when a line is about to be crossed. Good business judgment compels at least enough insight to know when the issue might become problematic, to attempt to assess risk within the wide range of possible outcomes.

Flipping Sides

If someone is now completely comfortable with marginalizing the importance of HHI and market concentration and condescending when speaking of Alcoa, that person has gone astray. Nobody can ever be comfortable with anything in antitrust law. Every court sees everything differently; every case has its own twists and turns. Take, for example, the attempted merger of Staples and Office Depot in 1997.(4)

The founder of Staples had one thing in mind when starting that company—to provide office products at lower prices and with greater availability than the previous vendor/business relationships had allowed. He saw opportunity and successfully built his office supply superstore chain across the United States.

When Staples attempted to buy Office Depot, the Federal Trade Commission balked. Although Staples, Office Depot, and Office Max had managed to change the world of office supplies, they also managed, according to the federal District Court, to create an entirely new market: consumable office supplies sold through superstores in metropolitan areas.

Prior to the invention of the office supply superstore, the market would have been categorized generally as office supplies.

Competition would have been seen coming from traditional small businesses, "box" stores such as Costco and Wal-Mart, and specialty stores that dealt with specific types of equipment like copiers and calculators.

The court noted that although the market for durable types of office equipment (from furniture to computers) was not greatly impacted by the existence of office supply superstores, the buying of consumable office supplies like paper and ink had changed dramatically since their inception. They further noted that in urban areas consumers had changed their behaviors to shop only in superstores for office supplies, rather than in any of the other available venues where some specific products might be purchased less expensively.

Once the court decided to identify a market as consumable products sold at office supply superstores in metropolitan areas, the market would by definition be highly concentrated. There are only a few "box" store chains like Costco or office supply superstores like Staples. It is somewhat surprising, then, that the court spent a great deal of its time looking at market concentration and HHI, since it had identified a market that by its nature (and by the court's own analysis) must have few competitors.

This case uses some of the reasoning in *Syufy* about barriers to entry. In *Syufy* the court considered certain industries that could be pre-emptive in nature, such as "heavy manufacturing or mining, which requires onerous front-end investments that might deter competition from all but the hardiest and most financially secure investors…or a business dependent on a scarce commodity, control over which might give the incumbent a substantial structural advantage." Retail is generally not described in those terms. None the less, it is the capital investment required for a superstore to be run competitively that caused the U.S. District Court for the District of Columbia to find that there were barriers to entry, and that the merger of Staples and Office Depot would be anticompetitive if allowed to proceed. It would have been difficult to predict the outcome of the *Staples* case by simply applying the feel and logic of the Syufy court, but this is typical in antitrust law. Prediction is futile.

Federal Trade Commission, Plaintiff, v. Staples, Inc. and Office Depot, Inc., Defendants (1997)

U.S. District Court for the District of Columbia (970 F. Supp. 1066)

Judge Thomas Hogan delivered the opinion of the court.

BACKGROUND

The FTC is an administrative agency of the United States organized and existing pursuant to the Federal Trade Commission Act…. The Commission is responsible, *inter alia* [among other things] for enforcing federal antitrust laws, particularly Section 7 of the Clayton Act, and Sections 5 and 13(b) of the Federal Trade Commission Act.

Defendants are both corporations which sell office products—including office supplies, business machines, computers and furniture—through retail stores, commonly described as office supply superstores, as well as through direct mail delivery and contract stationer operations. Staples is the second largest office superstore chain in the United States with approximately 550 retail stores located in 28 states and the District of Columbia, primarily in the Northeast and California. In 1996 Staples' revenues from those stores were approximately $4 billion through all operations. Office Depot, the largest office superstore chain, operates over 500 retail office supply superstores that are located in 38 states and the District of Columbia, primarily in the South and Midwest. Office Depot's 1996 sales were approximately $6.1 billion. OfficeMax. Inc....is the only other office supply superstore firm in the United States.

On September 4, 1996, defendants Staples and Office Depot, and Marlin Acquisition Corp. ("Marlin"), a wholly-owned subsidiary of Staples, entered into an "Agreement and Plan of Merger" whereby Marlin would merge with and into Office Depot, and Office Depot would become a wholly-owned subsidiary of Staples. According to the Agreement and Plan of Merger, the transaction would be structured as a pooling of interests, in which each share of Office Depot common stock would be exchanged for 1.14 shares of Staples' common stock. Pursuant to the Hart-Scott-Rodino Improvements Act of 1976,...Staples and Office Depot filed a Premerger Notification and Report Form with the FTC and Department of Justice on October 2, 1996. This was followed by a seven month investigation by the FTC.

* * *

On March 10, 1997, the Commission voted 4-1 to challenge the merger and authorized commencement of an action under Section 13(b) of the Federal Trade Commission Act...to seek a temporary restraining order and a preliminary injunction barring the merger. Following this vote, the defendants and the FTC staff negotiated a consent decree that would have authorized the merger to proceed on the condition that Staples and Office Depot sell 63 stores to OfficeMax. However, the Commission voted 3-2 to reject the proposed consent decree on April 4, 1997. The FTC then filed this suit on April 9, 1997, seeking a temporary retraining order and preliminary injunction against the merger pursuant to Section 13(b) of the Federal Trade Commission Act....

* * *

II. The Geographic Market

One of the few issue[s] about which the parties to this case do not disagree is that metropolitan areas are the appropriate geographic markets for analyzing the competitive effects of the proposed merger. A geographic market is that geographic area "to which consumers can practically turn for alternative sources of the product and in which the antitrust defendant faces competition."

* * *

III. The Relevant Product Market

In contrast to the parties' agreement with respect to the relevant geographic market, the Commission and the defendants sharply disagree with respect to the appropriate definition of the relevant product market or line of commerce. As with many antitrust cases, the definition of the relevant product market in this case is crucial. In fact, to a great extent, this case hinges on the proper definition of the relevant product market.

The Commission defines the relevant product market as "the sale of consumable office supplies through office superstores," with "consumable" meaning products that consumers buy recurrently, i.e., items which "get used up" or discarded. For example, under the Commission's definition, "consumable office supplies" would not include capital goods such as computers, fax machines, and other business machines, or office furniture, but does include such products as paper, pens, file folders, post-it notes, computer disks, and toner cartridges. The defendants characterize the FTC's product market definition as "contrived" with no basis in law or fact, and counter that the appropriate product market within which to assess the likely competitive consequences of a Staples-Office Depot combination is simply the overall sale of office products, of which a combined Staples-Office Depot accounted for 5.5% of total sales in North America in 1996…. The Court finds that the appropriate relevant product market definition in this case is, as the Commission has argued, the sale of consumable office supplies through office supply superstores.

The general rule when determining a relevant product market is that "the outer boundaries of a product market are determined by the reasonable interchangeability of use [by consumers] or the cross-elasticity of demand between the product itself and substitutes for it." Interchangeability of use and cross-elasticity of demand look to the availability of substitute commodities, i.e. whether there are other products offered to consumers which are similar in character or use to the product or products in question, as well as how far buyers will go to substitute one commodity for another.

Whether there are other products available to consumers which are similar in character or use to the products in question may be termed "functional interchangeability."

This case, of course, is an example of perfect "functional interchangeability." The consumable office products at issue here are

Federal Trade Commission, Plaintiff, v. Staples, Inc. and Office Depot, Inc., Defendants (1997)

Federal Trade Commission, Plaintiff, v. Staples, Inc. and Office Depot, Inc., Defendants (1997)

identical whether they are sold by Staples or Office Depot or another seller of office supplies. A legal pad sold by Staples or Office Depot is "functionally interchangeable" with a legal pad sold by Wal-Mart. A post-it note sold by Staples or Office Depot is "functionally interchangeable" with a post-it note sold by Viking or Quill. A computer disk sold by Staples-Office Depot is "functionally interchangeable" with a computer disk sold by CompUSA. No one disputes the functional interchangeability of consumable office supplies. However, as the government has argued, functional interchangeability should not end the Court's analysis.

The Supreme Court did not stop after finding a high degree of functional interchangeability between cellophane and other wrapping materials in the E. L. Du Pont de Nemours case. Instead, the Court also found that "an element for consideration as to cross-elasticity of demand between products is the responsiveness of the sales of one product to price changes of the other." For example, in that case, the Court explained, "if a slight decrease in the price of cellophane causes a considerable number of customers of other flexible wrappings to switch to cellophane, it would be an indication that a high cross-elasticity of demand exists between [cellophane and other flexible wrappings]; [and, therefore,] that the products compete in the same market." Following that reasoning in this case, the Commission has argued that a slight but significant increase in Staples-Office Depot's prices will not cause a considerable number of Staples-Office Depot's customers to purchase consumable office supplies from other non-superstore alternatives such as Wal-Mart, Best Buy, Quill, or Viking. On the other hand, the Commission has argued that an increase in price by Staples would result in consumers turning to another office superstore, especially Office Depot, if the consumers had that option. Therefore, the Commission concludes that the sale of consumable office supplies by office supply superstores is the appropriate relevant product market in this case, and products sold by competitors such as Wal-Mart, Best Buy, Viking, Quill, and others should be excluded.

The Court recognizes that it is difficult to overcome the first blush or initial gut reaction of many people to the definition of the relevant product market as the sale of consumable office supplies through office supply superstores. The products in question are undeniably the same no matter who sells them, and no one denies that many different types of retailers sell these products. After all, a combined Staples-Office Depot would only have a 5.5% share of the overall market in consumable office supplies. Therefore, it is logical to conclude that, of course, all these retailers compete, and that if a combined Staples-Office Depot raised prices after the merger, or at least did not lower them as much as they would have as separate companies, that consumers, with such a plethora of options, would shop elsewhere.

The Court acknowledges that there is, in fact, a broad market encompassing the sale of consumable office supplies by all sellers of such supplies, and that those sellers must, at some level, compete with one another. However, the mere fact that a firm may be termed a competitor in the overall marketplace does not necessarily require that it be included in the relevant product market for antitrust purposes. The Supreme Court has recognized that within a broad market, "well-defined submarkets may exist which, in themselves, constitute product markets for antitrust purposes." …With respect to such submarkets, the Court explained "because Section 7 of the Clayton Act prohibits any merger which may substantially lessen competition 'in any line of commerce,' it is necessary to examine the effects of a merger in each such economically significant submarket to determine if there is a reasonable probability that the merger will substantially lessen competition. If such a probability is found to exist, the merger is proscribed." There is a possibility, therefore, that the sale of consumable office supplies by office superstores may qualify as a submarket within a larger market of retailers of office supplies in general.

* * *

[T]he FTC presented evidence comparing Staples' prices in geographic markets where Staples is the only office superstore, to markets where Staples competes with Office Deport or OfficeMax, or both. Based on the FTC's calculations, in markets where Staples faces no office superstore competition at all, something which was termed a one firm market during the hearing, prices are 13% higher than in three firm markets where it competes with both Office Depot and OfficeMax. The data which underlie this conclusion make it compelling evidence. Prices were compared as of January 1997, which, admittedly, only provides data for one specific point in time. However, rather than comparing prices from only a small sampling or "basket" of goods, the FTC used an office supply sample accounting for 90% of Staples' sales and comprised of both price sensitive and non-price sensitive items. The FTC presented similar evidence based on Office Depot's prices of a sample of 500 items, also as of January 1997. Similarly, the evidence showed that Office Depot's prices are significantly higher, well over 5% higher, in Depot-only markets than they are in three firm markets.

* * *

The FTC also pointed to internal Staples documents which present price comparisons between Staples' prices and Office Depot's prices and Staples' prices and OfficeMax's prices within different price zones. The comparisons between Staples and Office Depot were made in August 1994, January 1995, August 1995, and May 1996. Staples' prices were compared with OfficeMax's prices in August 1994, July 1995, and January 1996. For each comparison, Staples' calculations were based on a fairly large "basket" or sample of goods, approximately 2000 SKUs containing both price sensitive and non-price sensitive items. Using Staples' data, but organizing it differently to show which of those zones were one, two, or three firm markets, the FTC showed once again that Staples charges significantly higher prices, more than 5% higher, where it has no office superstore competition than where it competes with the two other superstores.

* * *

This evidence all suggests that office superstore prices are affected primarily by other office superstores and not by non-superstore competitors such as mass merchandisers like Wal-Mart, Kmart, or Target, wholesale clubs such as BJ's, Sam's, and Price Costco, computer or electronic stores such as Computer City and Best Buy, independent retail office supply stores, mail orders firms like Quill and Viking, and contract stationers.

* * *

…Staples' own pricing information shows that warehouse clubs have very little effect on Staples' prices. For example, Staples' maintains a "warehouse club only" price zone, which indicates a zone where Staples exists with a warehouse club but without another office superstore. The data presented by the Commission on Staples' pricing shows only a slight variation in prices (1%–2%) between "warehouse club only" zones and one superstore markets without a warehouse club. Additionally, in May 1996, two price comparison studies done by Staples, first using 2,084 SKUs including both price

Federal Trade Commission, Plaintiff, v. Staples, Inc. and Office Depot, Inc., Defendants (1997)

sensitive and non-price sensitive items and then using only 244 SKUs of price sensitive items, showed that prices in the "club only" zones, on average, were over 10% higher than in zones where Staples competes with Office Depot and/or OfficeMax.

* * *

The Court has observed that office supply superstores look far different from other sellers of office supplies. Office supply superstores are high volume, discount office supply chain stores averaging in excess of 20,000 square feet, with over 11,000 of those square feet devoted to traditional office supplies, and carrying over 5,000 SKUs of consumable office supplies in addition to computers, office furniture, and other non-consumables. In contrast, stores such as Kmart devote approximately 210 square feet to the sale of approximately 250 SKUs of consumable office supplies. Kinko's devotes approximately 50 square feet to the sale of 150 SKUs. Target sells only 400 SKUs. Both Sam's Club and Computer City each sell approximately 200 SKUs. Even if these SKU totals are low estimates as the defendants have argued, there is still a huge difference between the superstores and the rest of the office supply sellers.

* * *

While it is clear to the Court that Staples and Office Depot do not ignore sellers such as warehouse clubs, Best Buy, or Wal-Mart, the evidence clearly shows that Staples and Office Depot each consider the other superstores as the primary competition.

For the reasons set forth in the above analysis, the Court finds that the sale of consumable office supplies through office supply superstores is the appropriate relevant product market for purposes of considering the possible anti-competitive effects of the proposed merger between Staples and Office Depot.

IV. Probable Effect on Competition

After accepting the Commission's definition of the relevant product market, the Court next must consider the probable effect of a merger between Staples and Office Depot in the geographic markets previously identified[.] One way to do this is to examine the concentration statistics and HHIs within the geographic markets. If the relevant product market is defined as the sale of consumable office supplies through office supply superstores, the HHIs in many of the geo-

Federal Trade Commission, Plaintiff, v. Staples, Inc. and Office Depot, Inc., Defendants (1997)

Federal Trade Commission, Plaintiff, v. Staples, Inc. and Office Depot, Inc., Defendants (1997)

graphic markets are at problematic levels even before the merger. Currently, the least concentrated market is that of Grand Rapids-Muskegon-Holland, Michigan, with an HHI of 3,597, while the most concentrated is Washington, D.C. with an HHI of 6,944. In contrast, after a merger of Staples and Office Depot, the least concentrated area would be Kalamazoo-Battle Creek Michigan, with an HHI of 5,003, and many areas would have HHIs of 10,000. The average increase in HHI caused by the merger would be 2,715 points. The concentration statistics show that a merged Staples-Office Depot would have a dominant market share in 42 geographic markets across the country. The combined shares of Staples and Office Depot in the office superstore market would be 100% in 15 metropolitan areas. It is in these markets [that] the post-merger HHI would be 10,000. In 27 other metropolitan areas, where the number of office superstore competitors would drop from three to two, the post-merger market shares would range from 45% to 94% with post-merger HHIs ranging from 5,003 to 9,049. Even the lowest of these HHIs indicates a "highly concentrated" market.

The HHI calculations and market concentration evidence, however, are not the only indications that a merger between Staples and Office Depot may substantially lessen competition. Much of the evidence already discussed with respect to defining the relevant product market also indicates that the merger would likely have an anti-competitive effect. The evidence of the defendants' own current pricing practices, for example, shows that an office superstore chain facing no competition from other superstores has the ability to profitably raise prices for consumable office supplies above competitive levels. The fact that Staples and Office Depot both charge higher prices where they face no superstore competition demonstrates that an office superstore can raise prices above competitive levels. The evidence also shows that defendants also change their price zones when faced with entry of another office superstore, but do not do so for other retailers. Since prices are significantly lower in markets where Staples and Office Depot compete, eliminating this competition with one another would free the parties to charge higher prices in those markets, especially those in which the combined entity would be the sole office superstore. In addition, allowing the defendants to merge would eliminate significant future competition. Absent the merger, the firms are likely, and in fact have planned, to enter more of each other's markets, leading to a deconcentration of the market and, therefore, increased competition between the superstores.

The Court generally accepts that per-store advertising costs, such as those incurred for a newspaper insert, will likely be lower in markets where Staples or Office Depot has a larger number of stores as those costs may be spread over a larger number of stores, and the defendants have provided some concrete evidence that the price differentials shown by the FTC may be somewhat affected by marketing costs. Donna Rosenberg, Vice President of Marketing Strategy at Staples, testified by declaration that Staples has the lowest average marketing costs per store in Staples/Office Depot areas and the highest marketing costs per store in Staples only areas. Exhibit H to her declaration shows, more specifically, that in 1996 Staples stores in three firm areas had an average marketing expense of [$]202,112. In Staples/Office Depot areas, Staples' stores had an average marketing expense of [$]185,905. …These numbers do suggest a correlation between the prices charged by Staples and marketing costs as average marketing costs are higher in the one firm markets than the three firm markets. However, the marketing cost evidence also shows that marketing costs are lower in Staples/Depot areas than in Staples/OfficeMax areas and, in fact, that costs are higher in Staples/OfficeMax areas than in the three firm markets, which does not correspond with the pricing trend. Staples generally charges lower prices where it competes with Office Depot than where it competes with OfficeMax and generally charges lower prices in three firm markets than in Staples/OfficeMax areas. In addition, the differences in marketing costs are not so large that they alone could account for the significant price differentials shown by the FTC.

V. Entry Into the Market

"The existence and significance of barriers to entry are frequently, of course, crucial considerations in a rebuttal analysis…[because] in the absence of significant barriers, a company probably cannot maintain supra-competitive pricing for any length of time." …Thus, the Court must consider whether, in this case, "entry into the…market would likely avert anticompetitive effects from [Staples'] acquisition of [Office Depot]" Id. at 989. If the defendants' evidence regarding entry showed that the Commission's market-share statistics give an incorrect prediction of the proposed acquisition's probable effect on competition because entry into the market would likely avert any anti-competitive effect by acting as a constraint on Staples-Office Depot's prices, the Court would deny the FTC's motion. The Court, however, cannot make such a finding in this case.

Federal Trade Commission, Plaintiff, v. Staples, Inc. and Office Depot, Inc., Defendants (1997)

The defendants argued [at] the hearing and in their briefs that the rapid growth in overall office supply sales has encouraged and will continue to encourage expansion and entry. One reason for this, according to Dr. Hausman's declaration, is that entry is more attractive when an industry is growing, because new entrants can establish themselves without having to take all of their sales away from existing competitors. In addition, the defendants' impressive retailing expert, Professor Maurice Segall, testified at the hearing that there are "no barriers to entry in retailing," and defendants pointed to the fact that all office superstore entrants have entered within the last 11 years.

In addition to this general testimony regarding entry, defendants emphasized specific examples of recent or planned entry. For example, defendants offered testimony from John Ledecky, Chairman and CEO of U.S. Office Products, regarding U.S. Office Products' acquisition of Mailboxes, Etc., an acquisition that was coincidentally announced the night before Mr. Ledecky's testimony in this case. Through this acquisition, U.S. Office Products, an organization or co-op of approximately 165 contract stationers located throughout the country, will acquire the 3300-unit Mailboxes, Etc. franchise operation. Defendants also offered testimony regarding Wal-Mart's plans to revamp and expand the office supply section in its stores. According to the deposition testimony of William Long, Vice President for Merchandizing at Wal-Mart, and David Glass, President and CEO of Wal-Mart, Wal-Mart will modify its office supplies department, called "Department 3," beginning in May 1997 and continuing through the summer. Though Mr. Long was not certain of the exact number of SKUs of office supplies Wal-Mart's new Department 3 will offer, he estimated the range to be 2,600 to 3,000 SKUs. Finally, defendants offered testimony regarding the general ability of mass merchandisers, computer superstores, and warehouse clubs to change store configurations and shift shelf space to accommodate new demands or popular products.

…There are problems with the defendants' evidence, however, that prevent the Court from finding in this case that entry into the market by new competitors or expansion into the market by existing firms would likely avert the anti-competitive effects from Staples' acquisition of Office Depot. For example, while it is true that all office superstore entrants have entered within the last 11 years, the recent trend for office superstores has actually been toward exiting the market rather than entering. Over the past few years, the number of office superstore chains has dramatically dropped from twenty-three to three. All but Staples, Office Depot, and OfficeMax have either closed or been acquired. The failed office superstore entrants include very large, well-known retail establishments such as Kmart, Montgomery Ward, Ames, and Zayres. A new office superstore would need to open a large number of stores nationally in order to achieve the purchasing and distribution economies of scale enjoyed by the three existing firms. Sunk costs would be extremely high. Economies of scale at the local level, such as in the costs of advertising and distribution, would also be difficult for a new superstore entrant to achieve since the three existing firms have saturated many important local markets. For example, according to the defendants' own saturation analyses, Staples estimates that there is room for less than two additional superstores in the Washington, D.C. area and Office Depot estimates that there is room for only two more superstores in Tampa, Florida.

The Commission offered Office 1 as a specific example of the difficulty of entering the office superstore arena. Office 1 opened its first two stores in 1991. By the end of 1994, Office 1 had 17 stores, and grew to 35 stores operating in 11 Midwestern states as of October 11, 1996. As of that date, Office 1 was the fourth largest office supply superstore chain in the United States. Unfortunately, also as of that date, Office 1 filed for Chapter 11 bankruptcy protection. Brad Zenner, President of Office 1, testified through declaration, that Office 1 failed because it was severely undercapitalized in comparison with the industry leaders, Staples, Office Depot, and OfficeMax. In addition, Mr. Zenner testified that when the three leaders ultimately expanded into the smaller markets where Office 1 stores were located, they seriously undercut Office 1's retail prices and profit margins. Because Office 1 lacked the capitalization of the three leaders and lacked the economies of scale enjoyed by those competitors, Office 1 could not remain profitable.

For the reasons discussed above, the Court finds it extremely unlikely that a new office superstore will enter the market and thereby avert the anti-competitive effects from Staples' acquisition of Office Depot. The defendants, of course, focused their entry argument on more than just the entry of additional superstores, pointing also to the expansion of existing companies such as U.S. Office Products and Wal-Mart. The Court also finds it unlikely that the expansions by

U.S. Office Products and Wal-Mart would avert the anti-competitive effects which would result from the merger.

The defendants' final argument with respect to entry was that existing retailers such as Sam's Club, Kmart, and Best Buy have the capability to reallocate their shelf space to include additional SKUs of office supplies. While stores such as these certainly do have the power to reallocate shelf space, there is no evidence that they will in fact do this if a combined Staples-Office Depot were to raise prices by 5% following a merger. In fact, the evidence indicates that it is more likely that they would not. For example, even in the superstores' anti-competitive zones where either Staples or Office Depot does not compete with other superstores, no retailer has successfully expanded its consumable office supplies to the extent that it constrains superstore pricing. Best Buy attempted such an expansion by creating an office supplies department in 1994, offering 2000 SKUs of office supplies, but found the expansion less profitable than hoped for and gave up after two years. For these reasons, the Court also cannot find that the ability of many sellers of office supplies to reconfigure shelf space and add SKUs of office supplies is likely to avert anti-competitive effects from Staples' acquisition of Office Depot. The Court will next consider the defendants' efficiencies defense.

VI. Efficiencies

Whether an efficiencies defense showing that the intended merger would create significant efficiencies in the relevant market, thereby offsetting any anti-competitive effects, may be used by a defendant to rebut the government's *prima facie* case is not entirely clear. The newly revised efficiencies section of the Merger Guidelines recognizes that, "mergers have the potential to generate significant efficiencies by permitting a better utilization of existing assets, enabling the combined firm to achieve lower costs in producing a given quality and quantity than either firm could have achieved without the proposed transactions." This coincides with the view of some courts that "whether an acquisition would yield significant efficiencies in the relevant market is an important consideration in predicting whether the acquisition would substantially lessen competition…. Therefore, …an efficiency defense to the government's *prima facie* case in section 7 challenges is appropriate in certain circumstances."

…The Court agrees with the defendants that where, as here, the merger has not yet been consummated, it is impossible to quantify precisely the efficiencies that it will generate. In addition, the Court recognizes a difference between efficiencies which are merely speculative and those which are based on a prediction backed by sound business judgment. Nor does the Court believe that the defendants must prove their efficiencies by "clear and convincing evidence" in order for those efficiencies to be considered by the Court.

Defendants' submitted an "Efficiencies Analysis" which predicted that the combined company would achieve savings of between $4.9 and $6.5 billion over the next five years. In addition, the defendants argued that the merger would also generate dynamic efficiencies. For example, defendants argued that as suppliers become more efficient due to their increased sales volume to the combined Staples-Office Depot, they would be able to lower prices to their other retailers. Moreover, defendants argued that two-thirds of the savings realized by the combined company would be passed along to consumers.

Evaluating credibility, as the Court must do, the Court credits the testimony and Report of the Commission's expert, David Painter, over the testimony and Efficiencies Study of the defendants' efficiencies witness, Shira Goodman, Senior Vice President of Integration at Staples. Mr. Painter's testimony was compelling, and the Court finds, based primarily on Mr. Painter's testimony, that the defendants' cost savings estimates are unreliable. First, the Court notes that the cost savings estimate of $4.947 billion over five years which was submitted to the Court exceeds by almost 500% the figures presented to the two Boards of Directors in September 1996, when the Boards approved the transaction. The cost savings claims submitted to the Court are also substantially greater than those represented in the defendants' Joint Proxy Statement/Prospectus "reflecting the best currently available estimate of management," and filed with the Securities and Exchange Commission on January 23, 1997, or referenced in the "fairness opinions" rendered by the defendants' investment bankers which are contained in the Proxy Statement.

* * *

In addition to the problems that the Court has with the efficiencies estimates themselves, the Court also finds that the defendants' projected pass through rate—the amount of the projected savings that the combined company expects to pass on to customers in the form of lower prices-is unrealistic. The Court has no doubt that a portion of any efficiencies achieved through a merger of the defendants

Federal Trade Commission, Plaintiff, v. Staples, Inc. and Office Depot, Inc., Defendants (1997)

would be passed on to customers. Staples and Office Depot have a proven track record of achieving cost savings through efficiencies, and then passing those savings to customers in the form of lower prices. However, in this case the defendants have projected a pass through rate of two-thirds of the savings while the evidence shows that, historically, Staples has passed through only 15–17%. Based on the above evidence, the Court cannot find that the defendants have rebutted the presumption that the merger will substantially lessen competition by showing that, because of the efficiencies which will result from the merger, the Commission's evidence gives an inaccurate prediction of the proposed acquisition's probable effect. Therefore, the only remaining issue for the Court is the balancing of the equities.

VII. The Equities

…There are two types of equities which the Court must consider in all Section 13(b) cases, private equities and public equities. In this case, the private equities include the interests of the shareholders and employees of Staples and Office Depot. The public equities are the interests of the public, either in having the merger go through or in preventing the merger.

The strong public interest in effective enforcement of the antitrust laws weighs heavily in favor of an injunction in this case….

* * *

The public equities raised by the defendants simply do not outweigh those offered by the FTC. In addition, given some of the Court's earlier findings, several of the public equities submitted by the defendants are without factual support.

* * *

Turning finally to the private equities, the defendants have argued that the principal private equity at stake in this case is the loss to Office Depot shareholders who will likely lose a substantial portion of their investments if the merger is enjoined. The Court certainly agrees that Office Depot shareholders may be harmed, at least in the short term, if the Court granted the plaintiff's motion and enjoined the merger. This private equity alone, however, does not suffice to justify denial of a preliminary injunction.

The defendants have also argued that Office Depot itself has suffered a decline since the incipiency of this action. It is clear that Office Depot has lost key personnel, especially in its real estate department. This has hurt this year's projected store openings. The defendants argue, therefore, that Office Depot, as a separate company, will have difficulty competing if the merger is enjoined. While the Court recognizes that Office Depot has indeed been hurt or weakened as an independent stand-alone company, the damage is not irreparable. The evidence shows that Office Depot, which of the three superstores has been the low-priced aggressive maverick of the group, would continue generating sales volume and turning a substantial profit. In reaching this conclusion, the Court credits one of the defendants' own expert witnesses, Steven Mandel, who testified that, in his opinion, Office Depot would be fine even if the merger did not go through.

CONCLUSION

Thomas Stemberg pioneered the office supply superstore concept in 1985. He created a deep discount chain selling a broad array of office supplies primarily to small businesses which theretofore were undeniably "paying through the nose" for office supplies. Staples was to be a high volume chain operating at low gross margins, with higher volume leading to still lower costs for consumers. Staples' pricing as well as the pricing of other office supply superstores which soon followed Staples' lead, revolutionized the office products industry, impacting all channels of office products retailing. By selling office products at 30 to 60% off list price, Staples and the other superstores worked as a catalyst that forced everyone else in the industry to focus on cutting their prices. In a relatively short period of time, the office supply superstores caused a general decrease in the price of office products across the board. That decrease continued as the superstores have increased their buying power, forcing manufacturers and suppliers to implement efficiencies in their own businesses in order to compete in the sale of their products.

In light of the undeniable benefits that Staples and Office Depot have brought to consumers, it is with regret that the Court reaches the decision that it must in this case. This decision will most likely kill the merger. The Court feels, to some extent, that the defendants are being punished for their own successes and for the benefits that they have brought to consumers.

* * *

Federal Trade Commission, Plaintiff, v. Staples, Inc. and Office Depot, Inc., Defendants (1997)

The Court once again commends counsel on both sides for their excellent performances in this matter and the tremendous efforts made on both sides. Though this was an extremely complex matter, the issues were clearly presented to the Court by counsel possessing superior advocacy skills. Counsel also exhibited a high degree of professionalism in their ability to resolve peripheral matters so that the Court could focus on the important issues presented by this action.

[The temporary restraining order and preliminary injunction barring the merger of Office Depot and Staples was granted.]

Where Staples' Judge Hogan is concerned with the pre-emption of new entrants into the office superstore market, Judge Kozinski, who wrote the *Syufy* case, might well have had a different perspective. Kozinski debunked the notion that efficient and aggressive competition are barriers to entry. Hogan's concerns about the Staples-Office Depot merger were at least in part based on the pre-emptive qualities of the efficiencies of those firms.

Kozinski would likely opine that the continued success of any superstore requires low-cost pricing to keep new entrants out, and in that context, keeping competition out means the market is functioning well.

On the other hand, Judge Hogan did have evidence that in non-competitive markets where only Staples was present, pricing was higher while no new entrants came in. None the less, to call Staples' profits supra-normal, given its discounting model, is a matter of serious debate. Antitrust law does not demand the leanest profit—just that firms be competitively restrained to normal profit in their relevant product markets.

Students of antitrust law might not have predicted the outcome of the *Staples* case in the wake of *Syufy*, but they can at least follow the court's reasoning in the case. As noted earlier, that is the only realizable goal in this antitrust area of legal study.

Notes

1. http://www.investorwords.com/3112/monopoly.html

2. Alan S. Blinder, William J. Baumol, & Colton L. Gale. *Microeconomics: Principles and Policy, Thomson Southwestern*, (2001).

3. *United States of America v. Syufy Enterprises; Raymond J. Syufy* (1990) United States Court of Appeals for the Ninth Circuit (903 F.2d 659)

4. *Federal Trade Commission, Plaintiff, v. Staples, Inc. and Office Depot, Inc., Defendants* (1997) (970 F. Supp. 1066)

Chapter 8
The Trouble with Trade Restraints

The Sherman Antitrust Act, enacted in 1890,(1) contains one of our nation's most enduring statutory schemes. Although subsequently enacted statutes have targeted monopoly-related problems, the impact of the Sherman Act remains the most far-reaching, and its history is by far the most interesting.

As was mentioned in the previous chapter, monopoly has always been an area of concern in free market systems (one of four distinct market failure areas), but in the early 1880s, a rather ingenious but anticompetitive multi-corporate structure had evolved and was threatening the American economy. Large business aggregates composed of would-be competitors in a given market had determined that cooperation would be more profitable than competition. There were no laws prohibiting collaboration, so industry leaders in various markets decided to delegate their power to control price, supply, and distribution to trustees. Essentially this meant that the competitors in the trust would no longer actually compete with each other and could use their combined strength to crush smaller competitors. A functional trustee set production limits and

pricing, and all the member companies played on the same playing field.

Standard Oil's legendary trustee was John D. Rockefeller, who is credited with inventing the trust form of price fixing when he formed the Standard Oil Trust in 1882. Standard Oil's trust organization allowed its affiliated oil companies (which were separate corporations located in different states) to be headed by the same board of directors. Consequently, that single board controlled over half of the entire oil industry, including its pricing and transportation. The Organization of the Petroleum Exporting Countries (OPEC) has attempted to replicate this model, and although oil prices today are supernaturally high and supplies are seriously stressed, OPEC is significantly less successful at controlling prices than Standard Oil was.

In line with the Standard Oil model, large trusts formed in many sectors including railroads, sugar, hops (beer), and coal. They became powerful enough to create a sense of political alarm, and the government responded by signing the Sherman Act into law in 1890. It is for this reason that laws governing anticompetitive behaviors were named "antitrust" laws.

Although the Sherman Act was not initially accepted by the U.S. Supreme Court as a tool with which the trusts could be unraveled, in 1911 (under the presidency of "trust-buster" Teddy Roosevelt), the Standard Oil Trust was ordered to be dissolved.(2)

Subsequent to the Sherman Act, Congress enacted other statutes geared toward fighting anticompetitive or monopolistic behaviors. It enabled the Antitrust Division of the Federal Trade Commission to regulate against monopolistic behavior, and the Antitrust Division of the Department of Justice to prosecute it.

Legal Monopolies

There are many types of legal monopolies. Some monopolies are authorized and then regulated in terms of the time they are allowed to exist, like the monopolies that are specifically granted in patents and copyrights. Under current law in the United States, patents last for twenty years from the date of filing. A patent must disclose the "recipe" for the patented invention, so at the end of the twenty-year legal monopoly, others can copy and lawfully compete against the original patent holder.

Although legal, patents are often a contentious form of monopoly. During the time that the patent is valid, the patent holder can and generally will charge supra-normal profits, if there is a receptive market for the product. Patents theoretically exist to encourage investment, job creation, and research. If competition can "free-ride," there is little incentive to invest in innovation. A period of excess profit is the intended effect of patent protection.

Nonetheless, the drug companies are frequently vilified for their exces-

sive profit-taking. Theirs is a consumer market where product demand is often correlated to quality of life or mortality. Although politicians often advocate regulation to constrain prescription drug pricing, there is reluctance to regulate in this arena because of the anticipated impact on shareholder wealth, employment, and corporate investment in new drug development.

In the Syufy case in the previous chapter, Judge Kozinski spoke about another type of lawful monopoly. He pointed out that the U.S. Supreme Court differentiated unlawful monopoly from the lawful monopoly that occurs as a consequence of "a superior product, business acumen, or historic accident." Microsoft's monopoly in the Windows operating system falls into this category.

Many statutory monopolies have been integrated into our society in ways that are generally tolerated. Trademarks and copyrights are ubiquitous. We are accustomed to and accept power utility monopolies although we rely on the pricing controls government imposes to keep them in line.

Labor unions are an integral part of the American landscape even though they are anticompetitive on the employee side in that they allow workers to collude on their salary requirements. They are specifically exempted from antitrust laws under the National Labor Relations Act. On the other hand, major league baseball team owners are permitted to collude and set salary caps that apply to all the competing teams in the league. Baseball has always been exempted from antitrust law.

Clearly not all monopoly is bad, but we carefully identify those we will tolerate in our economy and leave the rest to the Department of Justice and the courts to figure out.

Legal Monopsonies

Monopsonies are a kind of monopoly—historically they were interpreted to occur when there was only one buyer in a given market. As is the case with monopoly in general however, the courts do not require 100% of the market to find monopsony power. Monopsonies are inferred when there is pricing power upward—the power to control prices to levels below normal profit. Monopsonies that are not the subject of collusion are generally lawful. For individual buyers this point is obvious. A buyer should be able to accept or reject a product based on price even if that buyer is the only market for the product. That is part of the exercise of free choice.

The issue becomes more onerous when dealing with commercial entities. Consider the following example. Costco sells an enormous amount of Kirkland paper towels to its customers. The company that produces those towels for Kirkland (which is Costco's house brand) depends on Costco for most of its revenue. Costco clearly has pricing power with respect to that supplier and can constrain that supplier's profit by threatening to take its business elsewhere. This use of monopsony power is completely legal, and moreover, it significantly benefits consumers.

In fact, most large producers have similar relationships with smaller producers. IBM has many relationships with small producers for component parts. If IBM finds a producer who can produce a component part more cheaply than its existing supplier, it can "squeeze" the existing supplier for below-normal pricing or change suppliers and cause the existing supplier to go out of business. Like any shopper who looks for the best price, this is lawful behavior, it occurs frequently, and many domestic businesses have suffered closure as a consequence.

Still, monopsony power can in some circumstances be used unlawfully. The government successfully prosecuted the illegal use of monopsony power by Toys"R"Us, Inc. for anti-competitive restraints of trade. In overly simplified terms, Toys"R"Us attempted to keep out competition by controlling the distribution of toys by its suppliers to its competitors. Toys "R"Us is a major purchaser of toys in the United States, constituting up to 35 percent of the market for some of its suppliers. If Toys"R"Us were to discontinue purchasing toys from Mattel or Hasbro, those companies would suffer dramatic negative effect. On the other hand, as was noted above, Toys "R"Us is free to choose its suppliers as it decides.

What made the conduct of Toys "R"Us unlawful was its anticompetitive motivation and effect. It conditioned its willingness to purchase products from its suppliers on the agreement of those suppliers to refuse to supply warehouse stores like Sam's Club and Costco with competing products. Toys"R"Us played all of its suppliers against each other to keep goods from getting to the shelves of those who price lower. Consumers consequently paid more.

Although most of the time it is lawful for retailers to require exclusivity in exchange for their willingness to invest in selling a product, Toys"R"Us was attempting to garner exclusivity for products from all the major manufacturers in the toy industry.

The resulting behavior mimicked collusion among manufacturers to boycott certain retailers. Boycotts generally constitute unlawful behavior.

Deregulation

Monopolies are frequently (but not always) regulated, and this is especially true with respect to utility companies. The question of deregulating utilities is one that is politically revisited as power shifts to elected officials with differing views on the political economy. Utilities are often referred to as "natural monopolies," where competition harms rather than enhances efficiency. As a result, utilities generally are regulated *into* being pre-emptive monopolies, and *out* of being able to price monopolistically. In other words, government regulations operate bilaterally to protect the monopoly by prohibiting competition on the one hand, and to control monopoly profit-taking on the other.

As technology, resources, and social needs change, whether a given sector still should remain a governmentally sanctioned monopoly can become the subject of great debate. This happened in the 1990s, and the result of the debate was that the supply-side of energy—the price the power companies had to pay for the power they sold—was deregulated.

The Enron debacle pointed out the fragility of that form of deregulation, and how susceptible the energy supply is to manipulation. Because of deregulation, Enron was able to buy up electricity in California at low prices, and then sell that power out of that state, creating shortages in it. California consequently suffered huge energy price increases, rolling brown-outs, and industry recession in some sectors. In addition, Enron traders were filmed and recorded getting their power plants to artificially lower capacity or create congestion to further drive up prices.(3)

The deregulation of cable companies in the 1990s also caused substantial rate increases and consumer anger. Government presumed that competition would enter the field if cable companies were deregulated, but the presumption did not materialize, at least not in a timely manner. Prices skyrocketed. The barriers to entry were not adequately considered. Municipalities have little interest in allowing new cable operators to tear up streets and obstruct traffic in order to lay more cable. Even if permits were granted, laying cable is a process that takes years to complete. New technologies like broadband and satellite were not widely available at the time of deregulation. Only the re-imposition of pricing controls (within a year after deregulation) capped the spiral. Obviously, supervening technologies like broadband and satellite have evolved

since that time and have forced cable operators to price at competitive levels. Consequently, it is unclear whether price regulation of cable is still necessary, but the government is now highly sensitized to the risks involved in deregulating that utility.

There is one area where deregulation has significantly enhanced consumer pricing. Until early in the 1980s, AT&T controlled all local and long distance telephone services and was regulated both federally and locally. But in 1974, the Department of Justice took the dramatic step of suing to break up Ma Bell. A settlement agreement reached in 1982 compelled AT&T to sell off all of its local telephone companies and share use of the telephone lines with other providers of long distance services. This opened the door for competition in equipment sales, long distance, and local services.

Since the AT&T trust was busted, long distance telephone services have dramatically declined in price. Cell phone and Internet products have created new types of competition against traditional landlines and long distance services. Technology has exploded for both visual and audio communication. Consumers have unquestionably benefited greatly.

The Rule of Reason and *Per Se* Illegality

Section 1 of the Sherman Act appears on the surface to outlaw all trade restraints. It says in relevant part:

"Every contract, combination in the form of trust or otherwise, or conspiracy, in restraint of trade or commerce among the several States, or with foreign nations, is declared to be illegal."

However, not all trade restraints are harmful, and some are actually beneficial. Consequently, the U.S. Supreme Court has established two distinct rules to determine lawfulness or unlawfulness of restraints on trade.

The first is the "rule of reason," which was first articulated in the 1911 Standard Oil Trust case. The rule of reason limits the Sherman Act to forbid only *unreasonable* restraints of trade.

The second is *"per se* illegality," and it is applied to behavior that is potentially so harmful that it is considered unreasonable as a matter of law. No evaluation of reasonableness is required to find culpability on *per se* illegal conduct.

The courts have spent over one hundred years grappling with determining what behaviors are *per se* illegal and what restraints need to be analyzed for reasonableness under the rule of reason.

The current law holds that for the most part, if horizontal competitors engage in any form of collusion, price or non-price, their conduct will be considered *per se* illegal. On the other hand, if businesses in a vertical relationship engage in trade restraints, those behaviors will be evaluated under the rule of reason. In most cases, vertical restraints are considered reasonable as a matter of law.

A detailed explanation of horizontal and vertical trade restraints follows.

Vertical Trade Restraints

The area where the rule of reason is most often applied is in vertical trade restraints, where it would appear that there are no longer any *per se* illegal forms of conduct recognized in the law. Vertical trade restraints are those between manufacturers, suppliers, distributors, or other entities up and down the supply chain. In a typical, vertical price restraint, a retailer will be told the price at which it must sell a product to consumers, or risk being cut off from further supply.

Consumers do not like vertical price restraints because they interfere with shopping for bargains on specific brand-name merchandise. On the other hand, the macro-economy can generally benefit from vertical price restraints. Vertical integration in terms of exclusive distribution rights, franchises, and recommended pricing strategies is great for synergy and efficiency and, under the right circumstances, can promote inter-brand competition which is the higher goal in the market system.

Although the area of law is settled now, the courts and the legislative branch vacillated with regard to vertical trade restraints over the past 100 years. In the early 1900s, vertical restraints were initially *per se* illegal under the Sherman Act. After the establishment of the rule of reason in the 1911 Standard Oil case, the U.S. Supreme Court established the "Colgate Doctrine" (see the *U.S. v. Colgate* case that follows) in 1919, allowing a "back door" for vertical price restraining through which a manufacturer could deal or refuse to deal with a retailer who failed to sell at the manufacturer's recommended prices.(4)

U.S. v. Colgate & Co. (1919)

United States Supreme Court (250 U.S. 300)

Justice James Clark McReynolds delivered the opinion of the court.

…We are confronted by an uncertain interpretation of an indictment itself couched in rather vague and general language.…The indictment runs only against Colgate & Co., a corporation engaged in manufacturing soap and toilet articles and selling them throughout the Union. It makes no reference to monopoly, and proceeds solely upon the theory of an unlawful combination.… [I]t alleges:

> …[T]he defendant knowingly and unlawfully created and engaged in a combination with said wholesale and retail dealers, in the Eastern district of Virginia and throughout the United States, for the purpose and with the effect of procuring adherence on the part of such dealers (in reselling such products sold to them aforesaid) to resale prices fixed by the defendant, and of preventing such dealers from reselling such products at lower prices, thus suppressing competition amongst such wholesale dealers, and amongst such retail dealers, in restraint of the aforesaid trade and commerce among the several States, in violation of the act entitled 'An act to protect trade and commerce against unlawful restraints and monopolies,' approved July 2, 1890.

[In finding for Colgate, the trial court noted:]

> The retailer, after buying, could, if he chose, give away his purchase or sell it at any price he saw fit, or not sell it at all, his course in these respects being affected only by

the fact that he might by his action incur the displeasure of the manufacturer, who could refuse to make further sales to him, as he had the undoubted right to do.

[The finding of the U.S. Supreme Court is as follows:]

The purpose of the Sherman Act is to prohibit monopolies, contracts, and combinations which probably would unduly interfere with the free exercise of their rights by those engaged, or who wish to engage, in trade and commerce—in a word to preserve the right of freedom to trade. In the absence of any purpose to create or maintain a monopoly, the act does not restrict the long recognized right of trader or manufacturer engaged in an entirely private business, freely to exercise his own independent discretion as to parties with whom he will deal; and, of course, he may announce in advance the circumstances under which he will refuse to sell.

The judgment of the District Court must be Affirmed.

The Colgate Doctrine allowed producers to refuse to deal with retailers who did not cooperate with pricing suggestions, but in 1937, the law temporarily broadened to formally allow resale price restraints.

In 1937, Congress enacted the Miller-Tydings Act, which exempted from antitrust laws "contracts or agreements prescribing minimum prices for the resale" of articles purchased. This statute opened a "front door" through which vertical price restraints became completely legal. Miller-Tydings essentially replaced and expounded the Colgate Doctrine by allowing the establishment of "fair trade" pricing, where retailers were made functionally unable to compete with each other in terms of price on brand-name items. Under Miller-Tydings, price competition was focused exclusively on interbrand (as opposed to intrabrand) competition. Manufacturers implemented strategies to set their prices relative to other manufacturers, and controlled those prices through the retail distribution system. During this time, some interesting consumer practices evolved.

During the days of Miller-Tydings, consumers could not benefit from shopping around for fair traded items, since all stores charged functionally the identical price. As the new product lines were to come out, however, stores generally got permission from the manufacturers to sell off last-season items at sale prices. These sales were monumental events. Goods were set out on tables and customers would hoard piles of discounted product. At times, an item would be tried on and put back on the sale rack or table so many times that it would actually get worn out before it was ever bought. This was called being "shop worn," meaning the product was used up, even though nobody ever bought it.

This explains one of the metaphors in the Syufy case presented in the previous chapter. In that case, Judge Kozinski criticized the government's use of the *Alcoa* argument that efficient and aggressive competition could itself be a barrier to entry. Judge Kozinski referred to that argument as "a shopworn argument we had thought long abandoned...." It is a subtle insult, meaning that so many people "tried on" or looked at that argument, it was totally worn out even though nobody "bought" or adopted its reasoning.

In 1975, a congressional about-face occurred and Miller-Tydings was repealed. This reflects the national ambivalence toward resale maintenance arrangements. Consumers (voters) wanted competition between retailers, and they got it. "Suggested retail" pricing replaced fair trade pricing, and consumers could find widely varying prices for the same article in different stores.

Some manufacturers legitimately believed this intra-brand competition had a chilling effect over their distribution and sales. Retailers would back away from certain products where price-cutters were present. The consequence of the repeal of Miller-Tydings was a series of appellate cases about which standard (*per se* illegality or

rule of reason) the courts should apply to vertical restraints.

First, the Continental TV case established that the rule of reason applies to vertical nonprice restraints, and further indicated that such restraints are generally reasonable (lawful) under that rule. Retailers can consequently be given exclusive territories or rights of distribution without running afoul of the Sherman Act.

Then the Monsanto case allowed vertical price restraints to be examined under the rule of reason in the same manner as non-price restraints, and the courts have likewise indicated that they would generally be found reasonable. This brought back Colgate-style power to the marketplace. Nike, for example, currently refuses to restock retail outlets that discount their new-line products. Several other manufacturers of leading brands operate similarly. This behavior is lawful.

In 1997, the U.S. Supreme Court decided to apply the rule of reason to contractually imposed vertical price restraints where the restraint served as a ceiling, or maximum and not a minimum. Although manufacturers must still use the Colgate back door for vertically imposed price minimums to be absolutely comfortable with vertical price restraints, price ceilings are now subject to the rule of reason and are reasonable according to the State Oil case. Price floors will be subject to the rule of reason going forward, but we do not know if the court will generally find them reasonable or not.

In summary, in the area of vertical trade restraints, reasonableness will rule, and most restraints will be allowed.

Horizontal Trade Restraints

Horizontal trade restraints involve agreements or collusions between competitors. Horizontal trade restraints are, with few exceptions, *per se* illegal. Price-fixing, where competitors agree on minimum pricing, can be charged criminally or civilly. Even nonprice horizontal restraints, such as output restrictions or geographic divisions, are *per se* illegal because they are likely to have pricing effects.

Conduct that is *per se* illegal is perceived to be so injurious that its mere existence is sufficient for liability. Horizontal collusion is (with rare exception) irrebuttably threatening.

People sometimes confuse horizontal mergers (where one competitor acquires another) with horizontal restraints (where one competitor colludes with another). Mergers of competitors occur quite frequently, can produce efficiency and consumer benefit, and, when subject to Department of Justice review, are only prohibited if they are perceived to harm competition. Syufy was a case involving horizontal mergers.

Horizontal collusion can rarely offer consumer benefit, and can almost always cause some harm, which is why it is generally illegal altogether. But there are problems even in this established area of antitrust law, where exceptions seem to always poke through rules.

First, it is not always easy to see when a restraint is actually horizontal—sometimes they look rather vertical. Consider cases involving horizontal trade restraints imposed by trade associations. The trade association sets rules, so it looks like a separate entity that exercises some power over a group of competitors, not unlike a big retailer might do over a producer. However, trade associations are organizations comprised of member businesses that are engaged in the same area of trade. This is best described by example.

Consider the Solid Waste Association of North America (SWANA), which is a trade group whose members are in the business of disposing of solid waste. The voting members control the organization whose mission is to "advance the practice of environmentally and economically sound management of municipal solid waste."(5)

If SWANA decided to impose a pricing floor on solid waste disposal, it would be the same as if its competitor-members got together and colluded on price. The association and the members are legally indistinguishable from each other.

Until recently, the most famous member association case involved the National Collegiate Athletic Association (NCAA) and the sale of television rights for NCAA football games. The NCAA is an organization of colleges and universities that participate in intercollegiate sports. The NCAA is a not-for-profit trade association, having no power other than what the voting membership delegates to it.

So when the NCAA engaged in controlling and limiting the sale and pricing of NCAA football games to television networks, it was acting as a trustee would act, and the member schools were functionally engaging in horizontal trade restraints.

The problem is that it is virtually impossible to have a competitive sport without the teams colluding on the basic rules of the game, the times the games will be played, how the victor will be determined, and how certain revenues generated by multiple teams for (say) playoffs or other conjoined games will be divided. Calling all collusive conduct on the part of the NCAA *per se* illegal would end Division 1 intercollegiate athletics. A rule of reason had to be applied, and while the NCAA's restraint on television sales was considered illegal, that finding was based on the rule of reason and could theoretically have gone the other way.

The consequence of using the rule of reason in any horizontal restraint case means more uncertainty in antitrust cases, but only a little bit more. Most of the time horizontal collusion is *per se* illegal, and competitors will get in trouble for engaging in it. But certain context requires thinking outside that box, and antitrust law can only be rational when put in context. Athletics is one of those contexts that cries for exception, and has throughout our history.

Antitrust Law and Athletics

Baseball has a global exemption to antitrust law because, as one of our unique American sports, it evolved that way. But the other athletic organizations are not equally protected. The National Football League (NFL), National Basketball Association (NBA), and, as mentioned, the NCAA have limited protection. Non-statutory labor exceptions have been made (like for the NFL Player's Association) through which players have been given the right to organize (they are not covered under the National Labor Relations Act, so the players technically cannot form a union without a legal exception). There are other obvious exceptions as well, as the league teams must be able to collude on the fundamental logistics of the competition.

In 2010, a most interesting case was taken by the U.S. Supreme Court with respect to the NFL. In the midst of a union lock-out over salary caps and other conflicts between players and owners, a small clothing manufacturer (American Needle) took on the question of the legality of the NFL acting as a single legal entity (instead of each team acting on its own) with regard to branding of NFL team logos, trademarks, and intellectual property.

In *American Needle v. National Football League, et al.*, the court had to decide whether the NFL's single entity interest in promoting its member teams' logos and branded merchandise was in conflict with each individual teams' interests in promoting their own team "brands" as competitors. The court determined that teams do compete with each other for fans and for the sale of team merchandise, and that therefore they were all individual units for purposes of merchandising their branded merchandise and intellectual property. This meant that through the NFL, the teams were "acting in concert." Therefore, they were covered under the Sherman Act and were horizontally colluding on merchandising.

It is important to note that the only reason such conduct (competitors acting in concert to create a single entity) would not be *per se* illegal is because of the nature of the athletic industry and the need for a certain amount of collusion. In this NFL case, the conduct was not *per se* illegal because of the unique relationships of the teams, but it still may be unreasonable under the rule of reason. In the NCAA case referenced earlier in this chapter, a restraint on the sale of television rights by the NCAA was unreasonable and illegal under the Sherman Act. The reasonableness of the restraint of the NFL on team logos and merchandising was something the Supreme Court remanded to the trial court to determine in the American Needle case summarized below. As of the writing of this chapter, it is unknown what the trial court decided with respect to the reasonableness of the restraint in this case.

The syllabus of the Supreme Court Decision explains how the court reasoned through the complex issues in the case, noting in its final paragraph what types of collusions within the NFL would be inherently reasonable.(6)

American Needle, Inc. v. National Football League et al.

Supreme Court of the United States

Syllabus

Argued January 13, 2010—Decided May 24, 2010

Respondent National Football League (NFL) is an unincorporated association of 32 separately owned professional football teams, also respondents here. The teams, each of which owns its own name, colors, logo, trademarks, and related intellectual property, formed respondent National Football League Properties (NFLP) to develop, license, and market that property. At first, NFLP granted nonexclusive licenses to petitioner and other vendors to manufacture and sell team labeled apparel. In December 2000, however, the teams authorized NFLP to grant exclusive licenses. NFLP granted an exclusive license to respondent Reebok International Ltd. to produce and sell trademarked headwear for all 32 teams. When petitioner's license was not renewed, it filed this action alleging that the agreements between respondents violated the Sherman Act, §1 of which makes "[e]very contract, combination…or, conspiracy, in restraint of trade" illegal. Respondents answered that they were incapable of conspiring within §1's meaning because the NFL and its teams are, in antitrust law jargon, a single entity with respect to the conduct challenged. The District Court granted respondents summary judgment, and the Seventh Circuit affirmed.

Held: The alleged conduct related to licensing of intellectual property constitutes concerted action that is not categorically beyond §1's coverage.

(a) The meaning of "contract, combination…, or, conspiracy" in §1 of the Sherman Act is informed by the Act's "'basic distinction between concerted and independent action.'" because, unlike independent action, "[c]oncerted activity inherently is fraught with anticompetitive risk" insofar as it "deprives the marketplace of independent centers of decision making that competition assumes and demands." And because concerted action is discrete and distinct, a limit on such activity leaves untouched a vast amount of business conduct. That creates less risk of deterring a firm's necessary conduct and leaves courts to examine only discrete agreements. An arrangement must therefore embody concerted action in order to be a "contract, combination...or, conspiracy" under §1.

(b) In determining whether there is concerted action under §1, the Court has eschewed formalistic distinctions, such as whether the alleged conspirators are legally distinct entities, in favor of a functional consideration of how they actually operate. The Court has repeatedly found instances in which members of a legally single entity violated §1 when the entity was controlled by a group of competitors and served, in essence, as a vehicle for ongoing concerted activity. Conversely, the Court has found that although the entities may be "separate" for purposes of incorporation or formal title, if they are controlled by a single center of decision-making and they control a single aggregation of economic power, an agreement between them does not constitute a "contract, combination...or, conspiracy."

(c) The relevant inquiry is therefore one of substance, not form, which does not turn on whether the alleged parties to contract, combination, or conspiracy are part of a legally single entity or seem like one firm or multiple firms in any metaphysical sense. The inquiry is whether the agreement in question joins together "separate economic actors pursuing separate economic interests," such that it "deprives the marketplace of independent centers of decision making," and therefore of diversity of entrepreneurial interests and thus of actual or potential competition. If it does, then there is concerted action covered by §1, and the court must decide whether the restraint of trade is unreasonable and therefore illegal.

(d) The NFL teams do not possess either the unitary decision making quality or the single aggregation of economic power characteristic of independent action. Each of them is a substantial, independently owned, independently managed business, whose "general corporate actions are guided or determined" by "separate corporate consciousnesses," and whose "objectives are" not "common." They compete with one another, not only on the playing field, but to attract fans, for gate receipts, and for contracts with managerial and playing personnel. Directly relevant here, the teams are potentially competing suppliers in the market for intellectual property. When teams license such property, they are not pursuing the "common interests of the whole" league, but, instead, the interests of each "corporation itself." It is not dispositive, as respondents argue, that, by forming NFLP,

American Needle, Inc. v. National Football League et al.

they have formed a single entity, akin to a merger, and market their NFL brands through a single outlet. Although the NFL respondents may be similar in some sense to a single enterprise, they are not similar in the relevant functional sense. While teams have common interests such as promoting the NFL brand, they are still separate, profit maximizing entities, and their interests in licensing team trademarks are not necessarily aligned. Nor does it matter that the teams may find the alleged cooperation necessary to compete against other forms of entertainment. Although decisions made by NFLP are not as easily classified as concerted activity, the NFLP's decisions about licensing the teams' separately owned intellectual property are concerted activity and thus covered by §1 for the same reason that decisions made directly by the 32 teams are covered by §1. In making the relevant licensing decisions, NFLP is "an instrumentality" of the teams.

(e) Football teams that need to cooperate are not trapped by antitrust law. The fact that the NFL teams share an interest in making the entire league successful and profitable, and that they must cooperate to produce games, provides a perfectly sensible justification for making a host of collective decisions. Because some of these restraints on competition are necessary to produce the NFL's product, the Rule of Reason generally should apply, and teams' cooperation is likely to be permissible. And depending upon the activity in question, the Rule of Reason can at times be applied without detailed analysis. But the activity at issue in this case is still concerted activity covered for §1 purposes.

538 F. 3d 736, reversed and remanded.

STEVENS, J., delivered the opinion for a unanimous Court.

American Needle, Inc. v. National Football League et al.

Predatory Pricing

In its simplest legal definition, predatory pricing means pricing below cost in order to drive out a competitor. That, of course, means everyone has to agree on what "below cost" means. There are fixed and variable costs, as financial accounting courses explain. Fixed costs are those that would be incurred whether or not a single item is actually produced. Variable costs are those associated with each increment of production. The issue of what is below cost pricing in an antitrust case is the subject of great debate.

Suppose that a competitor is indeed pricing below variable cost and selling goods for less than each good cost to produce without consideration for the fixed cost component. The assumption might be that this competitor is unlawfully pricing as a predator to eliminate competition. That might be true, but this would not necessarily constitute unlawful predatory pricing. Competitors are allowed to price even below variable cost if they are doing so in order to compete.

If you are completely confused as to where the doctrine of predatory pricing would ever be useful in an antitrust action, you are not alone. There is little to grip in terms of an actionable legal theory. However, the precedents that establish the doctrine persevere because (like arguments in the *Alcoa* case), given the right set of variables, pricing can be used in an anticompetitive manner that can harm competition (and not merely competitors).

The following case, *Brooke Group v. Brown and Williamson Tobacco*, is a private cause of action. Brooke (known throughout the case as Liggett) brought an action against Brown and Williamson for predatory pricing.

Even though antitrust laws are designed to protect competition and not competitors, the law does allow competitors to bring the action against the predator or antitrust violator. Policy reasons do support this, because competitors are generally the first to see conduct that goes beyond competition into what Judge Kozinski refers to as "monkey business." Liggett, in the following case, definitely alleged monkey business on the part of Brown and Williamson.

The court in the *Brooke* case made several findings, not all of which are in the redacted version of the case below. Liggett was the first to enter into the generic cigarette market, competing with the big players by offering an inexpensive, "black and white" non-brand product for the lower middle-class cigarette smoker. These cigarettes cost up to 30% less than brand-named products, and began to usurp market share from the big tobacco companies. Brown and Williamson (makers of Benson and Hedges brand cigarettes and one of the smaller players at the time decided to compete directly in the generic cigarette market, and the price war between Brooke and Brown began. The case answers the question as to whether or not Brown was pricing as a predator.(7)

Brooke Group Ltd. v. Brown & Williamson Tobacco Corp. (1993)

United States Supreme Court (509 U.S. 209)

Justice Anthony Kennedy delivered the opinion of the court.

Cigarette manufacturing is a concentrated industry dominated by only six firms, including the two parties here. In 1980, petitioner (hereinafter Liggett) pioneered the economy segment of the market by developing a line of generic cigarettes offered at a list price roughly 30% lower than that of branded cigarettes. By 1984, generics had captured 4% of the market, at the expense of branded cigarettes, and respondent Brown & Williamson entered the economy segment, beating Liggett's net price. Liggett responded in kind, precipitating a price war, which ended, according to Liggett, with Brown & Williamson's selling its generics at a loss. Liggett filed this suit, alleging, *inter alia* [among other things], that volume rebates by Brown & Williamson to wholesalers amounted to price discrimination that had a reasonable possibility of injuring competition in violation of the [Robinson-Patman] Act.... Liggett claimed that the rebates were integral to a predatory pricing scheme, in which Brown & Williamson set below-cost prices...[to help preserve] Brown & Williamson's supracompetitive profits on branded cigarettes.

* * *

Held: Brown & Williamson is entitled to judgment as a matter of law.

(a) The Robinson-Patman Act, by its terms, condemns price discrimination only to the extent that it threatens to injure competition. A claim of primary-line competitive injury under the Act, the type alleged here, is of the same general character as a predatory pricing claim under...the Sherman Act: A business rival has priced its products in an unfair manner with an object to eliminate or retard competition, and thereby gain and exercise control over prices in the relevant market.... A plaintiff must prove (1) that the prices complained of are below an appropriate measure of its rival's costs and (2) that the competitor had a reasonable prospect of recouping its investment in below-cost prices.

…The inquiry is whether, given the aggregate losses caused by the below-cost pricing, the intended target would likely succumb…. If so, then there is the further question whether the below-cost pricing would likely injure competition in the relevant market. The plaintiff must demonstrate that there is a likelihood that the scheme alleged would cause a rise in prices above a competitive level sufficient to compensate for the amounts expended on the predation, including the time value of the money invested in it. Evidence of below-cost pricing is not alone sufficient to permit an inference of probable recoupment and injury to competition. The determination requires an estimate of the alleged predation's cost and a close analysis of both the scheme alleged and the relevant market's structure and conditions. Although not easy to establish, these prerequisites are essential components of real market injury.

* * *

The cigarette industry also has long been one of America's most profitable, in part because, for many years, there was no significant price competition among the rival firms. List prices for cigarettes increased in lockstep, twice a year, for a number of years, irrespective of the rate of inflation, changes in the costs of production, or shifts in consumer demand….

By 1980, however, broad market trends were working against the industry. Overall demand for cigarettes in the United States was declining, and no immediate prospect of recovery existed. As industry volume shrank, all firms developed substantial excess capacity. This decline in demand, coupled with the effects of nonprice competition, had a severe negative impact on Liggett. Once a major force in the industry, with market shares in excess of 20%, Liggett's market share had declined by 1980 to a little over 2%. With this meager share of the market, Liggett was on the verge of going out of business.

At the urging of a distributor, Liggett took an unusual step to revive its prospects: It developed a line of black and white generic cigarettes. When introduced in 1980, black and whites were offered to consumers at a list price roughly 30% lower than the list price of full-priced, branded cigarettes. They were also promoted at the wholesale level by means of rebates that increased with the volume of cigarettes ordered. Black and white cigarettes thus represented a new marketing category. The category's principal competitive char-

Brooke Group Ltd. v. Brown & Williamson Tobacco Corp. (1993)

acteristic was low price. Liggett's black and whites were an immediate and considerable success, growing from a fraction of a percent of the market at their introduction to over 4% of the total cigarette market by early 1984.

As the market for Liggett's generic cigarettes expanded, the other cigarette companies found themselves unable to ignore the economy segment. In general, the growth of generics came at the expense of the other firms' profitable sales of branded cigarettes. Brown & Williamson was hardest hit, because many of Brown & Williamson's brands were favored by consumers who were sensitive to changes in cigarette prices. Although Brown & Williamson sold only 11.4% of the market's branded cigarettes, 20% of the converts [to]…Liggett's black and whites had switched from a Brown & Williamson brand. Losing volume and profits in its branded products, Brown & Williamson determined to enter the generic segment of the cigarette market. In July, 1983, Brown & Williamson had begun selling Value-25s, and in the spring of 1984, it introduced its own black and white cigarette.

…Because Liggett's and Brown & Williamson's black and whites were more or less fungible, wholesalers had little incentive to carry more than one line. And unlike R.J. Reynolds, Brown & Williamson not only matched Liggett's prices, but beat them. At the retail level, the suggested list price of Brown & Williamson's black and whites was the same as Liggett's, but Brown & Williamson's volume discounts to wholesalers were larger. Brown & Williamson's rebate structure also encompassed a greater number of volume categories than Liggett's, with the highest categories carrying special rebates for orders of very substantial size. Brown & Williamson marketed its black and whites to Liggett's existing distributors as well as to its own full list of buyers, which included a thousand wholesalers who had not yet carried any generic products.

II

A

[W]hether the claim alleges predatory pricing under § 2 of the Sherman Act or primary-line price discrimination under the Robinson-Patman Act, two prerequisites to recovery remain the same. First, a plaintiff seeking to establish competitive injury resulting from a rival's low prices must prove that the prices complained of are below an appropriate measure of its rival's costs.

Brooke Group Ltd. v. Brown & Williamson Tobacco Corp. (1993)

...The second prerequisite to holding a competitor liable under the antitrust laws for charging low prices is a demonstration that the competitor had a reasonable prospect, or, under § 2 of the Sherman Act, a dangerous probability, of recouping its investment in below-cost prices. "For the investment to be rational, the [predator] must have a reasonable expectation of recovering, in the form of later monopoly profits, more than the losses suffered." Recoupment is the ultimate object of an unlawful predatory pricing scheme; it is the means by which a predator profits from predation. Without it, predatory pricing produces lower aggregate prices in the market, and consumer welfare is enhanced. Although unsuccessful predatory pricing may encourage some inefficient substitution toward the product being sold at less than its cost, unsuccessful predation is in general a boon to consumers.

That below-cost pricing may impose painful losses on its target is of no moment to the antitrust laws if competition is not injured: It is axiomatic that the antitrust laws were passed for "the protection of *competition*, not *competitors*."

* * *

These prerequisites to recovery are not easy to establish, but they are not artificial obstacles to recovery; rather, they are essential components of real market injury. As we have said in the Sherman Act context, "predatory pricing schemes are rarely tried, and even more rarely successful," and the costs of an erroneous finding of liability are high.

> [T]he mechanism by which a firm engages in predatory pricing—lowering prices—is the same mechanism by which a firm stimulates competition; because "prices in order to increase business often is the very essence of competition."

The judgment of the Court of Appeals is *Affirmed*. [The case against Brown and Williamson is dismissed, and Liggett takes nothing. Brown and Williamson did price below cost, but they will not be able to recoup their losses with supra-normal profits after pushing out Liggett because the rest of the industry will continue to keep them in line.]

There was no question that Brown and Williamson had priced below any measure of their own cost. Their rebates to retailers were alleged to have been higher than their prices. However, they still were not found liable.

As the Supreme Court indicated in the *Brooke* case, winning an antitrust case on a predatory pricing theory is not easy. Even though the trial jury had found *for* Brooke (Liggett), the trial judge entered judgment against them and for Brown and Williamson instead, indicating that the jury could not understand the complexity of the

antitrust laws at issue in the case. In fact, most lawyers cannot understand them—they are extremely convoluted.

However, predatory pricing was one of the two fundamental theories in the *antitrust trial of the century* against Microsoft for its anticompetitive conduct with regard to its browser, Internet Explorer, and its competitor's product, Netscape.

The second fundamental theory in the Microsoft case, which inextricably intertwined with the predatory pricing issue, was that of unlawful tying.

Unlawful Tying or Bundling

It has been noted above that certain monopolies are legal. For example, patents create allowable monopolies within the law. However, the monopolist who holds a legal monopoly must be careful not to leverage the power of the legal monopoly to expand it beyond its lawful bounds. One way that this occurs is when a monopolist has a legal monopoly and then requires that the consumer also buy another product in order to buy the monopolized one. This is called "tying" or "bundling," and as the words suggest, implies the tying together of two products when the consumer may only want the proprietary one.

An example may make this clearer. Assume that Raytheon holds trade secrets for the production of a guided missile that can target weapons caches that cannot be seen by satellite alone.

If, when the government places an order for these missiles, Raytheon compels the government to also buy certain fuel cells that are otherwise available on the open market, potentially, Raytheon would be engaging in unlawful tying. Raytheon has a legal monopoly on the missiles, but cannot extend that to fuel cells, especially if others can produce and sell those cells competitively. The converse is also true that Raytheon cannot, as a condition of sale, require that the government agree not to buy a competitor's fuel cells.

As would appear to be a pattern in antitrust law, the cases on unlawful tying are wholly inconsistent with each other, although the older cases hold little value in the courts today.

Two cases are frequently brought up in unlawful tying cases, and they both involve fast food. The first one is the Chicken Delight case. Chicken Delight was a predecessor of the Kentucky Colonel fried chicken empire, and their benchmark was free home delivery, which competed with the pizza home-delivery market.

The franchisees of Chicken Delight brought suit against the franchisor because they were being compelled to purchase generally traded items from the franchisor (ranging from cooking equipment to flour), which they could purchase cheaper on the open market. The Ninth Circuit Court of Appeals decided the case in 1971 and found that the franchisor unlawfully tied together the use of the Chicken Delight trade name (which was legally monopolized, or proprietary) with nonproprietary, generally available goods.

That case has not been followed by anyone since it was decided; however, it has not been overturned either. A more recent case (1997) was decided in the Third Circuit and involves a former franchisee of Domino's pizza that forfeited its franchise and became Queen City Pizza (which is why the case is named *Queen City Pizza v. Domino's*). In that case, Queen City sued Domino's on exactly the same grounds as the Chicken Delight franchisees sued their franchisor. Queen City objected to being compelled to buy sauce and other generically traded

canned goods in order to use the Domino's trade name. The Third Circuit Court of Appeals looked at the contractual nature of franchises and decided to uphold the contract as it was written. It was the right of the franchisor to determine how it wished to generate revenue and keep quality control over its franchisees. The appellate judge looked at the Chicken Delight arguments made by Queen City and found them to be without merit. Courts are significantly more likely to follow this Third Circuit case than the Chicken Delight case, and it is arguable as to whether the Ninth Circuit would reaffirm its precedent were it to be revisited today. Unlawful tying is not an oft-used cause of action.

However, the issue of unlawful tying became extremely important in the Microsoft case. At the time of the case, Microsoft had integrated its Internet Explorer browser into its Windows operating system and created a quagmire of antitrust issues for the Department of Justice's antitrust division. Microsoft engaged in both predatory pricing (since free can be considered below-cost) and unlawful tying. Though Microsoft fit neither cause of action perfectly, in the big picture with those theories both operating, its conduct was definitely anticompetitive and threatening.

Microsoft

Microsoft's history is one of great timing, ingenious programming, effective marketing, and shameless arrogance.

Microsoft has sued, been sued, robbed, been robbed, and has demonstrated the best and the worst of competition in industry. Its history is one of great innovation and great impudence. According to the online encyclopedia Wikipedia, Microsoft began at Harvard in a dorm room with co-founders Paul Allen and Bill Gates.

Microsoft cofounder Paul Allen was on his way to visit Bill Gates in his dorm room when he came across a magazine containing information about the Altair 8080. It was praised as the world's first microcomputer to rival commercial models. Days afterwards, Bill Gates called MITS (Micro Instrumentation and Telemetry Systems), creators of the Altair 8800, and informed them that he and others [had] developed a version of the programming language BASIC which ran on the Altair 8800 platform—neither Bill Gates or [sic] Paul Allen had touched an Altair 8800 computer, but MITS was very interested in possessing this new build, however.

After about eight weeks, when Gates and Allen finally believed that their product was ready for demonstration, Allen flew to MITS to unveil the new BASIC system. Allen had never handled an Altair, since Gates had done all of the actual product development, but the demonstration was successful and resulted in a deal with MITS to buy the rights to Allen's and Gates' BASIC for the Altair platform. Noticing an opportunity, Gates left Harvard University to pursue the market and eventually found [sic] Microsoft.(8)

The Altair BASIC (a quite innovative high-level programming and functioning language) constituted a worthy entry into the software market. The next part of the Microsoft story is not so pristine.

Gates did not develop the first generation of MS-DOS. He purchased an operating system from Tim Paterson of Seattle Computer Products for $50,000. Paterson had taken the then-most-popular operating system, Digital Research's CP/M, and in six weeks cloned what he named "QDOS," which stood for "Quick and Dirty Operating System." It copied the functionality of CP/M, but was sufficiently unique to be arguably legal. This was the operating system that Microsoft licensed to IBM. Fearing copyright violation issues, IBM ultimately offered both CP/M and QDOS (renamed as PC-DOS) on its PCs, but QDOS was significantly less expensive, and consequently significantly more popular. Digital Research ultimately did sue Microsoft for infringement—that case settled out of court.

Fast forwarding to the late 1990s, Microsoft had clearly become the world leader in terms of PC operating systems, having developed the Windows operating system as a derivative of MS-DOS. One could argue that Apple, with its Macintosh computer, should have been the market leader. Windows had in fact copied Apple's Macintosh graphics to provide PCs with a user interface very similar in form to the Macintosh. (Apple sued Microsoft for stealing the "look and feel" of their operating system, but that case also settled out of court.)

Microsoft's Windows was able to sweep past Macintosh in part because it was housed on computers that were much less expensive, and in part because PCs could interface more readily with the rest of the computing world than could the Macintosh. Also it was housed on computers that were manufactured by multiple producers, where only Apple produced the proprietary Macintosh.

There are some unique characteristics in the computer market that may seem obvious but need to at least be mentioned. In order for people to communicate with each other on computers, they need to have systems that can understand each other. The easiest way to do this is for people who want to "talk" to have the same operating system as each other. A child might sound

foolish if he were to say, "I got one 'cause he got one," but in this case that would actually constitute a valid reason. As a result, personal computer operating systems are especially vulnerable to the effects of market momentum. A good, affordable operating system, once entrenched, is not readily displaced.

Microsoft put itself in the middle of the PC explosion. It provided the operating system that most computer manufacturers included with their product. Microsoft's Windows monopoly is consequently completely and perfectly lawful, by virtue of what the courts would call both Microsoft's business acumen and historic accident.

However, as Microsoft continued to develop software and to beat off competitors, it arguably began to engage in anticompetitive conduct. There were rumblings many years before the Department of Justice brought its complaint that computer manufacturers were being strong-armed to install Microsoft Office on new PCs. It was rumored that manufacturers who declined were threatened with being denied licenses for the Windows operating system. The computer manufacturers would capitulate under such an ominous threat, and, presumably as a result, they put Microsoft Office or Microsoft Works on their products. The anticompetitive consequences to other spreadsheet or word processing software manufacturers were obvious. Those software competitors were being aced out of the market.

When Microsoft decided to enter into the browser market, Netscape was the clear market leader. The initial product release of Internet Explorer was, by all who used it, a seriously less desirable product than Netscape. However, Microsoft included Internet Explorer "free" with its operating systems. This raised the question of predatory pricing, but the issue on its own was not dispositive. Although "free" is at least theoretically below cost, it is not illegal to price below cost for competitive purposes. It is only unlawful if the purpose is to put competitors out of business and reap monopoly profits once they are gone. It is unclear that Microsoft, with an existing Windows monopoly, would have any greater ability to reap monopoly profit than it already could with its legal Windows operating system monopoly.

Netscape was compelled to provide its browser for free to stay in the market. Even an inadequate system that is free is a fierce competitor to one that carries a price. In addition, Windows was not particularly friendly to Netscape, making it more difficult for users to choose to download Netscape as opposed to using the already installed Internet Explorer.

The Department of Justice confronted Microsoft, which then entered into a settlement (consent decree) whereby Microsoft *agreed* to stop tying Internet Explorer with Windows, thereby ostensibly giving Netscape a chance to compete fairly (although

still without charging for their product). Then, in 1998, Microsoft introduced its new version of Windows (the now infamous Windows 98), and this operating system had an integrated version of Internet Explorer. Microsoft claimed that this was not the same as tying—it was just expanding the capability of its operating system, and this was good for everyone.

The Department of Justice (as you might expect) was not happy with Microsoft's rather technical distinction. The complaint against Microsoft was filed by May of 1998. The factual questions were complex, on issues that are difficult to prove one way or the other, since they focused on the intent of Microsoft. The factual disputes revolved around three things: 1) whether Microsoft intentionally developed its programming interfaces to favor Internet Explorer over Netscape, 2) whether Microsoft was using its Windows monopoly to compel computer manufacturers to favor Internet Explorer over Netscape, and 3) whether Microsoft's intent (in words taken from one of its own internal marketing videos) was to destroy the competition.

The legal questions in the case were less complicated. Depending upon the facts, the trial court would have to determine whether Microsoft was engaging in unlawful tying, predatory pricing, or both.

Everything came down to Microsoft's intent. If its purpose in tying Internet Explorer to Windows was to wipe out Netscape so that it could sell

Internet Explorer for monopoly level prices in the future, then its conduct was unlawful. If its motive for giving away Internet Explorer for "free" was to wipe out Netscape, then again, its conduct was predatory and unlawful. However, it is important to note that Microsoft could and did already sell Windows for monopoly level profit at monopoly equilibrium pricing, so motivation was not as obvious as it might have been if Microsoft could be shown to have had a greater opportunity to price higher with Internet Explorer than without.

The case might have gone more favorably for Microsoft had they been even a little bit less arrogant and a bit more honest. Microsoft claimed that its reason for integrating Internet Explorer into Windows was that the integration made Windows faster. They contended that removing Internet Explorer would slow Windows down substantially. According to Wikipedia, Microsoft Vice President James Allchin testified that a videotape demonstrating this slow-down was a seamless segment filmed on a PC. That proved to be completely false, and he was forced to revise his testimony that the tape had been edited from multiple PCs. When he re-ran an unedited tape, Microsoft was forced to drop its claim that Windows ran more slowly with Internet Explorer removed. This was only one of many distortions of truth in which Microsoft principals were caught. When caught, Microsoft would complain about government "nitpicking" or prosecutorial excess.

Judge Jackson, the trial judge in the Microsoft case, grew consistently more enraged at what he perceived to be the dishonesty of Microsoft's leadership. He gave comments to the media about the case that were extremely hostile to Microsoft, and his decision in the case was consistent with that hostility. He made findings that Microsoft was a monopolist that had engaged in unlawful tying of Internet Explorer to Windows. As a remedy, he ordered the company broken into separate companies.

Microsoft appealed, in part based on Judge Jackson's very public bias against it. Judge Jackson said in his own defense that Microsoft's own conduct created any bias he might be perceived to have, calling Microsoft "a company whose senior management is not averse to offering specious testimony to support spurious defenses to claims of its wrongdoing." The D.C. Court of Appeals overturned Judge Jackson's extraordinarily harsh remedy of breaking up the company but did affirm his findings that Microsoft acted as a monopolist in violation of antitrust law. The Court of Appeals remanded the case for further proceedings, but not to Judge Jackson, for whom it also had harsh words. Remember that the judiciary serves as the arbiter between the government and the private sector. It is the height of judicial impropriety to so publicly impart a bias.

The Microsoft case settled. The Department of Justice backed down in

2001 from the remedy ordered by Judge Jackson, and the parties reached a settlement shortly thereafter. The states who objected to the settlement have not been given support from the judiciary. Microsoft has slowly settled all of the antitrust actions brought against it in Europe and elsewhere. There are lingering questions about governmental policy, and whether it might be appropriate to reign in Microsoft's power and prevent other companies from becoming so central to the communications industry.

Some have argued that the Windows operating system is analogous to a natural monopoly that should be regulated. Others point out that there is similar concentration in the computer processor market held by Intel. Most would, however, note that there is no evidence that imposing governmental regulation on this innovative area of the free market would benefit consumers.

Antitrust law is not about ethics as much as it is about politics and fundamental economics. However, if there is an ethical lesson in this for managers, it should be about comportment. One might wonder why Intel has never been pursued by the government. I would surmise that part of the reason is that its management has exercised restraint and has never had the appearance of abusing its market position.

Notes

1. The Sherman Anti-Trust Act ,July 2 1890. Ch 647, 26 Stat 209.

2. *Standard Oil of New Jersey v. United States*, 221 U.S. 1 (1911)

3. "The Smartest Guys in the Room," documentary film, Alex Gibney, Director (2005).

4. *U.S. v Colgate*, (1919), 250 U.S. 300

5. www. SWANA.org

6. *American Needle, Inc. v. National Football League et al.* Argued January 13, 2010—Decided May 24, 2010, Syllabus, 130 S. Ct. 2201

7. *Brooke Group Ltd. V. Brown and Williamson Tobacco Corp* (1993), United States Supreme Court (509 U.S. 209)

8. Wikipedia, http://en.wikipedia.org/wiki/Microsoft#History

Chapter 9
Employment

The vast amount of statutory and common law regarding employment precludes a complete exploration of the content in one or two chapters. There is no single thematic approach that can tie the pieces together into a neat package in this body of law. Employment law has evolved over the past eight hundred years and, in America, has been heavily influenced by periodic political and economic upheavals.

Much of employment law is at least familiar in feel, because most people have been confronted with legal issues in the employment arena at some point in their lives. However, some employment law is counter-intuitive, and it is where intuition might not work that this chapter spends most of its time.

Because the Civil Rights Act and employment discrimination in general constitute such a large body of law, this text devotes this entire chapter to the topic.

Course and Scope

Before exploring the rights of employees, it is important to know the liabilities of employers. Understanding that can help give context to the circumscription that surrounds employee rights.

Under the centuries-old doctrine known as *respondeat superior*, which literally means "let the master answer," employers are liable for the acts of their employees when those acts are committed in the "course and scope" of employment. This liability was established during feudal times and was modeled around the master/slave relationship of the early British Commonwealth. From its inception, the notion of employer liability has been a practical rather than a moral solution to the problems caused when one person, while working for another, causes harm.

In the days when there were masters and slaves, the masters owned everything (including the slaves) and the slaves obviously owned nothing. If harm was done by a slave, no compensation could have been gotten from someone who by definition owned nothing. So the early common law imposed full liability on the master for all actions of the slave.

Not much has changed in this regard over the centuries since the doctrine of *respondeat superior* was established even though slavery has been abolished. Once an act is considered to have been in the course and scope of employment, the employer is liable for the consequences and has no defenses to a claim for damages.

The fight in the modern world now is what constitutes being in the "course and scope" of employment. To complicate things a bit further, the phrase "course and scope" is defined differently in different contexts.

Liability to Third Parties

Respondeat superior as a concept only applies to damages to non-employees, i.e., third parties. Consequently, harm to an employee in the course and scope of employment is treated differently than harm to an outsider. This can only make sense if one considers the context of how the law evolved. Although in feudal times a master would care for a slave for practical and moral purposes, he would not owe the slave compensation were the slave injured on the job. Harm to a slave was seen as harm to a master's own property; the master would suffer a loss if a slave were harmed, he might pay to have the slave "repaired," but he could not rationally owe his own property (the slave) anything. If the slave were to harm someone else, however, that person would have full recourse against the master.

Under the doctrine of *respondeat superior*, much has been litigated about what constitutes the "course and scope" of employment, and under what circumstances the employer can be held liable beyond that.

Some of the exclusions are obvious. If an employee happens to be at work when he or she manages to mastermind a robbery, the employer will not be liable for that robbery because no part of that action could be considered as part of the employee's job responsibility. Criminal conduct is generally considered to be outside the scope of employment.

If an employee is on Facebook while at work and posts a libelous comment about his former girlfriend, the employer would not be liable as this also would not be considered as being in the course and scope of employment. Intentional torts (civil wrongs) done for personal reasons while at work are generally not the employer's responsibility.

There are as many exceptions as rules in the application of the notion of "course and scope" of employment and many common law workarounds that impose employer liability even outside of that criterion. The important thing is to know where the problems might occur. There is no real way to predict outcomes when the cases have difficult factual situations, as the following cases, beginning with *Mary M. v. City of Los Angeles* (1), illustrate.

Mary M., Plaintiff and Respondent, v. City of Los Angeles, Defendant and Appellant

Supreme Court of California (54 Cal. 3d 202; 814 P.2d 1341; 285 Cal. Rptr. 99)

September 5, 1991

* * *

OPINION

* * *

The issue in this case is: When a police officer on duty, by misusing his official authority, rapes a woman whom he has detained, can the public entity that employs him be held vicariously liable for his misconduct? We conclude that the employer can be held liable under the doctrine of respondeat superior.

I. Facts

About 2:30 a.m. on October 3, 1981, plaintiff Mary M. was driving home alone when Sergeant Leigh Schroyer of the Los Angeles Police Department stopped her for erratic driving. Sergeant Schroyer was on duty as a field supervisor; he was assigned to supervise and train police officers patrolling the streets. He was in uniform, wore a badge and a gun, and was driving a marked black-and-white police car. When he detained plaintiff, he sent in a radio message that he was out of his vehicle conducting an investigation.

Sergeant Schroyer asked plaintiff for her driver's license; plaintiff gave it to him. He then asked her to perform a field sobriety test to determine whether she was under the influence of alcohol. Plaintiff, who had been drinking, did not do well on the test. She began to cry, and pleaded with Schroyer not to take her to jail. Schroyer ordered her to get in the front seat of the police car, but he did not handcuff her. He then drove to plaintiff's home.

After entering the house with plaintiff, Sergeant Schroyer told her that he expected "payment" for taking her home instead of to jail. Plaintiff tried to run away, but Schroyer grabbed her hair and threw her on the couch. When plaintiff screamed, Schroyer put his hand over her mouth and threatened to take her to jail. Plaintiff stopped struggling, and Schroyer raped her. He then left the house....

As a result of this incident, criminal charges were filed against Sergeant Schroyer, and a jury convicted him of rape. The trial court sentenced him to state prison.

Plaintiff then brought a civil lawsuit against both Sergeant Schroyer and his employer, the City of Los Angeles (hereafter the City), for damages arising out of the rape. Plaintiff's complaint originally asserted that the City was liable for negligence in employing Schroyer and that, as Schroyer's employer, the City was also vicariously liable under the doctrine of respondeat superior. At trial, however, plaintiff relied solely on the theory of respondeat superior. The jury returned a verdict for plaintiff, finding that "at the time of the events out of which this case arose" Sergeant Schroyer was "acting within the scope of his employment with the Los Angeles Police Department." The jury assessed general damages of $150,000 against the City.

...The City contends that...even if all conflicts in the facts and the inferences to be drawn from those facts are resolved in plaintiff's favor, Sergeant Schroyer was acting outside the scope of employment when he raped plaintiff.

We do not agree.

Conclusion

Our society has entrusted police officers with enforcing its laws and ensuring the safety of the lives and property of its members. In carrying out these important responsibilities, the police act with the authority of the state. When police officers on duty misuse that formidable power to commit sexual assaults, the public employer must be held accountable for their actions. "'It is, after all, the state which puts the officer in a position to employ force and which benefits from its use.'"

...The matter is remanded to the Court of Appeal for further proceedings consistent with this opinion.

The officer in the Mary M. case was convicted of rape and sentenced to prison accordingly. He never answered any of the civil claims brought against him and the City of Los Angeles. The case is counterintuitive because a rape is not something one would generally believe was committed in the "course and scope" of employment. The following case is more the norm in cases where sexual assault is present.(2)

Capitol City Foods, Inc. [Burger King] v. Superior Court (Mary T.) (1992)

5 Cal.App.4th 1042 , 7 Cal.Rptr.2d 418

Factual and Procedural Background

Mary T. began working at defendant's Burger King franchise in January of 1989. Vernon Johnson was the night shift supervisor. On January 29, Mary and a coworker asked Johnson to go with them for a drink. Johnson could not go then, but suggested another time. Mary and Johnson made arrangements to go out on the 31st. They both believed the coworker would accompany them. Neither Johnson nor Mary was scheduled to work that day, but unbeknownst to Johnson, Dan Singh had changed the schedule and scheduled Mary to work that day at 5 p.m. At that time Mary was still in training and had a flexible schedule as she learned the job alongside more experienced workers. On January 31, as arranged, Johnson picked up Mary, who was in her Burger King uniform, at a grocery store at 4 p.m.; the coworker did not show up. They drove around for 45 minutes, during which time Johnson made two phone calls. He called the Burger King and told Dan Singh that he should not have changed the schedule without Johnson's approval and that if Mary wanted to work she would come in late. He also called his parents' house. Johnson took Mary to his parents' house, where they had sexual intercourse. Johnson then dropped Mary off at an auto repair store, and he went to the Burger King. The next day Mary told the manager what had happened, and quit shortly thereafter.

Mary filed a complaint for sexual harassment, a form of sex discrimination...

Conclusion: [Burger King was not liable.] Nothing in the [law] imposes liability on a private employer for the acts of its supervisory employee while off-duty and acting on his own.

Although the sexual encounter between Mary T. and her night shift supervisor was initiated at work, the court found that any potentially offending conduct occurred away from the workplace and consequently not in the course and scope of employment.

Liability to Employees

It should be noted that in addition to discrimination (or discrimination-based harassment) claims, employees have recourse against employers under workers' compensation statutes for injuries in the course and scope of employment, and that workers' compensation laws exist in every state. The amount of damages an employee may receive as a result of a workplace injury is very restricted, and controlled by statute. Where a third party might receive millions, an employee might only be entitled to thousands.

As with *respondeat superior* claims, the employer is defenseless against a workers' compensation claim if the employee was injured in the course and scope of employment. Interestingly, the definition of course and scope for workers' compensation cases may be very different than the standard for third party claims under the doctrine of *respondeat superior* and tends to be much narrower. For example, if you are on your cell phone for work-related matters while driving to and from your workplace and are involved in an accident, you are excluded from coverage under workers' compensation, but your employer may still

be liable to third parties under the doctrine of *respondeat superior.*

One of the most interesting and controversial cases concerning the concept of *respondeat superior* is a 1996 case involving a woman manager at Saks Fifth Avenue in New York. According to the October 1996 newsletter of the National Organization of Women (NOW), the Saks manager "was raped in the store by a security guard…" and the store successfully argued that "the woman's only recourse was workers' compensation." NOW argued that Saks was treating the rape as if it "were a normal occupational hazard." The fact is that whether normal or not, the woman was in the course and scope of employment when the rape occurred, and based on accessible resources available at that time, Saks could not have known their security guard was dangerous. In New York (and most other states), the remedy of workers' compensation is exclusive no matter what the cause of the harm. (There were a number of efforts to change the law subsequent to this case to carve an exception for rape, but the author does not know whether any states have done so.)

The underlying problem that states deal with in setting policy in this arena is to not unduly penalize companies who have no actual fault in causing workplace injury, so that businesses are not shut down due to overwhelming insurance costs, etc. On the other hand, states do not want to unduly burden employees to have to prove employer fault when they want to recover damages for injuries that occur as a consequence of their job. Workers' compensation is a no-fault compromise legislative scheme.

Right to Work

Frequently students will ask about a devastating situation where they or someone to whom they are close has been fired from a job. They will say, "Since Arizona is a right-to-work state, I guess employers can do whatever they want."

Arizona is indeed a right-to-work state, but that has little to do with the issue. Surprisingly, the right to work is not about working at all. It is about paying union dues.

Under the National Labor Relations Act (NLRA), each state can choose from three limited options as to how it wants to regulate whether or not there will be compulsory union membership or dues requirements in unionized facilities. Twenty-nine states are "agency" or "union" shop states, where all employees in a unionized facility either have to join the union after a specified period of time (union-shop state) or at least begin paying some amount of union dues within that time (agency-shop state). The remaining twenty-one states are "right-to-work" states, where workers in unionized facilities do not need to either join the union or pay dues, unless they so choose. Although the phrase "right to work" implies ramifications beyond whether or not employees have to pay union dues, the fundamental union relationship in all states is basically the same.

In simple terms, here is how a collective bargaining unit (a union) works. The employees in a given group vote to be unionized, which means they elect to be represented as a group by a collective bargaining agent (type of union representative). Once certified through the NLRA process, that agent is the exclusive bargaining agent for the unit. Thus, no individual has the right to represent himself or herself once there is a certified bargaining agent. If an employee wants a salary increase, he or she can only get one if the union negotiates it. If an employee wants to assume more responsibility in the workplace, even that right is governed by the union agreement and cannot be exerted on a case-by-case basis.

On the other hand, if the employer wants to fire a worker, the employer is generally restricted by the union agreement as to how and why the worker can be terminated. Likewise, the employer cannot unilaterally cut salaries, add job responsibilities, or take away benefits.

In a right-to-work state, the first time the union is certified, more than fifty percent of the workers must have both voted for and committed to join it. However, over time, a shop may find that due to worker attrition or apathy, fewer than half the workers are members of the union. This does not mean the union is no longer the exclusive bargaining agent. It just means that the union is not getting paid very much in dues for its efforts, but it must still represent all members of the bargaining unit.

Here is how this works. Assume that you see some opportunities in your workplace, and you wish to speak to management directly about potential advancement. Assume further that you are not a member of the union (in a right-to-work state) but that you are working in a unit that has a certified bargaining agent. You may not speak to management in your own behalf, and if management speaks to you in this regard, they are violating the NLRA and committing an unfair labor practice. The policy reasons for this are complex and will not be covered here. The bottom line is that individuals in bargaining units are silenced with regard to most workplace-related issues, except to the extent that the union speaks for them.

Collective bargaining benefits workers in that the collective as a whole has more power than any individual and can compel more capitulation from the employer as a general rule. Unions generally advance the interests of the unit as a whole, but, for the most part, do not use meritocratic measures for individual reward. In other words, there is generally little short-term incentive to be the "best" in a union shop. On the other hand, most workers will get higher wages, more security, and more democratic voice about their conditions of employment if they are in a union than if they are not.

In summary, the "right to work" is simply the right not to be a member of the union and not to pay dues. Otherwise, union shops operate identically in all states. No matter whether your state is right-to-work, union, or agency-shop, if there is a union, it is the exclusive bargaining agent for the entire bargaining unit. It must represent even non-members in right-to-work states. Conversely, non-members do not have the right to negotiate for themselves if there is a certified bargaining unit.

At-Will Termination

Workers may be motivated to form and join unions in order to override the fundamental common-law employment relationship in the United States, which is the "at-will" relationship. Because most workers are not in a union, however, it is the "at-will" termination rules that largely apply to employment

situations, and this is a frequently misunderstood area of the law.

The at-will relationship provides that either the employer or the employee can terminate the employment relationship at any time, with or without cause, with or without notice. If there is a trade union agreement, terminations are governed under contract rather than under the common-law at-will doctrine. Absent a union agreement, unless there is a common-law or statutory exception (and there are very few), workers are vulnerable to the whims of the employer, and employers are vulnerable to their workers as well.

In theory, market factors should control employment relationships more effectively than regulation, and the law reflects that theoretical perspective. It would be foolish and inefficient for an employer to terminate its relationship with a productive, valuable employee, and one would assume that the "invisible hand" of self-interest would generally stop employers from such inefficiency and foolishness. Likewise, it would be foolish and inefficient for a worker to leave a good job where he or she was well treated.

Theory and practice, however, often conflict. The at-will doctrine implies an equality between employers and employees that is not realistic. Although both parties in an employment relationship need each other, an employer (especially a large corporate employer) generally will not suffer enormous hardship if an employee quits. However, an employee who is terminated may well suffer enormous hardship, ranging from losing his or her home to suffering from illness without the benefit of medical coverage.

The law has not evolved to completely accommodate the fundamental disequilibrium between employers and employees because a sweeping change in the doctrine would have deep and, many would argue, harmful effects on our market economy. Still, there is a hint of acknowledgment that the two sides of the coin are not equally weighted in the eyes of the law even in our Constitution. The Thirteenth Amendment anti-slavery provisions in the Constitution leave intact the unequivocal right of employees to quit a job at will. However, lawmakers and the courts have established limited statutory and common-law protections in various areas, including civil rights, which erode the at-will doctrine as it applies to employers.

Over time, additional rights have been given to workers, such as minimum wage, overtime pay, right to a safe workplace, and others that acknowledge the vulnerability of workers relative to employers.

The biggest exceptions to the at-will doctrine are found in the anti-discrimination statutes under the Civil Rights Act, but those will not be explored until the next chapter.

Public Policy Exceptions to the At-Will Rule

Public policy is defined as that which is perceived to be in the public interest, as evidenced directly or implicitly by statutes or common law.

States vary widely on what is known as the "public policy" exception to the at-will termination rule.

In oversimplified terms, in certain states under certain conditions, an employee may not be fired for reasons that are against public policy. This exception to the at-will rule is actually quite narrow.

In order for there to be a public policy issue that impedes an employer's at-will termination rights, there generally has to be a law that has been broken by the employer to the personal detriment of the employee. The public policy exception was never intended to cover all termination decisions of questionable morality. Most of the time, exceptions in the at-will doctrine for public policy reasons are statutory. For example, in virtually every state there are workers' compensation statutes that protect workers who are injured in the workplace. Those statutes generally prohibit employer retaliation in the event a worker files a claim after being injured. Assume that an injured worker is told that if he or she processes a workers' compensation claim, he or she will be fired. Assume further that the worker does process the claim and is, in fact, fired. The employer would at least theoretically be liable for an unlawful termination, and the at-will rule would be "overruled" by the anti-retaliatory provisions in the workers' compensation statute.

For those who have known people who have been terminated after filing a workers' compensation claim, it is important to note that having a right is not necessarily the same thing as being able to enforce it. Employers do sometimes circumvent the law and lay off or find other ways to terminate employees who have filed claims after being injured in the workplace. In Arizona, remedies for retaliation are difficult to pursue because there is insufficient incentive in terms of attorney fees to convince lawyers to commit to the practice of filing wrongful discharge claims on a contingency fee basis. (Contingency fees are payable only at the conclusion of a case and are based solely on the amount of money awarded to the complainant.) Most people involved in workers' compensation cases do not have the money to pay attorney fees out of their own pockets.

In states like California, where incentives are higher due to more accessible attorney fee awards by the labor board, a larger number of attorneys engage in the practice of filing contingency-fee claims against retaliation in workers' compensation cases.

Even in more protective states like California, however, there are many instances where unfairness may underlie a termination, and the at-will rule will still govern the situation. Consider the following hypothetical situation:

> You are fired after a trivial disagreement with your manager. You do not believe you have been insubordinate. In fact, you sense your supervisor picked a fight with you as an excuse to

terminate you so that she could hire her friend.

Under those facts, the at-will rule would still apply. Unless there are civil rights issues involved, the employer has no responsibility to prove that you did anything wrong, and a supervisor may hire a personal friend at will. Fairness is not legally required in hiring or firing in most instances.

Whistleblower Exceptions

The state of Virginia protects the at-will rule with strong judicial precedent. Whistleblowers are not protected against termination in Virginia unless specific statutory enactments provide such protection. The case of *April L. Dray v. New Market Poultry Products, Inc.* illustrates this point.(3)

April L. Dray v. New Market Poultry Products, Inc. (1999)

Virginia Supreme Court (258 VA 187)

Justice Christian A. Compton delivered the opinion of the court.

This is another case in which an employee seeks to create an exception to the Commonwealth's established employment-at-will doctrine in order to pursue a common-law claim for wrongful discharge.

In August 1997, appellant April L. Dray, the employee, filed a motion for judgment against appellee New Market Poultry Products, Inc., the employer, seeking damages for alleged wrongful termination of her employment. The employer filed a demurrer, which the trial court sustained in a May 1998 "Opinion and Order." The employee appeals.

Because a demurrer, which tests the legal sufficiency of the motion for judgment, admits the correctness of all material facts that are properly pleaded, we shall recite the facts set forth in the motion for judgment as if they are true.

The employee worked for the employer from August 1994 until she was "fired" on September 11, 1996. For about three months prior to her termination, the employee was a "quality control inspector" on the employer's production lines to assure that no adulterated poultry products were distributed.

April L. Dray v. New Market Poultry Products, Inc. (1999)

Two months prior to her termination, the employee "experienced difficulty" in getting other employees to follow proper sanitary rules. "When management ignored and failed to correct the noted deficiencies," the employee, "in conformance to her training and assigned duties…, informed the plant's on-site governmental inspectors." The inspectors "confirmed the unsanitary conditions," according to the allegations, and "forced" the employer to correct the deficiencies. Subsequently, the employee was told by her supervisor "that she would be fired if she ever again brought plant sanitary deficiencies to the attention of the…governmental inspectors."

In the week prior to the employee's termination, she and other quality control inspectors condemned as adulterated some poultry products based on improper work performed on the plant's "wash line." On the day of the employee's termination, a government inspector required the employer to "reprocess a large quantity of poultry product due to contamination by metal-laced ice."

The employer's management believed that the employee had informed the government inspector of this adulterated product. She was discharged for violating the "edict" that she not inform the inspectors of unsanitary conditions and adulterated poultry products.

When the employee asked the reason for her discharge, the employer's personnel supervisor informed her that "'it was not working out.'"

In her motion for judgment, the employee says she "states a common law claim for wrongful termination of employment in violation of the public policy of the Commonwealth of Virginia." Elaborating, the employee asserts the public policy relied upon is articulated by the Commonwealth in the "Virginia Meat and Poultry Products Inspection Act," Code Sections 3.1-884.17 through -884.36 (the Act).

She alleges the employer terminated her in contravention of the public policy she finds set forth in the Act that is applicable to her. As a result, she asserts, she has incurred damages for which she seeks recovery.

In sustaining the demurrer, the trial court held that the motion for judgment did not set forth a legally cognizable claim for wrongful discharge. The court ruled that the plaintiff had failed "to extrapolate" from the broad declaration found in the Act, of an intent to serve "the public good" generally, a specific public policy intended to benefit the class of individuals to which the plaintiff belonged. Thus, the court decided, the employee's claim did not qualify as an exception to the employment-at-will doctrine. The trial court was correct.

Virginia adheres to the common-law doctrine of employment-at-will. When a contract calls for the rendition of services, but the period of the contract's intended duration cannot be determined from its provisions, either party ordinarily is at liberty to terminate the contract at will upon giving reasonable notice of intention to terminate.

* * *

In *Bowman*, we applied "a narrow exception to the employment-at-will rule." We held that two bank employees, who were also stockholders of the bank corporation, had stated a cause of action in tort against the bank and bank directors when the employees were discharged after failing to heed a threat to vote their stock according to the wishes of their employer. We said that the public policy set forth…conferred upon the plaintiffs as stockholders the right to vote their shares "free of duress and intimidation imposed on individual stockholders by corporate management."

In the present case, the plaintiff seeks to mount a generalized, common-law "whistleblower" retaliatory discharge claim. Such a claim has not been recognized as an exception to Virginia's employment-at-will doctrine, and we refuse to recognize it today.

The Act upon which this plaintiff relies does not confer any rights or duties upon her or any other similarly situated employee of the defendant. Instead, the Act's objective is "to provide for meat and poultry products inspection programs that will impose and enforce requirements with respect to intrastate operations and commerce."

The plaintiff identifies two of the Act's provisions that she says articulate a public policy allowing her to evade the employment-at-will doctrine. She relies upon Code § 3.1-884.22, which forbids intrastate distribution of uninspected, adulterated, or misbranded meat and poultry products. She also relies upon Code § 3.1-884.25(2), which establishes criminal penalties for any person who "resists,…impedes,…or interferes" with state meat inspectors. These provisions do not secure any rights to this plaintiff, nor do any other provisions of the Act. Rather, the Act establishes a regulatory mechanism directed only to government inspectors and industry management.

In essence, the plaintiff claims she has been wrongfully terminated because she had a right to disregard management's requirements that she report to her company superiors, and not directly to government inspectors, when she believed she was acting to assure the safety of the employer's products. However, the Act affords plaintiff no express statutory right in this regard that is in specific furtherance of the state's public policy regarding inspections of meat and poultry products.

Consequently, we hold that the trial court did not err in sustaining the employer's demurrer. Thus, the judgment below will be Affirmed.

To sum up the preceding case, April Dray was a quality control inspector for New Market. In the course of her job, she noted that workers were not following sanitation rules, and she reported this to her employer. Her employer did not respond to her complaints, and so she notified the on-site governmental inspectors who allegedly agreed with her. April Dray's employers then told her that if she notified the inspectors again, she would be fired. When inspectors showed up again and found contamination problems, Dray was fired even though she claimed that she did not notify inspectors.

This is a factually unusual case in that Dray claims that she was fired in retaliation for blowing the whistle after being warned not to, but she also claims she did not, in fact, blow the whistle about the problem over which she was fired. Her claim depends upon the employer thinking she lied, and firing her for its misperception.

Dray claimed that her termination was unlawful because if she had notified the inspectors, (or, in this case, if management had erroneously believed she had done so) she should have been protected from termination under Virginia's public policy exception to the at-will doctrine. Unfortunately for Dray, Virginia has no such broad public policy exception to an employer's at-will termination.

Although the Virginia Meat and Poultry Products Act had been enacted to enforce sanitation requirements, it did not either compel or protect whistleblowers. That statute placed the burden of enforcement on government inspectors. The court found that absent specific protection in the statute, Dray did not have any claims under the Virginia common law.

Many would argue that Dray should be lauded for trying to protect the public, and perhaps she should. But, most states have given only targeted protection to whistleblowers rather than general sweeping insulation. The reason for this is that not all whistleblowing is good. It can be used by people who want to "get even" with a firm as readily as by those who want to serve the greater public good. In general, the words used to describe whistleblowers (narc, fink, rat, turncoat) reflect the social ambivalence we have towards people who "tell."

Public Policy Exceptions to Arizona's At-Will Doctrine

Despite the perception that Arizona, a right-to-work state, is very pro-employer, it has an interesting pro-worker history with regard to its common and statutory law surrounding the issue of at-will termination.

Arizona's Supreme Court was at the forefront of establishing employee rights when, in the 1980s, it identified employment manuals as contractual in nature. In its rather startling 1985 *Wagenseller* decision (*Wagenseller v. Scottsdale Memorial Hospital*) (4), the Arizona Supreme Court decided that an employer who provided a general employment handbook had created a contract under which the employee could have a cause of action for breach. At the time of *Wagenseller*, most companies gave new employees a manual or handbook that generally described conditions of employment and benefits, along with procedures for employee discipline and termination. Before this case, such handbooks were never perceived to be contractual in nature, and most companies freely changed or at least did not rigidly adhere to them. After *Wagenseller,* any guidelines or terms in an employee handbook, unless specifically noted to the contrary, superseded the doctrine of at-will termination.

In addition to the rights that the *Wagenseller* court established regarding employment handbooks, that case also created a public policy exception to the at-will doctrine that was debated afterward for more than a decade. Here is what happened in that case.

A staff nurse (Catherine Sue Wagenseller) at Scottsdale Memorial Hospital was encouraged to go with her supervisor and other nurses on a river-rafting trip. During that trip, and ostensibly back at a hospital function afterward, the nurses performed a skit where they "mooned" the audience while singing "Moon River."

Wagenseller refused to participate in this skit and alleged that she was terminated from her position as a nurse at Scottsdale Memorial Hospital because of that refusal. The supervisor did not follow the guidelines in the employee manual when terminating Wagenseller, although management later attempted to rectify the procedural error, which was not substantive.

Scottsdale argued that Wagenseller had been terminated at will and that there was no cause of action available for her under Arizona law. The Arizona Supreme Court disagreed.

The court looked at the immoral nature of compelling an employee to "moon" in order for her to sustain her job, and the court both established a public policy exception to the at-will doctrine in Arizona and found that the conduct of Scottsdale Memorial (if it were as Wagenseller stated) fell within that exception. The court relied only tangentially on an Arizona statute that banned public nudity, although it did not find that the conduct alleged in the case violated that statute.

Approximately ten years after the *Wagenseller* case, the legislature of the State of Arizona intervened, criticizing the Arizona Supreme Court's establishment of a public policy exception without any legislative grounds. However, the legislature simultaneously supported the actual outcome of the *Wagenseller* case. What the legislature was thinking in this regard is known, because it discussed *Wagenseller* openly in its preamble to what one could call "corrective legislation." This was a somewhat delayed "battle between the branches" of Arizona's government, where the legislature partially overruled the judicial branch's *Wagenseller* precedent by enacting legislation that both narrowed and defined the public policy exception to the at-will doctrine in Arizona.

It should be noted that in this statutory enactment, the legislature also significantly narrowed the contractual nature of employment manuals, requiring that a manual must recite the fact that it is a contract for it to be enforceable. Under *Wagenseller,* employers were obligated to negate the contractual nature of the employment manual or be bound by its terms, irrespective of changes or unusual circumstances.

The following is the legislative response that came a decade after the *Wagenseller* case. Although this "Intent" portion of the statute was declared unconstitutional for violating the separation of powers (the court cannot, according to the court, consider advisory comments from the legislature), it is a valuable bit of history to show that the legislature did indeed spell out its intent to abrogate (or nullify) at least one of the precedents set in *Wagenseller.*

Excerpt from Arizona Revised Statutes

Reference Title: employment protection

An Act

Amending Section 12-541, Arizona Revised Statutes; amending Title 23, Arizona Revised Statutes, by adding Chapter 9; amend-

ing Section 41-1461, Arizona Revised Statutes; relating to Employment

Be it enacted by the Legislature of the State of Arizona:

Section 1. Intent

A. The Arizona Supreme Court in the case of *Wagenseller v. Scottsdale Memorial Hospital*, 147 Ariz. 370, 710 P.2d 1025 (1985) (*en banc*), held that an employer may be held liable for civil damages if such employer discharges from employment an employee for a reason that is against the public policy of this state. The court also held that it had the independent authority to determine what actions of the employer violated the public policy of this state. The legislature affirms that an employer may be held liable for civil damages in the event it discharges from employment an employee for a reason that is against the public policy of this state. However, public policy is expressly determined by the legislature in the form of statutory provisions. While courts interpret the common law in accordance with Arizona Revised Statutes section 1-201, they are not authorized to establish a cause of action in connection with specific acts or omissions that constitute a violation of the public policy of this state.

…While as a policy matter, the court reached the correct conclusion, it lacked the authority to make such a holding under the Constitution of Arizona. It is the role of the legislature, the elected representatives of the citizens, and not the court, to establish the public policy of the state. The court in *Wagenseller* reached the correct holding because the alleged acts would violate the state's public indecency statute, Arizona Revised Statutes section 13-1402. However, the court had no authority to create a cause of action. It is the intent of the legislature that the public policy of the state is that the termination of an employee in retaliation for refusing to violate the public indecency or other laws of the state constitutes a violation of the Employment Protection Act, subjecting the employer to civil damages.

[Although the following statute was upheld, the preamble which is redacted above was itself thrown out as unconstitutional and a violation of the separation of powers. The Arizona Supreme Court held that it cannot take "advice" from the legislature with respect to its role in setting precedent, as it is a co-equal and separate branch of government. The statute itself, however, is constitutional and the Arizona courts have applied it since it passed.]

Excerpt from Arizona Revised Statutes

* * *

Sec. 3, Title 23, Arizona Revised Statutes, is amended by adding chapter 9, to read:

Article 1. General Provisions

23-1501. Severability of employment relationships; protection from retaliatory discharges; exclusivity of statutory remedies in employment

The public policy of this state is that:

1. The employment relationship is contractual in nature.

2. The employment relationship is severable at the pleasure of either the employee or the employer unless both the employee and the employer have signed a written contract to the contrary setting forth that the employment relationship shall remain in effect for a specified duration of time or otherwise expressly restricting the right of either party to terminate the employment relationship. Both the employee and the employer must sign this written contract, or this written contract must be set forth in the employment handbook or manual or any similar document distributed to the employee, if that document expresses the intent that it is a contract of employment, or this written contract must be set forth in a writing signed by the party to be charged. Partial performance of employment shall not be deemed sufficient to eliminate the requirements set forth in this paragraph. Nothing in this paragraph shall be construed to affect the rights of public employees under the constitution of Arizona and state and local laws of this state or the rights of employees and employers as defined by a collective bargaining agreement.

3. An employee has a claim against an employer for termination of employment only if one or more of the following circumstances have occurred:

(a) The employer has terminated the employment relationship of an employee in breach of an employment contract, as set forth in paragraph 2 of this section, in which case the remedies for the breach are limited to the remedies for a breach of contract.

(b) The employer has terminated the employment relationship of an employee in violation of a statute of this state. If the statute provides a remedy to an employee for a violation of the statute, the remedies provided to an employee for a violation of the statute are the exclusive remedies for the violation of the statute….

(c) The employer has terminated the employment relationship of an employee in retaliation for…the refusal by the employee to commit an act or omission that would violate the constitution of Arizona or the statutes of this state.

Although some other very limited protections are given to workers in other portions of this Arizona statute, the parts of the statute included in this chapter show that the Arizona legislature narrowed the *Wagenseller* precedent significantly:

- The presumption of employment handbooks being contractual is gone and now the intent that the handbook be contractual must be expressed in the document if it is to be enforced against the employer.

- The public policy exception to at-will termination is narrowed to cases where specific statutes have been violated.

- Whistleblower protection is narrowed and circumscribed.

The underlying concern that instigated the legislative response to *Wagenseller* is based on fundamental free market principles for both capital and labor. Overburdening employers with excessive legal hurdles discourages new capital from coming into the state and creating more jobs. More jobs offer more freedom of choice to employees. Those free-market priorities need to be balanced against employer over-reaching and fundamental notions of fairness, which is what both the *Wagenseller* court and the responding legislature attempted to do, although with somewhat different results.

Federal Worker Protection Statutes

State rules govern basic termination of employment. They do not govern the other conditions of employment, however. In the years of the Great Depression, the federal government passed a series of worker protection statutes that dominate American employment standards. The National Labor Relations Act referenced in the beginning of this chapter was passed in 1935 at the height of labor unrest in the United States. Among other things, it empowered labor unions, codified the right to strike, and imposed the obligation on employers to bargain with the unions in good faith.

Salaried versus Hourly Employees

In 1938, the federal government passed the Fair Labor Standards Act (FLSA), which provided protection for workers in and out of labor unions by setting minimum wage limits and rights to overtime pay for nonexempt employees. Since its inception, the Fair Labor Standards Act has been excepted, interpreted, revised, and revisited on a very regular basis.

The basic rule under the FLSA is that most workers are entitled to a minimum wage, which Congress has the right to adjust over time, and to "time and a half" overtime pay for any hours over 40 in a work week. While every employer would choose to make full-time employees "exempt" from overtime pay, the FLSA limits who can be exempted and who can really be a salaried employee. The FLSA designates seven categories of employee types that are exempted from hourly pay and/or overtime minimums. These categories, listed below, are somewhat vague, frequently overlap, and form the basis for most disputes under the FLSA.(5)

1) Computer analysts, engineers and programmers, and software engineers

2) Executives such as CEOs, Chief Financial Officers (CFOs), etc.

3) Administrators who exercise independent judgment with wide discretion in matters of significance to the enterprise

4) Learned professionals whose work is primarily intellectual and who have advanced knowledge in their field such as teachers, lawyers, doctors, and engineers

5) Creative professionals such as dancers or artists

6) Outside sales professionals

7) Highly compensated employees who do non-manual labor and earn over $100,000 per year.

Administrative and executive exempt employees do have a minimum salary, which is $455/week, but this is not broken down to an hourly rate for purposes of overtime pay, and though there is no overtime pay, there may be salary deductions for absences or hours away from work.

In addition to the categorical exemptions, there are specific statutory exceptions that apply to specific jobs that are excluded from minimum wage/maximum hours rules. For example, employees who work in movie theatres are entitled to minimum wage but not time and a half overtime pay. Home health care workers such as babysitters and companion caregivers are exempt from minimum wage or overtime requirements (unless state law intervenes).

The question of when there is a wage violation is contentious and often protracted.

In 2006, an innovative attorney named Mark Thierman (6) decided to challenge the exempt status of securities brokers and recruited a significant number of plaintiffs to join the case to pursue back pay for unpaid overtime.

Securities brokers have always been classified as exempt under the administrative exception in the FLSA. Thierman challenged that brokers are actually inside sales people working on commission, and consequently they do not fit the criteria of the administrative exception. They do not fit as outside sales people because they do not perform their job away from the workplace. And, he argued, they cannot be considered learned professionals because the educational requirements for brokers are not sufficiently extensive to meet that standard.

Most interesting was his argument that the brokers were not paid the necessary $455 per week when considering that they were required to pay their sales assistants out of commission, and some weeks they received no commission at all. Thierman argued that the $455-per-week requirement is not an average but a minimum distribution. However, the brokerages pointed out that brokers were allowed to draw against unpaid or future commissions in that amount each week.

Banks and brokerages were facing such enormous, potential back-pay claims that many jumped to settlement in order to control losses. Morgan Stanley, UBS, and Merrill Lynch cumulatively paid over $165 million in settlements in California rather than face California's labor-friendly wage board.

Upon request of the Securities Industry and Financial Markets Association (SIFMA, formerly the SIA), the Department of Labor (DOL) issued an advisory opinion on this matter. It claimed that brokers did fall under the administrative exemption because they "deal primarily with performance of office or nonmanual work directly related to the management or general business operations of the employer or the employer's customers, and exercise discretion and independent judgment." The DOL opinion is not law and is not binding upon the courts. However, the U.S. Supreme Court will generally defer to a well-considered DOL interpretation of the FLSA, and consequently the pursuit of the broker-overtime claims appears to have dissolved.

In virtually every industry, there are potential issues arising regarding exempt versus non-exempt employment. Experienced Human Resources (HR) managers are profoundly aware of and generally very cautious about categorizing exempt workers. But even the most seasoned HR manager cannot anticipate the outcome of a case where historical norms are ignored and an entire industry rebuffed.

In 2010, the United States Court of Appeals for the Second Circuit decided (in opposition to the decisions in other circuits) that pharmaceutical sales representatives working for the Novartis company do not fit under the outside sales (or any other) FLSA exemption, and that all Novartis representatives were entitled to back pay for any unpaid overtime. In 2011, the U.S. Supreme Court unexpectedly denied certiorari and declined the opportunity to review the case and unify all the circuits on this issue.(7)

A summary of the case follows:

In re: Novartis Wage and Hour Litigation

US Court of Appeals for the 2nd Circuit

Argued February 19, 2010 July 6, 2010.

I. BACKGROUND

...Plaintiffs alleged principally that under the FLSA and state law, they were entitled to overtime pay at the rate of one and one-half times their normal compensation for time worked in excess of 40 hours per week. The following facts are not in dispute.

A. Novartis's Use of Pharmaceutical Sales Representatives

To market its pharmaceuticals, Novartis has a team of "brand" managers who, cognizant of limitations imposed by the United States Food and Drug Administration ("FDA"), devise descriptions of the essential features of each Novartis drug. Marketing managers assist in the production of written promotional materials. Novartis has regional managers who are involved in hiring, firing, and business planning decisions, including working on marketing strategy with the marketing team. Reporting to the regional managers are district managers who supervise the Reps.

Under federal regulations, Novartis is prohibited from selling its prescription drugs directly to patients. Instead, Novartis typically sells its products to wholesalers, which sell them to individual pharmacies. Physicians write prescriptions that permit patients to purchase those products from pharmacies. Novartis employs some 6,000 Reps nationwide and assigns them to make what Novartis characterizes as "sales" calls on physicians.

Reps do not sell the Novartis products to physicians. Although Novartis advertises openings for Reps as sales positions, the Reps' duties do not include "the exchange of good[s] or services, contracting to sell any good or service, consigning for the sale of any good or service, or obtaining orders or contracts for the use of facilities."

Rather, in visits typically lasting no longer than five minutes, the Reps provide physicians with information about the benefits of particular Novartis pharmaceuticals and encourage the physicians to prescribe those products. Reps give physicians reprints of clinical studies reporting findings about the Novartis products. Reps also inform doctors as to whether Novartis products are among those for which insurers will pay, resulting in little or no cost to patients. The Reps give the physicians samples of drugs; these samples are not sold, and no money is exchanged. Indeed, selling drug samples is a federal crime. The goal of the Reps is to get physicians to say they will prescribe Novartis products for their patients.

To enable the Reps to reach that goal, Novartis puts them through a training program for several weeks. The training is extensive, ranging from instruction on the medical benefits of each Novartis drug— and the way in which Reps should present favorable scientific studies—to matters of technique as detailed as how they should hold their pens when showing Novartis's written material to physicians.

In the training program, a Rep is taught how to question physicians to determine why they may be hesitant about prescribing Novartis products and then to offer arguments to overcome their reluctance. Novartis instructs the Reps on four "social styles" that a given individual may have in interacting with others and teaches the Reps how to tailor their presentations to a physician's particular social style. Novartis has also hired consultants to observe its most successful Reps and incorporate their techniques into the training program.

Novartis sets the number of times per trimester a Rep must call on each physician and how often specific drugs should be promoted. For each product in each trimester, Novartis has a principal marketing message—its "core message"—developed by the Novartis brand managers, which Reps are instructed to convey to physicians on each call. Novartis gives the Reps written promotional materials developed by its brand and marketing managers, including posters, brochures, and laminated cards, to use on sales calls. The Reps do not play any part in formulating the core message or the written materials; nor do they play any part in devising Novartis's advertising. During training, Reps are required to engage in role-playing, using scripts to practice delivering the core message and parrying objections from physicians.

In re: Novartis Wage and Hour Litigation

Although the Novartis training material encourages the Reps to tailor their pitches to an individual physician, they are not allowed to deviate from the core message. They are not allowed to use any written materials other than those provided by Novartis. One Rep testified that Reps were expected to act like "robots" because of the limitations on what they could say during sales calls. If a physician asks a Rep a medical question for which Novartis has not prepared an answer, the Rep is required to refer the doctor to Novartis's medical department.

The Reps report to their district managers by telephone at least every week or two, and sometimes report or confer daily. In addition, once or twice a month, the district managers accompany the Reps on their visits to physicians. During these ride-alongs, the managers observe the Reps' meetings and critique their performance. Reps receive negative reviews if they deliver the Novartis core message in a way that violates FDA-imposed limitations or Novartis policies.

As the Reps do not make sales, they are trained to end their meetings with physicians with a "closing" in which they may ask, "Doctor, will you prescribe this product for your patients who suffer from [the appropriate medical conditions]?" They may also ask, "Doctor, do I have your commitment to prescribe it[?]" One Novartis district manager described this type of colloquy as a "persuasive sale" but acknowledged that there was no way to know whether any physician actually followed through on such a commitment. One Rep stated that a physician might answer affirmatively just to get the Rep out the door.

As to physicians who refuse to entertain office visits from Reps, Novartis instructs the Reps to use other techniques to make contact, such as showing up at hospitals early in the morning before medical rounds. Reps also organize meals and other programs for physicians where speakers promote Novartis products. For such programs, Novartis maintains a list of cooperating doctors, from which Reps must book speakers. Reps manage the budgets for these events, but do so within limits set by Novartis managers; Novartis sets a minimum number of such events that it expects each Rep to hold.

Novartis does not know how many prescriptions individual physicians write for its products. It subscribes to several services that provide it with information as to when prescriptions for Novartis products are filled at pharmacies that report such information to the services; this information identifies the prescribing physicians. Because the data are gathered from pharmacies, however, these reports represent only the number of prescriptions the reporting pharmacies filled, not all the prescriptions actually written. Further, because some 19,000 pharmacies do not report sales to these services, Novartis has data for only about 72% of all filled prescriptions. Novartis extrapolates from the reported sales in order to estimate the sales at non-reporting pharmacies, and it believes those estimates generate a fairly accurate picture of how many prescriptions are being filled at non-reporting pharmacies; however, the latter prescriptions cannot be traced to particular physicians.

Notwithstanding the absence of actual information as to the numbers of prescriptions for Novartis drugs written by particular physicians, the Reps, whose base wages are at least $455 a week, receive up to a quarter of their compensation as bonuses based on their performance with physicians. Given the limits of its ability to monitor physicians' actual prescriptions, Novartis sets goals for the number of prescriptions it hopes to have filled in a particular territory, and it pays a Rep a bonus when the number of filled prescriptions attributable to physicians in the Rep's territory exceeds the goal Novartis has set. Some Novartis Reps earn more than $100,000 a year. In 2005, Novartis Reps' total compensation averaged $91,539.

The FLSA provides that many employees must be paid one and one-half times their regular rate of compensation for time worked in excess of 40 hours a week, but provides that certain categories of workers are excluded from this requirement. Novartis Reps are expected to be in the field from 8 a.m. to 5 p.m. on work days; they eat lunch with physicians or while driving to or from their physician visits; and they attend the mandatory dinner programs, which sometimes prevent them from returning home before 9 or 10 p.m. Notwithstanding a standard week of five such nine-hour days plus the occasional evening work, Novartis does not give its Reps overtime pay. As is the practice throughout the pharmaceuticals industry, Novartis treats its Reps as exempt from the overtime pay requirement in the FLSA, as well as from comparable state-law requirements.

Outside Sales Exemption Discussion

…[W]here the employee promotes a pharmaceutical product to a physician but can transfer to the physician nothing more than free samples and cannot lawfully transfer ownership of any quantity of the drug in exchange for anything of value, cannot lawfully take an order for its purchase, and cannot lawfully even obtain from the physician a binding commitment to prescribe it, we conclude that it is not plainly erroneous to conclude that the employee has not in any sense, within the meaning of the statute or the regulations, made a sale.

Novartis points out that a number of district courts have held that pharmaceutical sales representatives are exempt from the FLSA overtime pay requirements as outside salesmen (and/or administrative employees). Those cases are, of course, not binding on us, and their reasoning does not persuade us that the Secretary's interpretations of the regulations should be disregarded. To the extent that the pharmaceuticals industry wishes to have the concept of "sales" expanded to include the promotional activities at issue here, it should direct its efforts to Congress, not the courts. Given the existing statute and regulations, we conclude that the district court should have ruled that the Reps are not outside salesmen within the meaning of the FLSA and the regulations.

Administrative Employee Exemption Discussion

…We see no evidence in the record that the Reps have any authority to formulate, affect, interpret, or implement Novartis's management policies or its operating practices, or that they are involved in planning Novartis's long-term or short-term business objectives, or that they carry out major assignments in conducting the operations of Novartis's business, or that they have any authority to commit Novartis in matters that have significant financial impact. Although Novartis argues that the Reps do commit Novartis financially when they enter into contracts with hotels, restaurants, and other venues for promotional events, "which may cost NPC thousands of dollars," the record reveals that the Reps have been given budgets for such events by the Novartis managers and that the Reps have no discretion to exceed those budgets. Nor have we been pointed to any evidence that the Reps have authority to negotiate and bind Novartis on any significant matters, or have authority to waive or deviate from Novartis's established policies and procedures without its prior approval. What Novartis characterizes as the Reps' exercise of discretion and independent judgment—ability to answer questions about the product, ability to develop a rapport with a physician who has a certain social style, ability to remember past conversations with a given physician, ability to recognize when a message has been persuasive—are skills gained and/or honed in their Novartis training sessions. As described in Part I.A. above, these skills are exercised within severe limits imposed by Novartis. Thus, it is undisputed that the Reps, …

- have no role in planning Novartis's marketing strategy;

- have no role in formulating the "core messages" they deliver to physicians;

- are required to visit a given physician a certain number of times per trimester as established by Novartis;

- are required to promote a given drug a certain number of times per trimester as established by Novartis;

- are required to hold at least the number of promotional events ordered by Novartis;

- are not allowed to deviate from the promotional "core messages";

- and are forbidden to answer any question for which they have not been scripted.

Novartis argues that the Reps exercise a great deal of discretion because they are free to decide in what order to visit physicians' offices, free to decide how best to gain access to those offices, free to decide how to allocate their Novartis budgets for promotional events, and free to determine how to allocate their samples. In light of the above controls to which Novartis subjects the Reps, we agree with the Secretary (of the Department of Labor) that the…freedoms advanced by Novartis do not show that the Reps are sufficiently allowed to exercise either discretion or independent judgment in the performance of their primary duties. Accordingly, we conclude that …the Reps are not bona fide administrative employees within the meaning of the FLSA and the regulations.

Conclusion: [Novartis pharmaceutical representatives are non-exempt employees, and must be paid overtime pay.]

Notes

1. *Mary M. v. City of Los Angeles, California* (1991) 43 Cal 3rd 202)

2. *Capital City Foods, Inc. (Burger King) v. Mary T.* (1992) 5 Cal. App. 4th, 1042

3. *April Dry v. New Market Poultry Products*, Virginia Supreme Court (1999) 258 VA 187

4. *Wagenseller v. Scottsdale Memorial Hospital*, (1985) 147 Arizona 370

5. Department of Labor Web site http://www.dol.gov/esa/regs/compliance/whd/fairpay/fs17a_overview.html

6. Touryalai, Halah. "Department of Labor to Brokers: No Overtime for You," Registered Rep: The Source for Investment Professionals (Online magazine). December 1, 2006.

7. *In re: Novartis Wage and Hour Litigation*, US Court of Appeals for the 2nd Circuit, Argued Febrary 19, 2010 July 6, 2010

Chapter 10
Discrimination

For most people, the word "discrimination" evokes images of social malfeasance. We see as oppressed a class of people whose plight has been caused by irrational bias. Although this type of class discrimination is unacceptable, there are forms of bias that are essential. Most would inherently discriminate against someone who is lazy, or someone who is dishonest. They would be biased against anyone who is disrespectful or inadequately skilled for the requirements of a business. The law permits bias—just not the kind of bias that has systemically oppressed certain classes of people who consequently have been disenfranchised

Therefore, there are certain classes of individuals that are called "protected." In the early days of civil rights law, these classes were called "suspect"—but that is misleading. What that word intended to imply was that actions against members of that class would be considered suspect (suspicious) in the law.

There are only seven protected classes under the Civil Rights Act (as it has been amended and augmented over the duration of its existence). These are:

1) Race (Title VII)

2) Color (Title VII—related to darkness of complexion: often commingled with race in the case precedents)

3) National Origin (Title VII)

4) Sex (Title VII—defined as gender, not orientation), which includes pregnancy (Pregnancy Protection Act)

5) Religion

6) Disability (Americans with Disabilities Act, "ADA")

7) Age (Age Discrimination in Employment Act, "ADEA")

The greatest area of exception to the doctrine of at-will termination is where a termination implicates the civil rights of a member of a protected class. Although the at-will doctrine would allow an employer to fire someone for any reason, with or without cause, with or without notice (with some policy exceptions noted in the last chapter), the employer cannot fire (or refuse to hire or fail to promote) individuals because they are members of a protected class. Employers can certainly fire someone who is *in* a protected class; they just cannot treat that individual adversely *because* he or she is in that class. One also cannot (without good reason) do something that negatively impacts a protected class even if that impact is wholly unintended. The protections for protected classes are not trivial.

The reason for the civil rights exception to at-will termination is obvious. In theory, in a free market employers should never discriminate based on anything other than employee qualifications. Employers should always select the best person for the job. That theory ignores the social realities of racism, gender bias, and other forms of prejudice that serve to compel those in power to act inefficiently. There is no better example of institutionalized racism than the *Griggs v. Duke Power* case, which will be summarized later in this chapter.(1)

Duke Power Company (now Duke Energy) was a major producer of electric power in North Carolina. Prior to the enactment of the Civil Rights Act of 1964, at Duke Power's Dan River plant, "Negro" employees were not allowed to work in any of the operating departments except the Labor department. All other departments, including Coal Handling and Maintenance, were staffed exclusively with white employees. The most sobering fact of all is that the highest paid person in the Labor department was paid less than the lowest paid person in any of the white departments. There was simply no way, regardless of work ethic, ability, excellence, or drive, for a black employee at Duke Power to earn as much

as any white employee in the company. No black employee at Duke Power, no matter how many years of service or competency in their work, could ever earn as much as an entry-level coal handler. An even more overwhelming fact is that Duke was one of the better employers for blacks in North Carolina at the time.

With the Civil Rights Act of 1964, racial discrimination in both the private and public sectors became unlawful. It cannot be said enough that not all discrimination became unlawful—only that which correlated to a statutorily identified class of individuals that Congress saw fit to protect. This is one of the most difficult concepts to accept, because it operates to permit unfairness in many other circumstances. At the time the first version of the Civil Rights Act was enacted, women were not included as a protected class.

As of this time, the Civil Rights Act has not been amended to include protection against discrimination on the basis of sexual orientation, although there are states and cities where such protections exist.

Obviously, there are many classes of individuals who are not protected under the Civil Rights Act. This is the case even when the bias is against something the individual cannot control or change. For example, an employer may discriminate on the basis of appearance. Ugly people are not protected. An employer may discriminate on the basis of a bad complexion. People with pimples are not protected.

An employer may discriminate on the basis of someone's weight as long as that person is not medically obese. Chubby people are not protected. An employer may discriminate on the basis of how good a person's credit is or even how someone appears on Facebook unless a protected class is indirectly harmed. Similarly, people who are homeless or just experiencing financial difficulties are not protected for those conditions. Neither the Civil Rights Act nor any other legal imposition attempts to rid either the public or private sector of all unfairness. At-will rules apply until discrimination hits a protected class (one of the seven mentioned earlier). That can happen intentionally or unintentionally, as will be discussed in the next section.

Types of Discrimination Claims

Disparate Treatment

Two types of discrimination are prohibited under the Civil Rights Act. The first is the most obvious—it is unlawful to intentionally discriminate against anyone or any group based on their protected status. This is known as disparate treatment.

Were an employer to fire, refuse to hire, or fail to promote an employee based on his or her being in a protected class the employer would be violating the Civil Rights Act and unlawfully engaging in disparate treatment. Most people fully understand this concept in practice. An employer with even a small number of brain cells would never say to an applicant or employee, "You can't have that job because you are black, and the other employees don't want to work with you."

This does not mean, however, that nobody treats protected-class members disparately. It does mean that today it is a bit more difficult to see it when it happens.

An employer or manager who is inclined to discriminate generally knows better than to admit it. He or she may say to the protected-class member, "You are not qualified for this job." That may be the real reason; but if it is obvious that other individuals with lesser qualifications are given the job, it may be that the employer is lying. The law refers to that kind of lie as a "pretext." The statement "you are not qualified" is a pretext for the real reason for the conduct, which is, "I don't want to hire your kind." In other words, it is not necessary for an employer to admit disparate treatment for the case to be actionable. Disparate-treatment claims are generally proven with circumstantial evidence rather than direct admissions of unlawful intent.

Not all disparate treatment is unlawful. If there is a "*bona fide* occupational qualification" that excludes one or more protected classes, it will be lawful if there is no less discriminatory alternative. For example, if the job is for a prison guard who oversees the women's showers, the women in those showers have a *bona fide* privacy interest, and the employer has the obligation to protect that interest. In such circumstances, excluding men would be lawful, even though that exclusion disparately treats men and discriminates on the basis of sex (gender), one of the protected classes.

Sexual Harassment (a Form of Disparate Treatment)

Frequently misunderstood, sexual harassment is actually a form of disparate treatment and not some separate problem under the law. In fact, if there is no disparate treatment involved (treating one gender differently from the other through sexual harassment), there is no unlawful conduct under the Civil Rights Act and no legal claim for harassment.

Several cases emphasize this point, but the following quotes from *Equal Employment Opportunity Commission v. Harbert-Yeargin* (2) summarize the matter most clearly.

> Although an employer may have some type of general duty, a failure to remedy complaints of sexual harassment that doesn't rise to the level of gender discrimination is not actionable under Title VII.
>
> * * *
>
> …[A] hypothetical…was recently addressed in *Holman v.*

Indiana…. Holman involved a married couple who worked in the same unit of Indiana's Department of Transportation. They alleged that their common male supervisor sexually harassed them both in violation of Title VII. In dismissing their claim, the Seventh Circuit stated that "Title VII does not cover the 'equal opportunity' or 'bisexual' harasser, then, because such a person is not *discriminating* [emphasis added] on the basis of sex." To hold otherwise, stated the court, "would change Title VII into a code of workplace civility."

The U.S. Supreme Court addressed the issue of same-sex sexual harassment in the *Oncale v. Sundowner* case. The case reaffirms the notion that an action for sexual harassment discrimination must be based on gender disparity and not merely unctuous or inappropriate conduct equally offensive to either sex. It is also always based on disparate treatment, since disparate impact claims rest on the notion that everyone is treated the same.

For Oncale, it would be an extraordinarily difficult burden to prove that the harassment levied against him was gender-based, but the case stands for the proposition that if he were able prove that, he would prevail even though the harassment was from someone of the same gender.

Oncale v. Sundowner Offshore Services, Inc. (1998)

Supreme Court of the United States (523 U.S. 75)

Justice Antonin Scalia delivered the opinion of the court.

This case presents the question whether workplace harassment can violate Title VII's prohibition against [discrimination because of sex], when the harasser and the harassed employee are of the same sex.

I

The District Court having granted summary judgment for respondent, we must assume the facts to be as alleged by petitioner Joseph Oncale. The precise details are irrelevant to the legal point we must decide, and in the interest of both brevity and dignity we shall describe them only generally. In late October 1991, Oncale was working for respondent Sundowner Offshore Services on a Chevron U. S. A., Inc., oil platform in the Gulf of Mexico. He was employed as a roustabout on an eight-man crew.... On several occasions, Oncale was forcibly subjected to sex-related, humiliating actions against him...in the presence of the rest of the crew. [Certain co-workers] also physically assaulted Oncale in a sexual manner, and [one] threatened him with rape.

Oncale's complaints to supervisory personnel produced no remedial action.... Oncale eventually quit—asking that his pink slip reflect that he "voluntarily left due to sexual harassment and verbal abuse." When asked at his deposition why he left Sundowner, Oncale stated "I felt that if I didn't leave my job, that I would be raped or forced to have sex."

Oncale filed a complaint against Sundowner in the United States District Court for the Eastern District of Louisiana, alleging that he was discriminated against in his employment because of his sex.

II

Title VII of the Civil Rights Act of 1964 provides, in relevant part, that "[i]t shall be an unlawful employment practice for an employer...to discriminate against any individual with respect to his compensation, terms, conditions, or privileges of employment, because of such individual's race, color, religion, sex, or national origin."

* * *

We see no justification in the statutory language or our precedents for a categorical rule excluding same-sex harassment claims from the coverage of Title VII. As some courts have observed, male-on-male sexual harassment in the workplace was assuredly not the principal evil Congress was concerned with when it enacted Title VII. But statutory prohibitions often go beyond the principal evil to cover reasonably comparable evils, and it is ultimately the provisions of our laws rather than the principal concerns of our legislators by which we are governed. Title VII prohibits "discriminat[ion]…because of…sex" in the "terms" or "conditions" of employment. Our holding that this includes sexual harassment must extend to sexual harassment of any kind that meets the statutory requirements.

* * *

Courts and juries have found the inference of discrimination easy to draw in most male-female sexual harassment situations, because the challenged conduct typically involves explicit or implicit proposals of sexual activity; it is reasonable to assume those proposals would not have been made to someone of the same sex. The same chain of inference would be available to a plaintiff alleging same sex harassment, if there were credible evidence that the harasser was homosexual. But harassing conduct need not be motivated by sexual desire to support an inference of discrimination on the basis of sex. A trier of fact might reasonably find such discrimination, for example, if a female victim is harassed in such sex-specific and derogatory terms by another woman as to make it clear that the harasser is motivated by general hostility to the presence of women in the workplace. A same-sex harassment plaintiff may also, of course, offer direct comparative evidence about how the alleged harasser treated members of both sexes in a mixed-sex workplace. Whatever evidentiary route the plaintiff chooses to follow, he or she must always prove that the conduct at issue was not merely tinged with offensive sexual connotations, but actually constituted *"discrimina[tion]* [emphasis added]…because of…sex."

Oncale v. Sundowner Offshore Services, Inc. (1998)

III

Because we conclude that sex discrimination consisting of same-sex sexual harassment is actionable under Title VII, the judgment of the Court of Appeals for the Fifth Circuit is reversed, and the case is remanded for further proceedings consistent with this opinion.

It is so ordered.

Disparate Impact

Disparate-impact discrimination is not the invidious type of discrimination that we generally envision when we think about civil rights violations. Disparate impact indirectly affects the protected class and is generally unintentional. When an employer sets a requirement, standard, or test (e.g., a height requirement) that is neutral as applied to different races, both genders, etc., that requirement may impact a protected class more than the majority. For example, a minimum six-foot height requirement would eliminate more women than men, and probably more Asians than whites. In *Griggs v. Duke Power* (1964), a high school diploma requirement had a disparate impact on blacks in the relevant applicant pool. Fewer blacks had diplomas than whites at that time in that area.

Again, merely because a requirement has a disparate impact on a protected class does not mean it is unlawful. Such a requirement may be legal if two conditions are met: (1) the standard, requirement, or test is reasonably necessary for the successful performance of the job, and (2) there is no less discriminatory alternative available. Just as disparate treatment may be legal if there is a *bona fide* occupational qualification, disparate impact may be (and often is) legal if there is a reasonable business necessity for the standard, requirement, or test.

A disparate-impact case does not generally carry punitive damages or penalties, because it is not the result of malicious intent. Recoveries are generally limited to compensation for the victims based on actual loss. This can still be an extraordinary amount of money if there are a large number of class members who are entitled to back pay or lost wages and/or who are entitled to get jobs that were previously denied.

The doctrine of disparate impact discrimination was established in the *Griggs v. Duke Power* case. Although a superficial reading might imply that Duke Power was being penalized for its history of pre-Civil Rights Act lawful discriminatory conduct, that is not the case. A summary of the landmark *Griggs* case follows:

Griggs v. Duke Power Co.

Supreme Court of the United States (401 U.S. 424)

Argued: December 14, 1970—Decided: March 8, 1971

Chief Justice Warren Burger delivered the opinion of the Court.

We granted the writ in this case to resolve the question whether an employer is prohibited by the Civil Rights Act of 1964, Title VII, from requiring a high school education or passing of a standardized general intelligence test as a condition of employment in or transfer to jobs when (a) neither standard is shown to be significantly related to successful job performance, (b) both requirements operate to disqualify Negroes at a substantially higher rate than white applicants, and (c) the jobs in question formerly had been filled only by white employees as part of a longstanding practice of giving preference to whites.

…All the petitioners are employed at the Company's Dan River Steam Station, a power generating facility located at Draper, North Carolina. At the time this action was instituted, the Company had 95 employees at the Dan River Station, 14 of whom were Negroes; 13 of these are petitioners here.

The District Court found that, prior to July 2, 1965, the effective date of the Civil Rights Act of 1964, the Company openly discriminated on the basis of race in the hiring and assigning of employees at its Dan River plant. The plant was organized into five operating departments: (1) Labor, (2) Coal Handling, (3) Operations, (4) Maintenance, and (5) Laboratory and Test. Negroes were employed only in the Labor Department, where the highest paying jobs paid less than the lowest paying jobs in the other four "operating" departments, in which only whites were employed. Promotions were normally made within each department on the basis of job seniority. Transferees into a department usually began in the lowest position.

In 1955, the Company instituted a policy of requiring a high school education for initial assignment to any department except Labor, and for transfer from the Coal Handling to any "inside" department (Operations, Maintenance, or Laboratory). When the Company abandoned its policy of restricting Negroes to the Labor Department in 1965, completion of high school also was made a prerequisite to transfer from Labor to any other department. From the time the high school requirement was instituted to the time of trial, however, white employees hired before the time of the high school education requirement continued to perform satisfactorily and achieve promotions in the "operating" departments. Findings on this score are not challenged.

The Company added a further requirement for new employees on July 2, 1965, the date on which Title VII became effective. To qualify for placement in any but the Labor Department, it became necessary to register satisfactory scores on two professionally prepared aptitude tests, as well as to have a high school education. Completion of high school alone continued to render employees eligible for transfer to the four desirable departments from which Negroes had been excluded if the incumbent had been employed prior to the time of the new requirement. In September, 1965, the Company began to permit incumbent employees who lacked a high school education to qualify for transfer from Labor or Coal Handling to an "inside" job by passing two tests—the Wonderlic Personnel Test, which purports to measure general intelligence, and the Bennett Mechanical Comprehension Test. Neither was directed or intended to measure the ability to learn to perform a particular job or category of jobs. The requisite scores used for both initial hiring and transfer approximated the national median for high school graduates.

The District Court had found that, while the Company previously followed a policy of overt racial discrimination in a period prior to the Act, such conduct had ceased. [emphasis added] The District Court also concluded that Title VII was intended to be prospective only, and, consequently, the impact of prior inequities was beyond the reach of corrective action authorized by the Act.

[We are] confronted with a question of first impression, concerning the meaning of Title VII. …

The objective of Congress in the enactment of Title VII is plain from the language of the statute. It was to achieve equality of employment opportunities and remove barriers that have operated in the past to favor an identifiable group of white employees over other employees. Under the Act, practices, procedures, or tests *neutral on their face, and even neutral in terms of intent* [emphasis added], cannot be

Griggs v. Duke Power Co.

maintained if they operate to "freeze" the *status quo* of prior discriminatory employment practices.

…What is required by Congress is the removal of artificial, arbitrary, and unnecessary barriers to employment when the barriers operate invidiously to discriminate on the basis of racial or other impermissible classification.

…On the record before us, neither the high school completion requirement nor the general intelligence test is shown to bear a demonstrable relationship to successful performance of the jobs for which it was used. …Rather, a vice-president of the Company testified, the requirements were instituted on the Company's judgment that they generally would improve the overall quality of the workforce.

The evidence, however, shows that employees who have not completed high school or taken the tests have continued to perform satisfactorily, and make progress in departments for which the high school and test criteria are now used.…

The Company's lack of discriminatory intent is suggested by special efforts to help the undereducated employees through Company financing of two-thirds the cost of tuition for high school training. But Congress directed the thrust of the Act to the consequences of employment practices, not simply the motivation. More than that, Congress has placed on the employer the burden of showing that any given requirement must have a manifest relationship to the employment in question.

Nothing in the Act precludes the use of testing or measuring procedures; obviously they are useful. What Congress has forbidden is giving these devices and mechanisms controlling force unless they are demonstrably a reasonable measure of job performance. Congress has not commanded that the less qualified be preferred over the better qualified simply because of minority origins. Far from disparaging job qualifications as such, Congress has made such qualifications the controlling factor, so that race, religion, nationality, and sex become irrelevant. What Congress has commanded is that any tests used must measure the person for the job, and not the person in the abstract.

Distinguishing between Types of Discrimination

Although this will be discussed again later in this chapter, for purposes of introducing the notion of disparate treatment, Hooters provides an easy example. When Hooters made the decision to hire only young, buxom, female employees, it was engaging in disparate treatment. There is no logical disparate-impact claim because the test or requirement directly excludes the protected class (men). This is sometimes difficult to see.

On the other hand, when Duke Power Company changed its policies toward black employees after the 1964 Civil Rights Act, it no longer disparately treated black employees. Its new policies disparately impacted them. Analyzing the facts of the *Duke* case will illustrate the point.

In 1955, Duke began to require all new hires to have high school diplomas, except for those in the (exclusively black) Labor department. In addition, existing employees who wanted to transfer from the Coal Handling department to any other inside department needed to have a high school diploma. When Duke first imposed this high school diploma requirement, it could not have had racial discrimination in mind, since the only area where blacks could work (Labor department) was excluded from it. Given that institutional racism already governed the roles that white and black workers could play, there was no need for racially imposed tests or criteria.

Approximately a year after the 1964 Civil Rights Act passed, Duke amended the transfer/hire requirements to allow that employees without a high school diploma could transfer as long as they scored sufficiently well on two general-intelligence/ability aptitude tests. This theoretically somewhat lessened the burden of transfer since applicants were able now (theoretically) to get a transfer without a high school diploma; however, the test adversely affected more black applicants than white. (Relatively fewer black applicants scored in the passing range compared to white applicants.)

The U.S. Supreme Court recognized that the requirements in the *Duke* case were neutral "on their face." They appeared to treat black and white applicants in the same manner. However, the court noted that the effect on the black, relevant applicant pool was significantly greater than on the white, and it questioned the necessity of the requirements. Although the U.S. Supreme Court appeared to agree that the requirements were imposed without any "intention to discriminate against Negro employees," the absence of discriminatory intent did not "redeem employment procedures or testing mechanisms that operate[d] as built-in headwinds for minority groups and [were] unrelated to measuring job capability."(1)

In conclusion, the court noted that if a test or requirement is to adversely impact a group that is protected under the Civil Rights Act, that test must be necessary, or in the courts own words, "must measure the person for the job and not the person in the abstract."

Although the difference between disparate impact and disparate treatment seems obvious in the abstract, the theories blur even for seasoned trial lawyers and judges. Such blurring can be fatal to a claim on appeal. It is important not to confuse or try to blend these two causes of action, since disparate treatment and disparate impact have different remedies, and each must be proven on its own grounds.

In the *Raytheon v. Hernandez* case in 2003 (3), Hernandez reapplied for his old position at Raytheon from which he had been fired for workplace misconduct. That misconduct was apparently related to Hernandez's drug abuse. Hernandez was precluded from rehire because of an unwritten Raytheon policy that employees fired for workplace misconduct are permanently ineligible for rehire.

Hernandez initially claimed that Raytheon treated him disparately because of his disability (drug addiction) and that any other stated reason for not rehiring him was pretext. His lawyer tried to amend the complaint to allege that the policy itself, though neutral on its face, imposed a disparate impact on disabled persons (drug addicts) who were more likely to be fired for work-

place misconduct related to drug abuse than other people were. Fortunately for Raytheon, this attempt to amend the complaint was done too late (there is a strict statute of limitations on Civil Rights claims). That amended complaint was dismissed.

However, the Ninth Circuit Court of Appeals combined or as the Supreme Court said "conflated" the two causes of action (disparate impact and disparate treatment) and found for Hernandez. The U.S. Supreme Court took exception to the Court of Appeals' assertion that Hernandez was *treated* disparately based on a neutral no-rehire policy that treated everyone the same.

Justice Thomas, writing for the majority in the Raytheon case, reversed the Ninth Circuit for confusing the two very different causes of action. A neutral, no-rehire policy is inherently non-discriminatory under the theory of disparate treatment—the employer is treating everyone the same when it acts neutrally. Raytheon's conduct could only have been problematical under a disparate impact theory, and that claim had been dismissed for its failure to have been timely filed. The case would have been significantly more cumbersome for Raytheon had the disparate impact claim been filed on time.

Lies, Damn Lies, and Statistics

The presence of distorted statistics in the workplace (i.e., more male managers than female or more white new hires than black, proportional to the relevant applicant pools) will often give rise to the notion that there must be something nefarious, either disparate impact or disparate treatment, going on.

Suspecting that a culture of male dominance at Wal-Mart (branded as Walmart) was causing women to be excluded from promotional opportunity, attorneys for a class of women at Walmart brought an action against that firm to show that this culture was operating in a discriminatory manner. The following case, decided by the U.S. Supreme Court in 2011, was the result.

Wal-Mart Stores, Inc. v. Dukes et al.

Supreme Court of the United States

No. 10–277. Argued March 29, 2011—Decided June 20, 2011

Justice Antonin Scalia delivered the opinion of the Court.

We are presented with one of the most expansive class actions ever. The District Court and the Court of Appeals approved the certification of a class comprising about one and a half million plaintiffs, current and former female employees of petitioner Wal-Mart who allege that the discretion exercised by their local supervisors over pay and promotion matters violates Title VII by discriminating against women. In addition to injunctive and declaratory relief, the plaintiffs seek an award of back pay. We consider whether the certification of the plaintiff class was consistent with Federal Rules of Civil Procedure…

A

Petitioner Wal-Mart is the Nation's largest private employer. It operates four types of retail stores throughout the country: Discount Stores, Supercenters, Neighborhood Markets, and Sam's Clubs. Those stores are divided into seven nationwide divisions, which in turn comprise 41 regions of 80 to 85 stores apiece. Each store has between 40 and 53 separate departments and 80 to 500 staff positions.

In all, Wal-Mart operates approximately 3,400 stores and employs more than one million people.

Pay and promotion decisions at Wal-Mart are generally committed to local managers' broad discretion, which is exercised "in a largely subjective manner." …Local store managers may increase the wages of hourly employees (within limits) with only limited corporate oversight. As for salaried employees, such as store managers and their deputies, higher corporate authorities have discretion to set their pay within pre-established ranges.

Promotions work in a similar fashion. Wal-Mart permits store managers to apply their own subjective criteria when selecting candidates as "support managers," which is the first step on the path to management. Admission to Wal-Mart's management training program, however, does require that a candidate meet certain objective criteria, including an above-average performance rating, at least one year's tenure in the applicant's current position, and a willingness to relocate. But except for those requirements, regional and district managers have discretion to use their own judgment when selecting candidates for management training. Promotion to higher office—*e.g.*, assistant manager, co-manager, or store manager—is similarly at the discretion of the employee's superiors after prescribed objective factors are satisfied.

B

…The named plaintiffs in this lawsuit, representing the 1.5 million members of the certified class, are three current or former Wal-Mart employees who allege that the company discriminated against them on the basis of their sex by denying them equal pay or promotions, in violation of Title VII of the Civil Rights Act of 1964.

Betty Dukes began working at a Pittsburg, California, Wal-Mart in 1994. She started as a cashier, but later sought and received a promotion to customer service manager. After a series of disciplinary violations, however, Dukes was demoted back to cashier and then to greeter. Dukes concedes she violated company policy, but contends that the disciplinary actions were in fact retaliation for invoking internal complaint procedures and that male employees have not been disciplined for similar infractions. Dukes also claims two male greeters in the Pittsburg store are paid more than she is.

Christine Kwapnoski has worked at Sam's Club stores in Missouri and California for most of her adult life. She has held a number of positions, including a supervisory position. She claims that a male manager yelled at her frequently and screamed at female employees, but not at men. The manager in question "told her to 'doll up,' to wear some makeup, and to dress a little better." The final named plaintiff, Edith Arana, worked at a Wal-Mart store in Duarte, California, from 1995 to 2001. In 2000, she approached the store manager on more than one occasion about management training, but was brushed off. Arana concluded she was being denied opportunity for advancement because of her sex. She initiated internal complaint procedures, whereupon she was told to apply directly to the district manager if she thought her store manager was being unfair. Arana, however, decided against that and never applied for management training again. In 2001, she was fired for failure to comply with Wal-Mart's timekeeping policy.

These plaintiffs, respondents here, do not allege that Wal-Mart has any express corporate policy against the advancement of women. Rather, they claim that their local managers' discretion over pay and promotions is exercised disproportionately in favor of men, leading to an unlawful disparate impact on female employees. And, respondents say, because Wal-Mart is aware of this effect, its refusal to cabin its managers' authority amounts to disparate treatment. Their complaint seeks injunctive and declaratory relief, punitive damages, and back pay. It does not ask for compensatory damages.

Importantly for our purposes, respondents claim that the discrimination to which they have been subjected is common to *all* Wal-Mart's female employees. The basic theory of their case is that a strong and uniform "corporate culture" permits bias against women to infect, perhaps subconsciously, the discretionary decision making of each one of Wal-Mart's thousands of managers—thereby making every woman at the company the victim of one common discriminatory practice. Respondents therefore wish to litigate the Title VII claims of all female employees at Wal-Mart's stores in a nationwide class action.

* * *

Wal-Mart Stores, Inc. v. Dukes et al.

[Redacted Summary of the Reasoning of the Court]

…In the landmark case of ours [*Watson v. Fort Worth Bank & Trust*] which held that giving discretion to lower-level supervisors can be the basis of Title VII liability under a disparate-impact theory, the plurality opinion *conditioned* that holding on the corollary that merely proving that the discretionary system has produced a racial or sexual disparity *is not enough.* "[T]he plaintiff must begin by identifying the specific employment practice that is challenged." That is all the more necessary when a class of plaintiffs is sought to be certified. Other than the bare existence of delegated discretion, respondents have identified no "specific employment practice"—much less one that ties all their 1.5 million claims together. Merely showing that Wal-Mart's policy of discretion has produced an overall sex-based disparity does not suffice.

Respondents' anecdotal evidence suffers from the same defects, and in addition is too weak to raise any inference that all the individual, discretionary personnel decisions are discriminatory. In *Teamsters v. United States*…, in addition to substantial statistical evidence of company-wide discrimination, the Government (as plaintiff) produced about 40 specific accounts of racial discrimination from particular individuals.

That number was significant because the company involved had only 6,472 employees, of whom 571 were minorities, and the class itself consisted of around 334 persons, The 40 anecdotes thus represented roughly one account for every eight members of the class. Moreover, the Court of Appeals noted that the anecdotes came from individuals "spread throughout" the company who "for the most part" worked at the company's operational centers that employed the largest numbers of the class members…. Here, by contrast, respondents filed some 120 affidavits reporting experiences of discrimination—about 1 for every 12,500 class members—relating to only some 235 out of Wal-Mart's 3,400 stores. More than half of these reports are concentrated in only six States (Alabama, California, Florida, Missouri, Texas, and Wisconsin); half of all States have only one or two anecdotes; and 14 States have no anecdotes about Wal-Mart's operations at all…. Even if every single one of these accounts is true, that would not demonstrate that the entire company "operate[s] under a general policy of discrimination," ...which is what respondents must show to certify a companywide class.

Conclusion: The broad-based claim made by the attorney for the three named Plaintiffs against Wal-Mart failed to identify a specific discriminatory employment practice uniformly applied to all members of the class and too few anecdotes from too few areas to present a valid class of individuals suffering from a common type of discrimination. Nothing precludes individual plaintiffs from pursuing their own claims or from forming smaller classes within regions where there are clear pervasive evidence of endemic gender-biased behavior. But the broad brush of a bad "culture" that may have created a statistical disparity at Wal-Mart is not going to meet the court's standards for a class action for employment discrimination.

Looking for the Protected Class

It is important to remember that even when a requirement is not reasonably necessary, it may still be lawful. Inessential tests or requirements are only problematic if they disparately impact a protected class. Therefore, before one decides that any requirement is unlawful, it is important that the protected class be identified. For example, if a height requirement appears in an ad that says, "You must be six feet tall to apply," there may not be a protected class. The Civil Rights Act does not protect short people.

If there is a protected class that is more significantly excluded than the majority, then there is a potential disparate impact claim. The impact must be real and not hypothetical. Although the height requirement example might theoretically exclude more women than men, there may be circumstances where the relevant applicant pool of women is not negatively impacted by the height requirement. If a protected class cannot be identified as disparately impacted, the requirement may be lawful even though it is gratuitous.

Less Discriminatory Alternatives

Assume that the height requirement discussed in the previous section did indeed cause a disparate impact by excluding more women than men, but that there was reasonable necessity for the requirement. It may seem that the employer should be off the hook, but that is not always true. If there are less discriminatory alternatives, a disparate impact claim may still lie. For example, if the reason for the height requirement was that employees must be able to reach high shelves in a warehouse, the use of stepladders is a reasonable, affordable alternative that would exclude fewer members of the protected class. Therefore, the requirement is unlawful, notwithstanding its being reasonable on the surface, because there is a less discriminatory alternative.

On the other hand, if the height requirement were imposed on commercial airline flight attendants who are required to be tall enough to be able to reach the overhead bins in the airplane, a stepladder would not be a reasonable option, and there would be no reasonable, less discriminatory alternative. Those who do not meet the height requirement in that circumstance would be legitimately excluded from employment despite the disparate impact.

In summary, a disparate impact must be real, not hypothetical. The disparate impact is lawful if the protected class is excluded by a test or standard that is reasonably necessary where there is no less discriminatory alternative.

Reasonable Accommodation

There are two protected classes, religion and disability, where employers may be required to make adjustments in the workplace to prevent a disparate impact. The requirement is that employers make a "reasonable accommodation" for the needs of the class.

Reasonable accommodation is a term of art, in that there is no bounded definition either in terms of dollars (how much an employer must spend to accommodate) or alterations to the job upon which one can make judgments with certainty. There are, however, some absolute employer rights. An employer is never required to hire an employee who (once reasonably accommodated) still cannot do the job, whether the reason for that inability is disability, religion, or any other protected reason.

Employers vary widely on how they deal with the issue of reasonable accommodation. One of the most generous corporate extremes can be found in the *Quaker Oats* case.(4) Quaker Oats Company employee Bradley Ciha was seriously injured in a motorcycle accident after he left work from an on-call weekend visit. He became a quadriplegic as a result of those injures. The Quaker Oats company went well beyond what any court would have compelled as a reasonable accommodation. Quaker developed a new materials supervisor position for Ciha that involved the use of an adaptive device attached to a modified computer by which Ciha was able to review inventory and purchase supplies and materials on behalf of Quaker Oats. Had the materials supervisor job already existed and the computerized adaptations been easily implemented, Ciha may have had a legal right to that accommodation. However, there is never an obligation for an employer to create a new job based on someone's disability, even when that disability is related to work done for the employer.

Ciha eventually sued Quaker Oats and won worker's compensation for his medical and custodial needs. The court acknowledged Quaker's extraordinary accommodations for Ciha's employment, but appropriately separated the two issues of accommodation and worker's compensation.

Most firms cannot afford to accommodate to the extent that Quaker accommodated Ciha, although incidents of corporate generosity in this regard are not uncommon. More common, however, are the types of situations and corporate response found in the following *Costco* case.

Kimberly M. Cloutier v. Costco Wholesale Corp. (2004)

United States Court of Appeals, First Circuit (390 F.3d 126)

Judge Kermit V. Lipez delivered the opinion of the court.

[U.S. Supreme Court denied certiorari in June 2005]

Kimberly Cloutier alleges that her employer, Costco Wholesale Corp. (Costco), failed to offer her a reasonable accommodation after she alerted it to a conflict between the "no facial jewelry" provision of its dress code and her religious practice as a member of the Church of Body Modification. She argues that this failure amounts to religious discrimination in violation of Title VII. The district court granted summary judgment for Costco, concluding that Costco reasonably accommodated Cloutier by offering to reinstate her if she either covered her facial piercing with a band-aid or replaced it with a clear retainer. We affirm the grant of summary judgment, but on a different basis. We hold that Costco had no duty to accommodate Cloutier because it could not do so without undue hardship.

I

We set forth the relevant facts from the summary judgment record, viewing them in the light most favorable to Cloutier. Kimberly Cloutier began working at Costco's West Springfield, Massachusetts store in July 1997. Before her first day of work, Cloutier received a copy of the Costco employment agreement, which included the employee dress code. When she was hired, Cloutier had multiple earrings and four tattoos, but no facial piercings.

Cloutier moved from her position as a front-end assistant to the deli department in September 1997. In 1998, Costco revised its dress code to prohibit food handlers, including deli employees, from wearing any jewelry. Cloutier's supervisor instructed her to remove her earrings pursuant to the revised code, but Cloutier refused. Instead, she requested to transfer to a front-end position where she would be permitted to continue wearing her jewelry. Cloutier did not indicate at the time that her insistence on wearing her earrings was based on a religious or spiritual belief.

Costco approved Cloutier's transfer back to a front-end position in June 1998, and promoted her to cashier soon thereafter. Over the ensuing two years, she engaged in various forms of body modification including facial piercing and cutting. Although these practices were meaningful to Cloutier, they were not motivated by a religious belief.

In March 2001, Costco further revised its dress code to prohibit all facial jewelry, aside from earrings, and disseminated the modified code to its employees. Cloutier did not challenge the dress code or seek an accommodation, but rather continued uneventfully to wear her eyebrow piercing for several months.

Costco began enforcing its no-facial-jewelry policy in June 2001. On June 25, 2001, front-end supervisors Todd Cunningham and Michele Callaghan informed Cloutier and another employee, Jennifer Theriaque, that they would have to remove their facial piercings. Cloutier and Theriaque did not comply, returning to work the following day still wearing their piercings. When Callaghan reiterated the no-facial-jewelry policy, Cloutier indicated for the first time that she was a member of the Church of Body Modification (CBM), and that her eyebrow piercing was part of her religion.

The CBM was established in 1999 and counts approximately 1000 members who participate in such practices as piercing, tattooing, branding, cutting, and body manipulation. Among the goals espoused in the CBM's mission statement are for its members to "grow as individuals through body modification and its teachings," to "promote growth in mind, body and spirit," and to be "confident role models in learning, teaching, and displaying body modification." The church's website [sic], apparently its primary mode for reaching its adherents, did not state that members' body modifications had to be visible at all times or that temporarily removing body modifications would violate a religious tenet. Still, Cloutier interprets the call

Kimberly M. Cloutier v. Costco Wholesale Corp. (2004)

to be a confident role model as requiring that her piercings be visible at all times and precluding her from removing or covering her facial jewelry. She does not extend this reasoning to the tattoos on her upper arms, which were covered at work by her shirt.

After reviewing information that Cloutier provided from the CBM website, [the supervisor] instructed Cloutier and Theriaque to remove their facial jewelry. They refused. The following day, Cloutier filed a religious discrimination complaint with the Equal Employment Opportunity Commission (EEOC)....

When Cloutier returned to work for her next shift on June 29, 2001, she was still wearing her facial jewelry. She met with Mark Shevchuk, the store manager, about her membership in the CBM and the EEOC complaint. During the course of the meeting, Cloutier suggested that she be allowed to cover her eyebrow piercing with a flesh-colored band-aid. Shevchuk rejected the suggestion and told Cloutier that she had to remove the piercing or go home. She left.

Theriaque also returned to work wearing her facial jewelry on June 29, 2001 and was reminded of the dress code. She asked whether she could wear clear plastic retainers in place of her jewelry to prevent the piercings from closing. The parties disagree as to whether Costco accepted this arrangement immediately or after several weeks of consideration. For purposes of our summary judgment analysis, we accept Cloutier's contention that Theriaque wore the retainers to work for several weeks unnoticed before Costco gave her permission to do so.

Although Cloutier learned during the week of July 2, 2001 that Theriaque had returned to work with retainers, she...chose to wait [at home] for her EEOC complaint to be resolved rather than following suit. During the week of July 7, 2001, Cloutier inquired of her superiors whether she could use vacation time to cover her absences and was told that she had been suspended. The following week, on July 14, Cloutier received notice in the mail that she had been terminated for her unexcused absences resulting from noncompliance with the dress code. She claims that this was her first notice that Costco had decided not to grant her request for an accommodation that would reconcile the dress code with her religious requirement of displaying her facial jewelry at all times.

The parties remained in contact after Cloutier's termination through the EEOC mediation process. During a meeting on August 10, 2001,

Costco offered to let Cloutier return to work wearing either plastic retainers or a band-aid over her jewelry (the same accommodation that Cloutier had suggested prior to her termination). Shevchuk repeated the offer in a letter dated August 29, 2001, asking Cloutier to respond by September 6, 2001.

Although there is some dispute as to whether Cloutier attempted to respond to Costco's offer before the deadline, she now maintains that neither of the proffered accommodations would be adequate because the CBM's tenets, as she interprets them, require her to display all of her facial piercings at all times. Replacing her eyebrow piercing with a plastic retainer or covering it with a band-aid would thus contradict her religious convictions. ...Cloutier asserts that the only reasonable accommodation would be to excuse her from Costco's dress code, allowing her to wear her facial jewelry to work. Costco responds that this accommodation would interfere with its ability to maintain a professional appearance and would thereby create an undue hardship for its business.

The EEOC determined in May 2002 that Costco's actions violated Title VII of the Civil Rights Act of 1964. It found that Cloutier's refusal to remove her facial jewelry was "religiously based as defined by the EEOC," that Costco did not allow her to wear her facial jewelry at work, and that there was no evidence that allowing her to wear the jewelry would have constituted an undue hardship. Based on this determination, Cloutier filed a suit against Costco in federal district court in August 2002 alleging a Title VII violation....

The district court granted Costco's motion to dismiss....

* * *

In granting summary judgment on the Title VII claim, the court stressed that "the search for a reasonable accommodation goes both ways. Although the employer is required under Title VII to accommodate an employee's religious beliefs, the employee has a duty to cooperate with the employer's good faith efforts to accommodate."

* * *

Cloutier now appeals, arguing that the court erred in finding no violation of Title VII...and that disputed material facts made summary judgment inappropriate. Summary judgment is appropriate when, viewing the record in the light most favorable to the nonmoving party, the court finds that there are no genuine issues of material fact in

Kimberly M. Cloutier v. Costco Wholesale Corp. (2004)

dispute and that the moving party is entitled to judgment as a matter of law.

II

On appeal, Cloutier vigorously asserts that her insistence on displaying all her facial jewelry at all times is the result of a sincerely held religious belief. Determining whether a belief is religious is "more often than not a difficult and delicate task," one to which the courts are ill-suited. Fortunately, as the district court noted, there is no need for us to delve into this thorny question in the present case. …[T]he facts here do not support a finding of impermissible religious discrimination.

* * *

A. Title VII

Title VII of the Civil Rights Act of 1964 prohibits employers from discriminating against employees on the basis of, among other things, religion. Under Title VII, an employer must offer a reasonable accommodation to resolve a conflict between an employee's sincerely held religious belief and a condition of employment, unless such an accommodation would create an undue hardship for the employer's business.

* * *

We follow the district court in assuming, *arguendo*, that Cloutier established a *prima facie* case sufficient to shift the burden to Costco to demonstrate that it offered a reasonable accommodation or that it could not do so without suffering undue hardship.

1. Reasonable accommodation

The parties dispute when Costco first offered Cloutier an accommodation, but we view the facts on summary judgment in the light most favorable to Cloutier. Cloutier was terminated on July 14, 2001. She maintains that Costco did not extend any offer of accommodation until August 10, 2001, approximately one month later….

* * *

2. Undue hardship

Cloutier asserts that the CBM mandate to be a confident role model requires her to display all of her facial piercings at all times. In her view, the only reasonable accommodation would be exemption from the no-facial-jewelry policy. Costco maintains that such an exemption would cause it to suffer an undue hardship, and that as a result it had no obligation to accommodate Cloutier.

An accommodation constitutes an "undue hardship" if it would impose more than a *de minimis* cost on the employer. This calculus applies both to economic costs, such as lost business or having to hire additional employees to accommodate a Sabbath observer, and to non-economic costs, such as compromising the integrity of a seniority system.

Cloutier argues that Costco has not met its burden of demonstrating that her requested accommodation would impose an undue hardship. She asserts that she did not receive complaints about her facial piercings and that the piercings did not affect her job performance. Hence, she contends that any hardship Costco posits is merely hypothetical and therefore not sufficient to excuse it from accommodating her religious practice under Title VII.

"...[I]t is possible for an employer to prove undue hardship without actually having undertaken any of the possible accommodations...." It can do so by "examining the specific hardships imposed by specific accommodation proposals." Here, Costco has only one proposal to evaluate (allowing Cloutier to wear and display her body jewelry as she demands) and has determined that it would constitute an undue hardship.

The district court acknowledged that "Costco has a legitimate interest in presenting a workforce to its customers that is, at least in Costco's eyes, reasonably professional in appearance." Costco's dress code, included in the handbook distributed to all employees, furthers this interest....

It is axiomatic that, for better or for worse, employees reflect on their employers. This is particularly true of employees who regularly interact with customers, as Cloutier did in her cashier position. Even if Cloutier did not personally receive any complaints about her appearance, her facial jewelry influenced Costco's public image and, in Costco's calculation, detracted from its professionalism.

Kimberly M. Cloutier v. Costco Wholesale Corp. (2004)

Costco is far from unique in adopting personal appearance standards to promote and protect its image. As the D.C. Circuit noted, "Perhaps no facet of business life is more important than a company's place in public estimation.... Good grooming regulations reflect a company's policy in our highly competitive business environment. Reasonable requirements in furtherance of that policy are an aspect of managerial responsibility."

* * *

Affirmed.

In the *Costco* case, the court determined that it was not reasonable to force Costco to change its appearance code based on an employee's religious preference. This is consistent with other cases where uniforms could be required despite religious preferences to the contrary. Even in this regard, however, the cases are not wholly in accord. An employer who did not allow a Jewish employee to wear a skull cap (yarmulke) was considered by one appellate court to be unreasonable in failing to accommodate that employee's religious preference. Much depends upon the tenets of the religion and how blatant or obvious the grooming departure is from the standards set by the enterprise.

Finally, in the *Costco* case, the court quotes a precedent indicating that customer preference may be the basis for grooming standards. It says this in a convoluted way—that "it is not the law that customer preference is…insufficient…." The reason for this indirect language is that there are situations where customer preference is definitely

not a sufficient basis for discriminatory behaviors. For example, a customer preference for white waiters over black ones is certainly not a basis for hiring only white waiters. That customers will have discriminatory biases in a society where prejudice has had a long history is inevitable. However, it would only serve to perpetuate unlawful discrimination if customer preference were sufficient to exempt employers from civil rights requirements.

So, how did Hooters get away with hiring only women waitresses, thereby disparately treating men on the basis of their gender? Hooters claimed that it was not selling food as much as it was selling sex. Identifying itself as a "Playboy" club equivalent, Hooters has identified its product with the sale of sexual imagery, and that is at least theoretically legal. In the same way that a strip club can impose *bona fide* requirements that its dancers be female and have certain body types, Hooters requires that its waitresses have attractive breasts. The EEOC has dropped its charges of gender bias against

Hooters for discriminating in its hiring of wait staff, and settled for alternative jobs being held by male staff including bar tending, cashiering, hosting, and back-room work. The notion of what types of job requirements are *bona fide* or reasonable, and what types are not, is at times contentious. Generally, reason prevails, and if the job rationally compels a specific gender or race, that will be permitted.

Affirmative Action

The history of affirmative action through the courts is long and somewhat tortured. Though the concept of affirmative action is frequently confused with general notions of equal opportunity, they are very different and often conflict with each other. The fundamental problem with acting "affirmatively"—which means specifically pursuing members of an underrepresented protected class for either admission to school or employment— is that it does exactly the opposite of what equal protection demands: it uses race, gender, or any other protected class status to differentiate candidates.

Affirmative action was initiated as an accelerator, to speed up integration in the schools and workplaces in order to more rapidly and efficiently remedy the effect of biases that had dominated prior to the Civil Rights Act of 1964. It did not take long, however, for conflicts to surface.

In 1978, Allan Bakke (5) brought the first successful "reverse discrimination" lawsuit against the University of California (UC) for its medical school admissions policy at its Davis campus. Bakke was a 30-year-old, white male who was not a particularly strong medical school candidate. However, minority students with quantitatively lower scores than his were admitted the year he was denied. Bakke successfully challenged the dual admissions process that protected 16 slots exclusively for minority applicants under UC Davis' affirmative action program. The U.S. Supreme Court found that a quota system, whether it sets minimum or maximum levels, is inherently offensive to the Constitution and the Civil Rights Act.

The 1979 U.S. Supreme Court case, *United Steelworkers v. Weber* (6), was the second case on affirmative action to reach the Supreme Court, and it dealt with employment rather than school admissions, which had been the subject of Bakke's case. Brian Weber was a white, unskilled steelworker employed at Kiser Steel. Weber's case was based on his being denied a training opportunity for which minority applicants were favored under the union's collective bargaining agreement. Weber did not win his claim, but the court set two important precedents in that case. First, it differentiated workplace affirmative action from college or academic affirmative action. Second, the case indicated that in order for an employer to act affirmatively, it must have had a demonstrable history of bias against the protected class. Kaiser Steel had statistics that bore a long history of racial bias, and so its affirmative action plan was validated.

In the intervening decades, affirmative action has been narrowed to the edge of extinction. In the now famous University of Michigan cases, the U.S. Supreme Court decided in two separate but concurrently argued cases that held:

1) undergraduate programs may not award "points" for minority status in admissions decisions, but

2) law schools may consider race among a host of other variables when considering admissions on a case-by-case basis. Race may not, however, be the dispositive factor.

In June of 2007, the U.S. Supreme Court decided the *Parents involved in Community Schools v. Seattle School District*.(7) Although this case deals with a school desegregation plan and not an employment case, the language of the case addresses affirmative action in both employment and admissions, and it significantly alters the ability of either academic or workplace leadership to implement affirmative action plans.

The Seattle School District's affirmative action plan classified children as white or nonwhite and used those racial classifications as "tiebreakers" to allocate slots in particularly desirable high schools.

The U.S. Supreme Court indicated that although remedying the effects of past discrimination is a compelling interest that might allow an affirmative action plan to exist, that interest did not apply in Seattle. This is because the Seattle schools in question are largely new and were never formally segregated. That there are many all-white schools as a matter of economic diversity in the district was found to be irrelevant.

Perhaps most counterintuitive was that the court said that the benefits of racial diversity in schools is not a constitutionally sufficient reason to act affirmatively. In other words, racial balance is not a constitutionally valid objective, nor is desegregation in the absence of historical discrimination.

As the law now stands, affirmative action is limited to remediation of intentional past discrimination and may not be used as a tool to promote integration. Although precedents regarding employment and academic affirmative action have followed separate lines, the law of the *Seattle School District* case is wholly consistent with the language of *Weber*, which it quotes liberally. One can expect that employment practices that correlate directly to affirmative action will be reevaluated over the next several years in accordance with this opinion.

On a final note, affirmative action was always meant to be a temporary measure to remediate past sins of systemic, entrenched discrimination. In the 2003 (law-school related) *Grutter v. Bollinger* case (8), Justice O'Connor reiterated that race-conscious affirmative action plans must be limited in time. She wrote, "The Court expects that 25 years from now, the use of racial preferences will no longer be necessary to further the interest approved today." The clock is most certainly ticking.

Notes

1. *Griggs v. Duke Power Co.*, 401 U.S. 424 (1971)

2. *EEOC v. Harbert-Yeargin, Inc.*, 266 F.3d 498 (Sixth Circuit Court of Appeals, 2001)

3. *Raytheon v. Hernandez*, US Supreme Court, 540 US 44, (2003)

4. *Quaker Oats Co. v. Ciha*, 552 N.W.2d 143 (Iowa 1996)

5. *Regents of the University of California v. Bakke*, 438 U.S. 265 (1978)

6. *United Steelworkers of America v. Weber*, 443 US 193 (1979)

7. *Parents involved in Community Schools v. Seattle School District*, 127 S. Ct. 2738 (2007)

8. *Grutter v. Bollinger*, 539 U.S. 306 (2003)

Appendix A
Legends of Corporate America's "Bad Guys"

Introduction

The new millennium brought a wave of accounting scandals that were, to some degree facilitated by an abundance of information that left balance sheets overly complicated and opaque. Frauds attributed to the executive leadership at both Enron and MCI were based on disclosures surrounded by so much confusing information that the facts underneath the disclosures were completely obscured. The end of the 20th and beginning of the 21st centuries introduced the crumbling of Fortune 100 corporations and the transition of guilty executives from lofty perches to prison cells. This chapter will discuss one great scandal of the last millennium, several scandals from the embryonic 21st century, and the heroes and villains (generally the same people) underneath them.

Morality and Markets: Michael Milken and Junk Bonds

Our American culture is generally conflicted about wealth. We both revere it and resent it. We eschew greed, but admire people like Warren Buffet and Bill Gates who have accrued inordinate personal fortunes. Our American dream includes winning the lottery or otherwise getting rich quick, but we demand economic value for our dollar, and our market system depends on it.

To some degree, these conflicts underlie many of the morally questionable decisions that have plagued this 21st century at its onset. The term "morally questionable" is used rather than "immoral" because the issues involved in corporate scandals are generally not black and white. If there is a clear lesson to be learned in reviewing the stories that follow, it is that there can be devastating consequences for failing to question the moral as well as legal component of a business judgment.

Bonds are generally secured by an asset. Corporate bond issues, for example, are frequently secured by the buildings that the bond proceeds financed. In theory, in the event of a default, the aggregate bond holders have an asset of comparable value to fall back on. In reality, there are lots of different types of bonds, and many provide little or no backup in the event of a default.

Some bonds, called debentures, are completely unsecured, with no asset underlying them. Other bonds are under-secured. A bond holder's interest in an under-secured bond might be subordinate to the interests of another debt holder, or the asset itself might be worth significantly less than the aggregate value of the bond issue. Bonds that are either under-secured or debenture have come to be known as "junk bonds."

The expression "junk bonds" became part of the American vocabulary in the 1980s, when billions of dollars of unsecured or under-secured debt flooded the American market. The junk bond was for the 1980s what subprime mortgages have been at the start of this millennium—instruments that appeared to provide high yields well beyond their correlated risk, but that ultimately proved to be devastatingly risky for both investors and the economy.

Investors rely on rating agencies like Moody's that rate bonds for their risk levels. Under Moody's system, bonds rated AAA are the least risky. Since markets demand that risk and reward operate in unison, junk bonds are rated low as an indication of high risk, and consequently pay a lot more interest than fully secured bonds. Unfortunately, as is often the case when a type of investment becomes extremely popular, both institutional and individual investors can get distracted from focusing on the risk side of the equation, and this is what happened when the

fervor of junk bond investment reached its peak in the 1980s.

A significant percentage of the junk bonds of the 1980s were purchased by savings and loan institutions, which were bank-like entities that provided depositors with government-insured savings accounts similar to those offered by banks insured by the Federal Deposit Insurance Corporation (FDIC). Although there is wide disagreement as to the role that the collapse of the junk bond market played in the failure of the savings and loan industry, the two events were proximate in time, and many have argued the connection.

Michael Milken, who worked for the firm Drexel Burnham Lambert, built the junk bond market from a small and uninviting niche market in the 1970s to a devastatingly large giant in the 1980s.

Milken believed and preached that low-rated bonds were not as risky as they appeared because factors such as leadership and growth potential were not included in the Moody's rating system. Milken passionately argued that those excluded factors were actually better predictors of bond safety than historical performance and underlying assets—the primary factors in Moody's ratings. Milken had support from some academicians with regard to his assertions. Some economists had used mathematical models to show that the high premiums on junk bonds exceeded the interest rates warranted by the actual risk of default. From

1970 through 1987, Milken infused his vision of the low risk of high-yield, low-rated bonds into the market. When the bottom fell out of the junk bond market in 1988, Michael Milken fell from grace, transitioning from hero to villain in the blink of a default-laden eye.

According to the facts reported in Daniel Fischel's book, *Payback,* (1) Michael Milken went to work for Drexel (ultimately Drexel Burnham Lambert) in 1970, when it was a third-tier bank in relatively poor financial condition. In 1973, his salary was a modest $52,000 per year, but he had negotiated a "bonus" of 35 percent of all profits related to high-yield bond sales. He had to pay his own staff from this percentage, but the financial incentives only matched his personal passion. Both provided overwhelming impetus to expand the high-yield/high-risk bond markets. This 35-percent bonus structure remained in place until Milken's fall in 1988.

Initially, Drexel's growth in the junk bond market was related to both pent-up, unmet demand and the remarkable sales ability of Milken. Between 1970 and 1983, Drexel went from a bank with minimal profit to a billion-dollar giant with $150 million in profit. Much of that profit was attributable to junk bonds, and it is estimated that more than $40 million went directly to Milken's pocket for his bonus.

In 1983, Milken and Drexel decided to follow Bear Sterns' lead and use

the high-risk bond business to finance mergers and acquisitions—more specifically, to finance hostile takeovers.

In Chapter 6 of this book, there was discussion of how hostile takeovers occur. The acquirer goes to the open market to try and get enough shares of the target to get control of that company without the approval of the target's board of directors. In order to get shares, the acquirer needs to offer a higher price than the current trade price to compel people to sell their stock. If the price goes up too high, theoretically the acquirer has to give up the hostile attempt.

Milken correctly believed that he could convince institutional purchasers of bonds to fund takeovers with bond proceeds. In fact, Milken was able to convince investors that bonds could safely finance 100 percent of an acquirer's costs of acquisition, with the acquisition itself as the sole security for those bonds.

He promoted the leadership ability of the would-be acquirers, and espoused their ability to increase revenues sufficiently to pay the acquisition debt.

Some firms have, at least to date, survived their leveraged buyouts. Revlon is one firm that was taken private with high-yield bonds, and its story is illustrative.

When Ronald Perelman made his first overture to buy Revlon, it was trading at $45 per share. Perelman was able to get control of the company but ended up offering and paying $58 per share, a significant premium over the earlier $45 trade price. All of the $700 million it took to purchase Revlon was raised by Milken and Drexel through the issuance of junk bonds. Perelman took the company private in 1985.

Revlon itself had to absorb the obligation to pay the $700 million of bond debt that Perelman leveraged to fund his purchase. It has never again been the profitable company it was prior to the leveraged buyout. Revlon went public again in 1996, although Perelman still controls a majority of the shares. It now trades at $1.20 per share.

Revlon is actually a junk bond success story relative to others. Many companies defaulted on their bond debt in 1988 and 1989, and more have done so since. They were burdened by impossible debt loads.

For Milken, however, the financial returns of the junk-bond-funded leveraged-buyout era were incredible. In 1987 alone he was paid $550 million for his percentage of the profits of Drexel's high-yield bond sales. Prior to using unk bonds for leveraged buyouts, his bonus was less than 10 percent of that amount.

By 1988, Milken was astronomically wealthy, but several of the bonds that he had so passionately endorsed (and some claim had guaranteed) had become valueless. Allegations abounded of market manipulation, insider trading, and fraud.

Rudy Giuliani (who subsequently became Mayor of New York City and ran for the Republican nomination for president in 2007) built his career by going after white-collar criminals while he served as the United States Attorney for the Southern District of New York. Giuliani went after both Drexel and Milken for securities fraud.

Using junk bonds for leveraged buyouts was not illegal (nor is it now). But investors alleged that they had been duped and misled by Milken and Drexel, and these allegations precipitated Giuliani's campaign to attempt to charge the parties criminally.

Drexel pled guilty to securities manipulation and that plea put it out of business. Drexel defaulted on over $100 million of debt when it went bankrupt.

Milken entered into a plea bargain, but only after four years of court battles. He never pled guilty to any charges based on junk-bond-related securities fraud or insider trading. In his plea bargain, he admitted guilt to relatively minor but very shady stock transfers with Ivan Boesky and also admitted to conduct resulting in tax fraud.

The questions of whether or not Milken was guilty of defrauding investors, misrepresentation, market manipulation, or insider trading will never be resolved by consensus. His defenders will claim that Milken heroically created shareholder wealth and compelled the market to price stocks at their true value by engineering successful leveraged buyouts. They will further allege that criminally he was only guilty of minor technical infractions. Those who vilify him would argue that he was responsible for the savings and loan collapse and for the destruction of jobs and productivity in corporate America. Both sides speak a piece of the truth.

Significantly, the fundamentals of Milken's strategies are legal. The free market depends upon the wisdom of investors to understand risk and constrain their portfolios accordingly.

Americans, however, are poor losers who generally look for blameworthiness. Milken was most definitely not the only one who built a huge fortune with the sale of risky securities, but he was by far the most prominent and the least repentant about the consequences.

Milken's plea bargain initially (and unexpectedly) yielded a ten-year sentence, but that sentence was reduced, and he was freed in 24 months. He is permanently banned from any work in the securities industry.

And the Junk Security Beat Goes On

Ben Stein's book, *License to Steal: The Untold Story of Michael Milken and the Conspiracy to Bilk the Nation*, presents the argument that Milken's sale of junk bonds to savings and loan institutions was tantamount to committing a fraud on the nation.(2) At the time Stein wrote his book, the cost to the American taxpayer to cover savings and loan deficits was considered astronomical.

However, 2008 losses in subprime, mortgage-backed securities (some of which are guaranteed by the U.S. government) are expected to be geometrically higher than those incurred during the junk bond debacle. No single person is being held accountable for the sub-prime mortgage debacle, but there are many victims. Several large mortgage lenders, including Countrywide and First Mag-

nus, went bankrupt in late 2007 and early 2008. Criminal complaints have been filed in many mortgage fraud cases and two hedge fund operators working for Bear Sterns have been indicted.

In March 2008, Bear Sterns collapsed when the market for its mortgage-based securities (collateralized debt obligations or CDOs) evaporated. Though only anecdotally related, Bear Sterns was the firm that preceded Drexel Burnham as the first to offer junk bonds to fund a leveraged buyout.

One other interesting anecdote with respect to the junk bond era relates to one of the biggest scandals of this millennium. When Enron was struggling with its finances in the mid-1980s, a junk bond deal with Milken pulled the company out of the fire.

Enron

The name Enron evokes a number of images, virtually none of them positive, at least not now. The company and its three top leaders have been vilified, two (Jeff Skilling and Andrew Fastow) are serving long jail terms, and Enron's former Chief Executive Officer (CEO), Ken Lay, is dead from a heart attack he suffered shortly after his trial and conviction.

The stories of Lay, Skilling, and Fastow raise serious questions about ethics and corporate morality in general. Many people assert that Lay and Skilling were able to self-delude until the company's collapse was imminent. Fastow, a bit lower on the executive grid, was more obvious in his self-dealing, but clearly was enabled by his superiors.

The story of Enron and its leadership is extraordinarily complex, which is partially why the conduct persisted so long. At first, Enron's aggressive financial positioning was praised as forward-thinking and heroic. In 1987, a reporter for Forbes wrote an article about Lay titled "Orderly Mind in a Disorderly Market." The article lauded Enron as being perfectly poised for a deregulated energy market and Lay as the "man to watch."(3) Wall Street analysts jumped onto the bandwagon, and Enron became their darling.

Indisputably, Lay took some extraordinary risks in the early days of

Enron, and these paid off handsomely. He was unparalleled in terms of his expertise in the natural gas markets. By the early 1990s, after several "hiccups" and great luck, Enron had legitimately become a significant force in all areas of the energy industry.

As discussed at the beginning of this chapter, the reason why risky investments pay so well is that risks are…risky. The higher the potential return, the more likely the investment will fail. As Enron's business began to suffer the downside of risk-taking, the leadership became more questionable in how it utilized aggressive financing mechanisms. These deals ultimately led to Enron's downfall. Enron was able to conceal its creative accounting despite supposedly making full disclosures of what it was doing. The leadership did this by providing an abundance of information that was, for the most part, incomprehensible.

Enron's Disclosure

The following is the disclosure in the second quarter 10-Q SEC Filing (mandatory quarterly report to SEC) that Enron filed regarding off-books partnerships and Fastow's interest in 2000. Fastow's name is never mentioned, but he was the senior Enron officer and the general partner in the "Related Party Transaction" that is disclosed below.

Enron Corporation 10-Q SEC Filing (11/14/2000)

Notes to Consolidated Financial Statements

* * *

7. Related Party Transactions

In the first nine months of 2000, Enron entered into transactions with limited partnerships (the Related Party), whose general partner's managing member is a senior officer of Enron. The limited partners of the Related Party are unrelated to Enron.

During the first quarter of 2000, Enron and the Related Party entered into an agreement to terminate certain financial instruments that had been entered into during 1999. In connection with this agreement, Enron received approximately 3.1 million shares of Enron common stock held by the Related Party. A put option, which was originally entered into in the first quarter of 2000 and gave the Related Party the right to sell shares of Enron common stock to Enron at a strike price of $71.31 per share, was terminated under this agreement. In return, Enron paid approximately $26.8 million to the Related Party. The agreement closed in April 2000. Additionally, in the first quarter of 2000, Enron advanced to the Related Party $10 million, at a market rate of interest, which was repaid in April 2000.

In the second quarter of 2000, Enron sold a portion of its excess dark fiber inventory to the Related Party in exchange for $30 million cash and a $70 million note receivable that matures in seven years and bears a market rate of interest. Enron recognized gross margin of $67 million on the sale.

In the second and third quarters of 2000, Enron entered into transactions with the Related Party to hedge certain merchant investments and other assets. As part of the transactions, Enron (i) contributed to newly-formed entities (the Entities) assets valued at approximately $1.2 billion, including 3.7 million restricted shares of outstanding Enron common stock, $150 million in Enron notes payable, the right to receive up to 18.0 million shares of outstanding Enron common stock in March 2003 (subject to certain conditions) and (ii) transferred to the [E]ntities assets valued at approximately $309 million, including a $50 million note payable and an investment in an entity that indirectly holds warrants convertible into common stock of an Enron equity method investee. In return, Enron received economic interests in the Entities, $309 million in notes receivable and a special distribution from the Entities in the form of $1.2 billion in notes receivable, subject to changes in the principal for amounts payable by Enron in connection with the execution of additional derivative instruments. In addition, Enron paid $123 million to purchase share-settled options from the Entities on 21.7 million shares of Enron common stock. The Entities paid Enron $10.7 million in the third quarter to terminate the share-settled options on 14.6 million shares of Enron common stock outstanding at June 30, 2000.

In the third quarter of 2000, Enron entered into derivative transactions with the Entities with a combined notional value of approximately $1.2 billion to hedge certain merchant investments and other assets. Enron's notes receivable balance was reduced by $36 million as a result of premiums owed on derivative transactions. Enron recognized revenues of approximately $60 million related to the derivative transactions, which offset market value changes of certain merchant investments. In addition, Enron recognized $10.2 million and $1.5 million of interest income and interest expense, respectively, on the notes receivable from and payable to the Entities.

Management believes that the terms of the transactions with related parties were reasonable and are representative of terms that would be negotiated with unrelated third parties.

Analysts and investors ostensibly read the disclosure, but most had no idea what they read. The underlying assumption under which analysts operate is that if something is disclosed, it must be all right. Enron management could legitimately reply that they always disclosed all of their transactions. Subsequently those disclosures became the genesis of the term "opaque" when used to describe securities filings.

Off the Books—the SPE

Even if one can believe that the disclosure gave all the essential information for any investor who wanted to analyze it, what Enron specifically omitted was that Andrew Fastow, then Chief Financial Officer (CFO) of Enron, was the general partner in the referenced "Related Party." Fastow pocketed an estimated $40 million overnight for his nominal role in the off-the-books arrangement described in the disclosure.

The type of partnership described in the "Related Party Transactions" section of the disclosure is generally legal if appropriately used. Known as a separate partnership entity (SPE), this type of partnership functions as a financing mechanism and not an operating business. In *Power Failure* (3), a hypothetical example is described as to how a legitimate asset-backed SPE might work. The following paraphrases and elaborates on that hypothetical.

Assume that a heavy-equipment company, (we will call it "Heavy") transfers (sells) its fleet of dump trucks into an SPE.

Heavy then sells the SPE to investors. The SPE leases the trucks back to Heavy, and the lease payments made by Heavy to the SPE provide the investors with their return.

Investors have security because their equities are backed by the value of the dump trucks. They have income from Heavy's lease payments. Meanwhile, without actually selling off the trucks or borrowing money against them, Heavy has raised money from what the investors have paid for the SPE. Although it no longer owns the dump trucks, Heavy has retained their use, gotten capital with which to expand its business, and, most importantly, has no debt on its balance sheet.

The efficiency of this type of financing arrangement for Enron was enormous. SPEs allowed Enron to avoid having to issue more of its own stock to raise capital, which would have required going through the registration requirements of the SEC—a long and expensive process. The SEC analysts were also inclined to ask substantive questions and require clearer disclosures that might have made the SPEs more transparent. That might well have impacted the willingness of investors to jump on board.

Sales to the SPEs always showed a profit to Enron and enhanced their balance sheet. Banks and other investors were enamored with Enron SPEs because they appeared to be an unending source of short, turn-around profit.

Rereading the disclosure, there are bright warning signs hidden under the huge volume of words. Consider the following segment:

"In the second quarter of 2000, Enron sold a portion of its excess dark fiber inventory to the Related Party in exchange for $30 million cash and a $70 million note receivable that matures in seven years and bears a market rate of interest. Enron recognized gross margin of $67 million on the sale."

This looks like an asset-backed security, where Enron sold dark fiber inventory to an SPE, and then sold shares of that SPE to investors. It got $30 million in cash from that, but it accrued $100 million in revenue based on the cash plus the $70 million note. That is how they generated a "profit" of $67 million. However, the only way that the SPE could pay that $70 million note to Enron was to sell the dark fiber inventory back to Enron. Either Enron was going to have to buy the fiber back at the inflated prices from which they had taken their large profit, or the SPE was going to default on its note because it had no independent source of revenue. Meanwhile, Enron was going to show profit from unpaid interest that it accrued on the note owed by the SPE. More importantly, the next part of the disclosure reveals that Enron had grown well past the typical asset-backed SPE described in the dump truck hypothetical. In its final year, Enron was backing SPEs with their own stock (or derivatives of it). Consider the next segment of the disclosure:

> "In the second and third quarters of 2000, Enron entered into transactions with the Related Party to hedge certain merchant investments and other assets. As part of the transactions, Enron (i) contributed to newly-formed entities (the Entities) assets valued at approximately $1.2 billion, including 3.7 million restricted shares of outstanding Enron common stock, $150 million in Enron notes payable, the right to receive up to 18 million shares of outstanding Enron common stock in March 2003…. In return, Enron re-

ceived economic interests in the Entities, $309 million in notes receivable and a special distribution from the Entities in the form of $1.2 billion in notes receivable."

This is what Sherron Watkins, the whistleblowing Enron internal accountant, referred to as the "smoking gun" that could not be extinguished. Here is what was actually being disclosed:

- Enron had transferred to the SPE $150 million in debt, along with rights to Enron restricted stock and derivatives in the second and third quarters of 2000.

- Enron took a profit of $60 million for the sale of the SPE.

- The only assets the SPE owned as a result of this transaction were Enron stocks and derivatives and Enron debt.

- The SPE owed Enron $1.2 billion plus interest, which showed on Enron's books as an asset.

- The SPE would only be able to repay its huge debt to Enron if it sold its Enron stock for more than the $1.2 billion it owed.

In theory, as long as Enron's stock kept going up in value, the SPE could eventually sell off Enron stock and pay its debt to Enron. In other words, under the best of circumstances, Enron could continue to feed off itself by diluting its own shares through the SPE until it legitimately earned revenue from operations. That did not happen.

Enron shares dropped, the SPEs defaulted, Enron went bankrupt, and the prosecutions began.

The government viewed the investment banks as enablers because they knew that Enron was inflating its income with these entities. Citibank and Merrill Lynch were prosecuted for securities fraud by New York's Attorney General Elliot Spitzer when the Enron house of cards collapsed.

Fastow

As prosecutions against Enron executives began to move forward, Andrew Fastow did not go down without a fight. Still, he was the first one to enter into a plea bargain. This is not surprising, as he would have been the easiest to convict. He had been the seller/architect of all of Enron's most questionable deals and had been the general partner in one of the final and most egregious SPE transactions. He also pocketed an estimated $40 million for his general partnership role, without disclosing his identity to the Enron shareholders. Fastow was the CFO of Enron in 2000. Obviously, he knew that there was a conflict of interest in his role as general partner in the Related Party Transaction because he had gotten the Enron board of directors to waive the conflict. The omission of his name and his personal profit from any footnote in Enron's quarterly report could not credibly have been argued as oversight. The government's case against Fastow had little room for doubt, reasonable or otherwise.

On the other hand, Fastow's rationale for pocketing so much capital was not completely indefensible in context. If he did not become general partner, the SPE would have had to pay someone else to step into the position, and that person would have been paid the same bizarre compensation. He had facilitated overnight fortunes in Enron's SPEs for many others, including an allegedly unwitting Enron attorney named Kristina Mordaunt. She had been invited to invest in one of the SPEs, had put in $5800, and less than two months later was paid out with a check for $1,000,000. (Mordaunt came forward on her own and was not criminally prosecuted, but her assets—including her home—were seized in federal forfeiture actions after the scandal broke.) People did not invest in partnership interests in Enron SPEs for small returns.

Fastow ultimately appeared repentant and entered into a plea bargain with the government. He agreed to, and did, testify against Skilling and Lay in exchange for leniency, and his testimony was considered the most critical in garnering convictions against them. Fastow began serving a six-year sentence in prison in 2006, and he will serve two additional years under house arrest after that. He will be a free man in 2014. Prior to his sentencing, Fastow's wife had to serve a year in jail for signing their joint income tax return, which contained misrepresentations about their joint income.

Skilling

Lay first brought Jeff Skilling to Enron in 1990, having recruited him from McKinsey and Co., an intellectually-charged corporate think tank that primarily served as a consulting firm to large publicly traded corporate clients. Skilling had been the youngest person to ever become a partner at McKinsey and Co., and Lay respected his keen mind and aggressive attitude.(3)

By 1994, Harvard Business School had published a case study on Skilling lauding his brilliantly innovative mind. Skilling had by then established Enron as a leader in the natural gas trading business. Goldman Sachs went so far as to say Enron was undervalued, given its potential under Skilling. Lay and Skilling were considered "The Smartest Guys in the Room."(4)

In 2001, Lay stepped aside as CEO, and Skilling was made President and CEO. Lay remained at Enron as Chairman. However, by 2001, Enron was already starting to unravel. Skilling lasted in the CEO position a mere six months and then left, claiming that the stress and pressure on him were too great. The investment community was suspicious. Analysts did not believe that Skilling would leave his dream job only six months after assuming it unless there were serious troubles within Enron.

As Enron's collapse became an issue of political significance, Skilling was called to testify under a Congressional subpoena and was questioned rigorously by Representatives whose constituents were harmed. Skilling insisted that under the Financial Accounting Standards Board rules, Enron's accounting was aggressive but legal. He asserted that the SPEs (at least as he claims he was informed about them) were lawful entities. He claimed that Enron's collapse was caused by the equivalent of a "shareholder run on the bank."

In some ways, his was not a completely indefensible position. The illegality of the SPEs is not and has never been entirely clear. The criminal convictions that ultimately occurred rested (at least in part) on the assumption that no risk was ever transferred to the SPEs. Skilling argued that the structuring documents proved that risk did transfer. Fastow testified that although on paper this was true, Skilling always guaranteed investors that they would not lose a dime if they invested in an SPE. This assertion was disputed by Skilling, but, in the long run, the jury believed Fastow.

There is another way in which Skilling's arguments can be seen as logical. As a practical matter, if (as Skilling asserts) the shareholders had not sold their stock, the share prices would not have plummeted. If the shares had retained their value, the SPEs would have been able to pay their debt to Enron. If that had happened, Enron would have had capital to continue on. From that perspective one could in fact blame the entire debacle on shareholder hysteria. This may seem far fetched, but a recent issue of the online version of *The Economist* magazine included an article indicating that Skilling's argument has economic credibility.(5) Of course, with any house of cards, if nothing moves and the wind doesn't blow, the house can theoretically keep standing.

That logic notwithstanding, the statistics are overwhelmingly against the house of cards being able to stay standing over the long haul.

From a moral perspective, the complete shadiness of the SPEs, the huge payoffs to insiders, and the overall obfuscation of Enron's earnings (or lack of earnings) over the years under Skilling's leadership cannot be defended. Even if the disclosures told all, the information was delivered amidst so much haze that only the most insightful investigator—who believed there was a reason to investigate—would have seen that Enron had not netted black ink strictly from operations for several years.

In October 2006, after being charged with a variety of crimes related to stock manipulation, fraud, and misrepresentation, Skilling was sentenced to over 24 years in prison. He has been incarcerated since. However, he has appealed the convictions and his sentence. The Fifth Circuit Court of Appeals has already overturned several of the Enron convictions, including the one against Arthur Anderson, the accounting firm that was put out of business by Enron prosecutors and,

only after its demise, was exonerated. Prosecutors have engaged in arguable conduct in their own right with respect to disclosures they made (and failed to make) to the defense during the Enron trials. Skilling's chances of winning at least some of his arguments on appeal are considered good.

Lay

Ken Lay was a consummate statesman. His warmth, brightness, and general charisma augmented his superlative knowledge of natural gas and energy. During most of Enron's existence, the world embraced Lay as a critically important authority in his field. Everyone liked him.

But Lay's appearance covered other aspects of his personality that were less than comforting in a business leader. Lay was an enormous risk-taker. In the early years, Lay's risk-taking paid off and helped build Enron into a behemoth in the natural gas industry. But given the nature of risk, one is likely to lose more often than win when taking really big risks, as ultimately happened with Enron.

Lay's personal financial decision-making was equally edgy. Although he earned massive amounts of money as Enron's CEO, in the end he was bordering on bankruptcy. He had leveraged huge investments by buying on margin. His controversial sale of Enron stock just prior to the bottom falling out was indisputably tied to his needing huge sums of money to pay the margin calls on his devaluing investments. The notion that someone so wealthy would even bother to wager so recklessly on margin has bewildered many who have studied Ken Lay since the Enron debacle.

Many people, including purported whistleblower Sherron Watkins, were inclined to believe that Ken Lay did not fully understand the complex SPEs or the seriousness of Enron's financial problems. Arthur Anderson, Enron's external auditors, had approved the SPE deals and the black-ink financial statements. Even upon re-examination after Watkins expressed her concerns, outside counsel had written to Lay that although public awareness about the SPEs might be embarrassing, nothing that Enron did appeared to be illegal.

On the other hand, Lay's history had indicated that he was not tied to a strong moral compass. He had allowed two former employees to continue working at Enron in the 1980s after it was proven that they had stolen money and "cooked books" to conceal their own self dealing. When Lay did not have them fired, some believed that the reason was that the two had actual-

ly made money for Enron while doing their dastardly deeds. (A year later, those same employees were again found to be keeping two sets of books, at which point they were fired and ended up in jail.)

Finally, Lay's financial conduct as CEO was extremely questionable. Over his tenure at Enron, Lay had borrowed $81 million dollars from the company, which he repaid in Enron stock, avoiding disclosure about his use of the stock and by-passing tax issues. When a CEO makes the corporate coffer his personal piggy bank, criminal prosecutions will generally follow.

Lay was convicted of various stock manipulation, fraud, and insider trading crimes but died of a heart attack before he was sentenced. Many who knew him mourned his loss, but few of his professional friends were willing to speak about this publicly. He had become a pariah—any friend of Lay's was likely to be indicted. He died a failed leader, with (literally) a broken heart.

There Were Bad Guys Everywhere

Accounting and financial scandals of the new millennium brought down WorldCom, Adelphia, Dynegy, and Tyco, among others.

Bernard Ebbers and WorldCom

In 1997, *Time Magazine* wrote of Bernard Ebbers, Founder, President,

and CEO of WorldCom, Inc., the following:

"Bernie Ebbers runs one of the most successful companies in the telecommunications business. But who would have known that this native Canadian had dropped out of college twice (before graduating from Mississippi College) and worked as a milkman by day and a bouncer by night. Ebbers began with a long-distance-resale company, LDDS (Long Distance Discount Service), then started devouring smaller firms (two valuable assets include MFS Communications and Uunet). What emerged was WorldCom, now one of the largest Internet carriers in the world and one of the biggest players in the telecommunications industry."(6)

Ebbers was sentenced to 25 years in prison in September 2005.

Ebbers was different than the Enron gang. Though he may well have been greedy and was indisputably self-indulgent, Ebbers did not make money from the accounting misrepresentations for which he was sentenced. It is the opinion of most that WorldCom had been pillaged before the first misstatement was filed.

Massive stock options had been granted to the WorldCom executives along with huge salaries and other perquisites. The SEC corporate monitor Richard Breeden (7) noted that WorldCom's Board of Directors appeared to spend its time trying to enrich Ebbers and the other executives, rather than representing the shareholders. Most egregious was the fact that Ebbers had been allowed to borrow over $400 million from WorldCom with only his own WorldCom shares as collateral.

Other executives were paid over $238 million in "retention bonuses" that were distributed without standards or supervision. None of this, however, was criminal.

What was criminal was the accounting trick used by WorldCom to make the bottom line appear significantly healthier than it was after the company started to suffer losses. Beginning in about 2000 and continuing through 2002, WorldCom was suffering financial stress from both competition and debt-load. WorldCom was primarily in the business of selling long distance line connections to local telephone companies. Historically, WorldCom had expensed its "line connection" costs, but changed its accounting in 2000 in order to conceal the company's serious financial weakness. Instead of expensing its costs, WorldCom began amortizing those expenses, taking only a percentage of the expense in the year it was incurred. It also inflated revenues by immediately accruing sales that were not to occur until a later time.

According to former CFO Scott Sullivan, Ebbers was insistent that WorldCom do what it needed to do to "hit the numbers," which Sullivan understood to be a command to falsify the documents. Sullivan, who implemented the plan to misstate the financial documents, claims he repeatedly told Ebbers that the numbers were wrong, but that Ebbers ignored him. Ebbers testified in his own behalf, claiming he knew nothing about the fraud, and that he did not understand the nuances of accounting.

Ebbers barely finished college with a degree in Physical Education. It is believable that he did not understand the accounting nuances, but the jury in his criminal trial also believed he was aware of the real financial condition of WorldCom.

Many agree that Ebbers was a victim of his own ego, unable to face Wall Street's disappointment. His had been an inordinate rise to the top in a telecom sector that he virtually invented after the breakup of AT&T. It is not unreasonable to assume that he was unwilling to publicly admit failure. Added to that was the $400 million that he owed WorldCom that was secured only by his stock in the company. If MCI stock plummeted, a margin call would have resulted, which would have forced Ebbers to try to find enough personal assets to sell off to repay the enormous loan. Financial stress and ego are two very powerful motivators. On the other hand, Ebbers did not sell one share of WorldCom stock after the misstatements. Where Ken Lay sold Enron in abundance to cover his margin calls, Ebbers held onto every share and option, placing himself identically to shareholders in terms of interest.

Ultimately, the misstatements in WorldCom's financial statements amounted to over $11 billion dollars in unreported loss. The company was forced into bankruptcy and shareholder wealth evaporated. Analysts have opined that had the truth been revealed from the onset, WorldCom would have at least lived to revive itself another day. Verizon subsequently purchased WorldCom (renamed MCI) out of bankruptcy.

Former WorldCom CFO Scott Sullivan, who designed the accounting scam, is serving five years in prison for his role in WorldCom's collapse. Ebbers, on the other hand, is serving twenty-five years and will not be eligible for parole until he is in his late 80's. He voluntarily relinquished all of his personal assets ($45 million) to the investors prior to his conviction. His appeals have all been exhausted, and he is now serving his time—what commentators have called a probable life sentence—in a medium security federal penitentiary. One appellate judge noted that there are murderers who have lesser sentences than Ebbers, but his sentence has been upheld and is consistent with the federal sentencing guidelines.

Dennis Kozlowski and Tyco

Tyco is an electronics company that produces component parts ranging from circuits to fiber optics for a very wide variety of consumer and industrial products. Kozlowski joined Tyco in 1975 and helped grow the company significantly during his time as CEO. He was widely lauded as a successful and irreplaceable leader of his company.

Kozlowski's case is unusual in that Tyco continues to thrive and never collapsed as a result of stock manipulation or fraud. It is also unusual in that the amount of crass behavior and self-indulgence that Kozlowski engaged in while CEO was beyond anything a publicly traded company had ever seen in its top leadership.

Most notorious in depicting Kozlowski's excesses was a party that he gave his wife for her fortieth birthday, half of which was paid for by Tyco. The party took place on the island of Sardinia and was videotaped. The tape showed an ice sculpture of the statue of David with vodka coming out of its penis into the fountain bowl. It also showed a birthday cake in the shape of a woman's breasts, with sparklers coming out of the nipples. The reaction of both Tyco shareholders and the public in general to this video was immediate and inflamed.

The jury in Kozlowski's trial was not allowed to see the most inflammatory scenes in the birthday video, but they were able to see enough. Warren Buffet and other financial leaders were in the video, all of whom were flown to Sardinia at Tyco's significant expense. Jurors were able to observe guests and entertainers in briefs and togas dancing around the pool in hedonistic fashion and Kozlowski dancing with his wife while being entertained by Jimmy Buffet, who was hired to perform at the party. Kozlowski's defense was that the party was a hybrid of both business and personal purpose.

To bolster his argument, he presented un-rebutted testimony that Barbara Jacques, Tyco events coordinator, had been the one to plan the entire event.

Had this party been Kozlowski's only problem, the case probably would not have been tried. In more substantive claims, Kozlowski was accused of stealing over $100 million in unauthorized bonuses from the company and selling $400 million of his own shares of Tyco at inflated values. His defense to the unlawful bonuses was that although he awarded them to himself, it was in the form of deferred compensation, so he never actually received the bonuses before he was tried. He also noted that the only way to liquidate his shares in Tyco without selling off a lot of stock and harming share value was to borrow against his stock ownership—which he claimed was the standard practice of all CEO's in similar circumstances at the time.

The jury was not convinced by either the legitimacy of the business purpose of the birthday party nor Kozlowski's other defenses, instead deciding that he was guilty of grand larceny and fraud charges (the corporate equivalent of pirate-style looting). Kozlowski was sentenced in New York state court to 8–25 years (New York still allows judges the right to give sentences in ranges). He is in a New York State medium security prison and will not be eligible for parole for at least six years.

John Rigas and Adelphia

After Adelphia Communications unexpectedly went bankrupt in 2004, investigations revealed inflated corporate earnings statements and the improper use of funds by both CEO John Rigas and his son Timothy, who served as CFO. Although the most incendiary newspaper accounts of fraud focused on Rigas' purchase of a $15,000 umbrella stand, it is likely that the 34 or more condos and vacation homes that Rigas bought for himself with corporate money played a more significant role in the jury's convictions.

John Rigas had run Adelphia Communications for 50 years prior to its bankruptcy. He was convicted of 18 counts of fraud-related falsifying of financial statements and pilfering corporate funds. Rigas was in poor health and 80 years old at the time he started his 15-year sentence in 2007. (His son, Timothy, age 49, was sentenced to serve 20 years.)

Eliot Spitzer

In the final ironic note that resonates in this first decade after the year 2000, Eliot Spitzer, the New York attorney general who aggressively pursued white collar criminals and became governor of New York on an anti-corporate corruption platform, has had to step down as governor because of his own scandalous behavior.

That Spitzer engaged the services of very high-priced prostitutes was fodder for newspaper headlines. Underlying the possibility of white collar criminal behavior was that he attempted to launder the money paid to the escort service that provided the prostitutes to him. Attempting to stay below the $10,000 cash transfer radar that forces banks to disclose transactions, Spitzer's high-dollar cash transfers qualified as "suspicious activities" that prompted an investigation.

It is obvious that when Spitzer transferred the cash he did not do so to fund terrorists or launder money for any truly evil crime. He did, however, attempt to secretly move cash to an illegal business, and in so doing, violated federal money laundering statutes.

Although he has not yet been charged with money laundering, he has stepped down as governor and has been publicly humiliated with disclosures about his very personal sexual misconduct. Many applaud his humiliation as proper retaliation for his intentionally embarrassing "perp walks" where executives were handcuffed and paraded in front of cameras on the way to their indictments. Others feel that the move toward executive accountability for which Spitzer was at least nominally an advocate is seriously hindered with this scandal.

The Common Thread

Although every corporate scandal was unique and a creature of its own corporate culture, there are some common threads. A certain type of arguable behavior took hold in a small way, and soon it was integrated into the corporate culture as acceptable. Then it quantitatively leapt out of control: Rigas' personal excess, Enron's SPEs, and even Ebbers' ego were all enabled in small bits first.

In virtually every case, the deeds were legally defensible in the eyes of the perpetrators, who never thought about getting caught because they (at least initially) failed to think about being wrong. Using the law in its most technical form, they rationalized behaviors and never considered the moral issue underneath.

Patrick Kuhse, an ethics lecturer and former white collar convicted felon, uses the acronym SUDs, which stands for "seemingly unimportant decisions." All of the corporate scandals discussed in this chapter started with SUDs.

Note

1. Daniel Fischel, *Payback: The Conspiracy to Destroy Michael Milken and His Financial Revolution*, HarperBusiness (1995).

2. Benjamin Stein, *License to Steal: The Untold Story of Michael Milken and the Conspiracy to Bilk the Nation*, Simon and Schuster (1992).

3. Mimi Swartz and Sherron Watkins, *Power Failure*, Random House (2003).

4. "The Smartest Guys in the Room," documentary film, Alex Gibney, Director (2005).

5. Economist.com, March 18, 2008.
   http://www.economist.com/business/displaystory.cfm?story_id=10873801

6. Time Digital Archives: http://www.time.com/time/digital/cyberelite/11.html.

7. "Restoring Trust," report to the U.S. District Court prepared by Richard Breeden, corporate monitor.
   http://fl1.findlaw.com/news.findlaw.com/hdocs/docs/worldcom/corpgov82603rpt.pdf

Appendix B
When Litigation Gets Out of Hand

If the law's purpose is to provide social certainty and justice, it achieves that purpose very imperfectly, limited by the mere mortals who pass, interpret, and implement it.

Fairness is elusive. Inflexible law can create as much injustice as it avoids because it applies the same standard to widely divergent circumstances. Too much flexibility creates vulnerability to the whims of judicial power. And the absence of law (such as will be evident in the following case) leaves us floundering in the attempt to pursue any form of justice at all.

The following story illustrates the imperfection of the U.S. legal system as it was in the 19th century, but it should also serve to create unease about the imperfection of the system as it is now.

The courts are a last resort for justice. The outcome of a case cannot be anticipated with certainty, and the cost and time associated with the pursuit of a legal remedy are not to be underestimated. Ethics, good judgment, and rational compromise must operate the social conscience if things are to proceed efficiently and fairly. But when those fail, sometimes even justices of the highest courts in the land can get caught in a quagmire.

A Story about Law, Sex, Murder, and Madness

All lawsuits involve a story with at least one victim or potential victim. The harm can be as varied as the human experience—someone may have been physically hurt, defrauded, or maligned with libel. In the U.S. system of justice, justice is the one thing that is absolutely not guaranteed. On the other hand, a battle between adversaries is.

Precedent is set when a legal question is sufficiently controversial that one of the parties asks an appellate (or supreme) court to give finality to the answer. In 1883, with a wide cast of rich, powerful, and somewhat bizarre characters, a legal conflict began that instigated at least 100 separate proceedings, both criminal and civil. It lasted for almost a decade and created more precedents than any case in American jurisprudence had before it and perhaps has since.(1) This chapter recounts the intersecting stories of the scorned Sarah Althea Hill Terry, former Senator William Sharon, former California Chief Justice David Terry, and former U.S. Supreme Court Justice Stephen Field. As it happens, it is also the grand story of some fascinating precedents in American law.

Once upon a Time

William Sharon, the U.S. Senator for the state of Nevada between 1875 and 1881, lived a relatively charmed existence for most of his life. He was born in 1821 in Ohio, went to college, became a lawyer, moved to California in 1849, and invested in real estate. He acquired significant holdings, became a banker, and then moved to Nevada in 1864 to manage a new branch of a bank in which he owned a significant interest. He served six years in the U.S. Senate until 1881, and right after that his life became more than interesting.

As seems to be the case with some men of wealth and power (see Appendix A, re Spitzer), Sharon's life lost some of its perfect charm following a sexual indiscretion. After Sharon's wife of many years died, he took a mistress by the name of Sarah Althea Hill—subsequently referred to as the "Rose of Sharon" in newspapers of the day. In 1880, Sarah Althea Hill (called Althea or Allie by those who were close to her) was considered quite beautiful, and Sharon was sufficiently taken with her to form a liaison and move her into a suite in the Grand Hotel, one of several San Francisco hotels he owned. He was still serving as the U.S. Senator from Nevada at this time, so presumably love blossomed as much in his absence as in his presence

for many of the first months of their affair. He wrote several letters to her of an affectionate nature, with the salutation "Dear Allie" or "Dear Miss Hill" preceding the content. In late 1881, however, when Sharon's Senatorial responsibilities were coming to an end, the affair became stormy and contentious.

Althea was disinclined to let the relationship go and would not leave voluntarily, so Sharon had her evicted from the Grand Hotel in dramatic fashion in December 1881. He gave her $7500 (the equivalent of approximately $150,000 today), and she signed a receipt marked "paid in full."(2) History indicates that he did not demonstrate an inclination to go without the companionship of a woman for any length of time, and the next mistress moved in shortly thereafter.

Althea tried for several years after her eviction to get back together with Sharon, but to no avail. Her closest friend in San Francisco was an African-American woman who went by the name Mammy Pleasant, and who apparently practiced voodoo. She tried to help Althea use that black art to reunite the lovers. Although Mammy Pleasant's power in the art of voodoo was insufficient to bring William Sharon back to Althea, evidence suggests that she came up with an alternative plan. Mammy (with the unwitting help of her attorney friend George Tyler) helped Althea develop a story that she and Sharon were secretly married, and that Althea was entitled to a divorce. This would mean she was also entitled to alimony and a share of Sharon's fortune.

A contract of marriage dated August 25, 1880, (later adjudicated in federal court to be a forgery) was brought first to the press, together with letters that Sharon had sent to Althea during their affair, slightly altered to read "Dear Wife" instead of "Dear Allie."

This seemingly shallow trick instigated years of litigation and ended in nothing less than murder and madness. Such is the stuff that sets enduring precedents.

The First Lawsuits

Sharon was appalled at the assertions (and financial demands) made by his former mistress, and he refused to consider any settlement of the matter. Things started to accelerate out of control when a warrant was issued for Sharon's arrest for the crime of adultery, and he was forced to pay $5,000 bail. At that time, adultery was a criminal offense, and Althea's claim of marriage, if true, made crimes out of Sharon's relationships with his subsequent mistresses.

Althea was the beautiful darling of the press. She claimed that all she wanted was to be formally acknowledged as the "Sen's wife." He was rich, ruthless, and the target of envy. In the press, she was the winner, hands down.

An outraged Sharon filed a complaint against Althea in federal court, asking that the marriage contract be declared a forgery. The complaint was filed in October 1883. A month later, Althea sued Sharon for divorce in the Superior Court of California.

Technically, both the California state court and the federal court had jurisdiction over the claims that were respectively filed with them. Sharon claimed he was a citizen of Nevada, and, under federal diversity jurisdiction, he had the right to file a federal claim. There is a right of "removal" from state to federal court in most controversies where the litigants are all from different states, and the dollar amount of the controversy meets a statutory minimum. During the time of this case, the amount in controversy needed to be $3,000. Although today the amount must exceed $75,000, there was so much money at risk in the Sharon/Hill case that it even exceeded today's minimums without any adjustment for inflation.

For reasons beyond the scope of this chapter, there is no jurisdiction in federal court for an action for divorce. Two separate courts had independent jurisdiction to adjudicate the underlying facts of this dispute.

By 1884 there were at least six different lawsuits and criminal actions that had been brought, all of which stalled as the state divorce action proceeded. In addition to the adultery charges against Sharon, concurrent with the divorce and fraud actions, a federal grand jury had indicted Althea with criminal charges of perjury, forgery, and conspiracy. The reporter who "broke" the story to the press after unsuccessfully trying to get money from Sharon was also charged with perjury in federal court. In response, he filed a slander suit against Sharon. Civil and criminal actions were significantly more intertwined at that time in American jurisprudence than they are today.

Althea's lawyers were clever. They successfully used every technique legally available to stall all federal proceedings until they adjudicated their claim in state court. The divorce trial began in March 1884 and continued for ten months until the day before Christmas that year. Althea's answer to the federal charges was not even filed until after the state trial ended.

On the day after Althea's divorce action began, attorney David Terry became a member of her defense team. She could not have found a more aggressive advocate nor, for that matter, a better character for this story.

David Terry

With so much money at stake, and so much press both in her behalf and against an unpopular Sharon, Althea assembled a dream team of attorneys that even O.J. Simpson would envy. David Terry was to play the most significant role, both on her team and in her life, from the minute he became involved in her case.

Terry was a perfect lawyer for the wild, wild West. He was physically large—over six feet three inches tall, weighing 220 pounds. Born in 1823, he "read" the law (which essentially means he studied it independently while working in a law office) and was admitted to the Texas state bar at the age of 22, in 1845.

Though Terry was brilliant, he was also a violent man. Dow Votaw's research (2) indicates that between 1849 and 1855, there are accounts of several incidents of assault committed by Terry with a knife or an axe. Despite this, or perhaps in deference to it, Terry was elected to the California Supreme Court in 1855. He stabbed a man named Sterling Hopkins a year after that appointment, but the man survived, and no sentence was imposed. Votaw opines that had Hopkins died, Terry would have been hanged.

Despite all the violence, or again perhaps because of it, Terry became the Chief Justice of the California Supreme Court in 1859. This is a testament to his political acumen, his intelligence, and the fact that the West was really that wild. The position of Chief Justice did not serve to mitigate Terry's tendency to violence. He stepped down a year later in order to fight a duel with U.S. Senator David C. Broderick, whom he killed in that altercation. Broderick was an anti-slavery Republican, and Terry was a pro-slavery Democrat. The duel was the result of hostile words between them on the slavery issue. Terry was acquitted of all charges related to the incident.

Of significance is that Broderick was close friends with another California Supreme Court Justice by the name of Stephen Field. Stephen Field was a bright and strong-willed jurist who served on the California Supreme Court both prior to and while Terry was Chief Justice. Field remained a California justice until 1863 when Abraham Lincoln appointed him to the U.S. Supreme Court, on which he served for almost 35 years. Field despised Terry for both his political views and for his killing of Broderick.

Adding fuel to the fire, Terry later helped defeat Field's bid for a presidential nomination. Field turned out ultimately to be the source of Terry's downfall, but that will be discussed at more length later in the story.

Despite his propensity for violence, by 1880 Terry had assumed a more unifying statesmanlike role in California politics and legal practice. He was a successful lawyer, and (as noted earlier) became a member of Althea's defense team in 1884.

This trial was a forum well-suited to Terry in many ways. Witnesses, parties, and attorneys came to court armed, and weapons were brandished along with rhetoric during the proceedings. Testimony was lurid, covering everything from the dried pigeon Althea wore around her neck as a voodoo charm to try and re-win Sharon's affection to the ungentlemanly manner by which Sharon threw Althea out of the Grand Hotel. The media reported daily on the trial.

Terry's Brilliant Strategy

David Terry knew that Sharon was rich and powerful with the ability to file an appeal of an unfavorable judgment and stall its imposition interminably. Consequently, in addition to continuing the strategy of delaying federal action, Terry figured out a brilliant strategy with which to proceed in the California case. He made a motion for temporary alimony and attorney

fees after the trial was concluded but prior to the decree being entered.

This move was clever in both timing and purpose. Judge Sullivan, the California trial court judge in the divorce action, had indicated that his judgment would favor Althea. Despite his finding that Althea had lied significantly during the trial, he found her fundamental assertion of the existence of a marriage to be truthful, and he announced his intention to find in her behalf on Christmas Eve 1884. However, his judgment was not entered as a decree for almost two months (this is an administrative function that often took several months in those days). Taking advantage of that interim period between the Christmas Eve announcement and the filing of the decree from which an appeal could be taken by Sharon, Terry made his motion for temporary support in January 1885.

Terry's aggressive legal strategy was going forward at the same time he suffered a personal tragedy. Having been a loyal family man through all of his life, he suffered the death of his wife in early 1885. This will become a significant part of the story a bit later.

Final judgments can be appealed and stayed (held in abeyance) pending appeal, but interlocutory (or temporary) judgments were not subject to appeal at that time. Specifically, temporary orders for alimony could not be appealed, nor could orders for interim attorney fees. A temporary order could go on until the decree became final with all appeals exhausted, without any appellate review on its own merits.

Judge Sullivan issued a temporary order for spousal support in the amount of $2500 per month to support Althea pending a final adjudication of the case, and attorney fees in the amount of $60,000 pending a final determination of total fees. This was an incredible sum (the modern equiva-

lent of $50,000 per month for alimony, and almost $200,000 for just interim attorney fees). Sharon had only paid Althea $500 per month for her support when she was his supposed wife. In addition, her attorneys were operating strictly on a contingency fee basis (no longer permissible in California divorce cases), and were only entitled to a percentage of the final judgment. They had no right to interlocutory or interim fees under their contract with Althea.

Although the basis for the interlocutory award was very arguable, the matter was (at least in theory) not subject to appeal. Terry counted on that loophole with initial success.

Just days after entering this generous temporary order, Judge Sullivan entered his final decree from which an appeal was immediately taken. Judge Sullivan was adamant that, pending appeal, Sharon pay the temporary alimony and attorney fees. However, Sharon's lawyers acted persuasively on their client's moral outrage. Their appeal to the California Supreme Court commingled both the temporary orders and the final decree. Even though the temporary order was technically not subject to appeal, the California Supreme Court set a new precedent and stayed the implementation of the temporary order and the permanent decree pending appeal. With that new precedent, *interlocutory orders in California courts became subject to appeal under extraordinary circumstances*. This remains the law today.

Meanwhile, Sharon's federal action was finally moving forward.

Making a Federal Case of It

As noted earlier, even though it was filed first, the federal case did not begin until after the California trial court had entered its decree. Terry tried to get the federal matter thrown out altogether on the grounds that California had already adjudicated the divorce, so the matter was moot (not legally relevant). The federal court refused to give up jurisdiction, noting that its action had begun prior to the filing of the California case. It would not advantage Althea's attorneys for their dilatory (delaying) tactics. A second trial on the validity of Althea's marriage contract was underway.

Federal courts at that time operated very differently than they do today. *Sharon v. Hill* had actually been filed in the Federal Circuit Court rather than a Federal District Court as would happen today. Federal Circuit Courts functioned in different ways depending upon the territory and were not exclusively for appeals at that time. More interesting in this case, testimony was not heard by either of the judges who rendered an opinion. Instead, an Examiner listened to the witnesses in deposition-like hearings, with hand-scripted court reports of the testimony for judges to review later.

By the time the federal hearings began in front of the court Examiner, Althea had become more erratic in her already odd behavior. She came to court each day with a small black satchel. In that satchel she carried a small black gun, which she would remove from the satchel and point threateningly when the proceedings appeared to be adverse to her interests. She alternately pointed the gun at hostile witnesses, Sharon's attorneys, and at the Examiner himself when things were not going well for her. She accompanied the physical gesture with disruptive and histrionic threats. Though Terry verbally defended her conduct, other members of her defense team actually joined in with threatening words of their own.

Even in 1885, carrying a gun and using it to intimidate witnesses in a federal court proceeding was illegal, but the Examiner was somewhat powerless, being something like a clerk in judicial stature. In August 1885, Althea's violent outbursts became so threatening that the Examiner was forced to suspend hearings, and the matter was brought before the Presiding Justice of the Circuit Court. That presiding judge was Justice Stephen Field, archenemy of the same David Terry who was now actively participating with Althea's defense team, although at this point less violently than his client.

It would never have occurred to anyone that Field should recuse himself based on a significant personal conflict with an attorney in the case. In fact, Field never admitted personal animus, although the newspaper accounts of their mutual dislike provides significant evidence to that effect.

How it was that Field, now a U.S. Supreme Court Justice, was the presiding judge of the Circuit Court is a matter of interesting judicial history. In those days, a Justice's appointment to the U.S. Supreme Court carried with it the obligation to "ride a Circuit" and adjudicate proceedings and appeals on the road for part of the year. Justice Field was fulfilling this part of his judicial obligation when the Sharon/Hill matter came before him.

Justice Field ordered that Althea be disarmed, forcibly if necessary, and that for the remainder of the proceedings a U.S. Marshall sit beside her and keep her under control. The federal proceedings were concluded on September 29, 1885. The next day William Sharon died, never knowing what the federal court would decide. The story, however, most certainly did not end with his demise.

In December 1885, two months after the federal case concluded, and al-most exactly one year after Judge Sullivan had indicated he would enter a judgment in favor of Althea, two federal judges (neither of whom was Justice Field) found that the marriage documents were forged. Those federal judges entered a decree in favor of the now-deceased William Sharon. The judges particularly blamed Mammy Pleasant for the entire fraud, referring to her as a "scheming, trafficking, crafty old woman."

Neither Terry nor other members of Althea's defense team appealed the federal court's decision, although later Terry claimed he had filed appeal papers that were lost in the federal system. At the time of the judgment, however, it is quite possible that Terry and the other defense attorneys were not overly concerned with the federal matter because California was not deferring to that court's power. The California case was moving forward, and Terry reasonably could have believed that Judge Sullivan's decree would be upheld.

But something else might have distracted Terry from attention to the legal proceedings at the time. One month after the conclusion of the federal trial, in January 1886, David Terry married Sarah Althea Hill.

Rulings and Reversals

Although Sharon was now dead, his son elected to pursue the fight in his father's place. He partially blamed his father's death on the outrageous accusations that Althea had levied against him. Knowing his father would never have conceded, the son vowed to continue the passionate fight.

Terry, on the other hand, was now a husband who perceived his role not only as Althea's legal counsel, but as the defender of his wife's honor. In every facet, this lawsuit was now personal for him.

Things remained relatively quiet for two years while the California appeal rested in the state Supreme Court. In January 1888, the dreams of David Terry and Althea Hill Terry appeared to come true. The California Supreme Court affirmed Judge Sullivan's decision in favor of Althea. The only alteration the California Supreme Court made to Judge Sullivan's decree was that the alimony be reduced to $500 per month. Althea's share in Sharon's estate would be so much larger than the alimony award, the Terrys were totally unconcerned. Alimony would have stopped at the date of their marriage to each other anyway.

Following this apparent victory for the Terrys, the administrator of Sharon's estate filed a petition in March 1888 to revive the federal decision that had been entered just after Sharon's death. That petition also made a procedural request that would be devastating to the Terrys if granted. It asked that the decision of the court in which the first action was filed (which was federal court, because Sharon's initial complaint preceded Althea's by a month) should govern the outcomes in both the federal and state actions.

At this point, Althea's luck in terms of favorable court decisions began to

evaporate. The revived federal case was heard by none other than Justice Stephen Field. The Terrys came to the courthouse August 14, 1888, to hear that Field would revive the federal decree claiming the marriage contract was forged and use the opportunity to enjoin the California courts from exercising any jurisdiction over the matter.

Chaos in the Courtroom

As one might imagine, Althea did not take the reading of Judge Field's decision very well. Screaming at Judge Field before he could complete the reading of his opinion, she loudly demanded to know for how much he had been bought by the Sharons. According to newspaper accounts, she then appeared to lose all control.

Field ordered her removed from the courtroom, and then Terry joined the fray prohibiting any man from touching his wife. Althea seemed to be reaching in her little black satchel (where her trusty gun was located), when Marshalls had no choice but to grab her. Terry had to be subdued by several Marshalls until his wife was safely out of the courtroom. As soon as they released him, he grabbed a nine-inch-long knife from his pocket and went chasing after those who were restraining her.

A diminutive man by the name of David Neagle managed to wrest the knife out of Terry's hand while Marshalls simultaneously were attempting to restrain him. As far as any records reflect, Neagle had no formal role in the proceedings, and his presence is not something readily explained. What is known is that Terry's reputation preceded him, and all those who knew him and Althea rightfully feared that there might be violence at the reading of Field's opinion. Many were on hand to try and control the situation.

After the violent outbursts and attempted assaults in his courtroom, Field sentenced both Althea and Terry to jail for contempt of court. Her sentence was for 30 days, his was for six months. The jail terms served to accelerate the deterioration of Althea's mind and to exacerbate Terry's already enormous rage. He loudly proclaimed (and the newspapers all reported his comments) that he would have Field horsewhipped, and if Field protested that, he would then kill him. His threats were heard by many, and some say encouraged.

Terry appealed both his and Althea's sentences, but to no avail. Although he had friends on the U.S. Supreme Court, his effort to get his sentence overturned was rebuked. His request to then-President Cleveland for a commutation was ignored. He was not even let out a month early for good behavior as was the custom. The actual reasons for that are unknown, but he blamed Field for that as well.

Continuing the Fight

Throughout the jail term and following into the middle of 1889, the Terrys continued to fight. In January 1889, while David Terry was still in jail, Althea moved to have a receiver (third party) appointed to take charge of the Sharon estate in her behalf.

Because of the federal injunction issued by Field prohibiting California from exercising any jurisdiction over the matter, Althea was forced to continue the legal battle without Terry's formal representation even after he was released from jail. Neither Terry nor the other lawyers could appear with her for fear that Field would have them all arrested and thrown in jail for contempt of court for ignoring his injunction. Instead, the lawyers advised her in the background. On June 3rd, she appeared to have some success. Judge Sullivan granted her request for a receiver on that day, ignoring the federal injunction.

Notwithstanding that apparent victory, Judge Sullivan was treading on thin ice. A month prior to his appointing the receiver for Althea, the U.S. Supreme Court had affirmed Field's decision and established the federal court's right to enjoin (stop) the state from taking further action in the case. This ruling set the precedent that *in a case where there is an unreconciled conflict between concurrent state and federal jurisdiction, the forum where the first complaint was filed will govern.*

The California Supreme Court did not wait for Sullivan's order to be appealed by Sharon's people. Instead, in an unusual resurrection of an old appeal, they reviewed unresolved matters stemming from Sharon's appeal of

Judge Sullivan's 1885 refusal to grant him a new trial. On July 17, 1889, the California Supreme Court decided to functionally overturn their earlier decision, citing (rather belatedly) a California statute that invalidated secret marriages. Althea's hopes for a share in the Sharon estate were dashed.

California Wasn't Big Enough for the Both of Them

At this point, all who knew both Field and Terry knew that Field had reason to fear. The Terrys issued threat after threat, the newspapers reported quotes voraciously, and the matter garnered significant speculation and gossip. The attorney general of the United States cautioned Field not to travel to northern California until tempers calmed, but Field refused to even consider such a notion. He was encouraged to carry a gun, but declined that as well. However, he agreed to have a deputized U.S. Marshall accompany him for his own protection. The person chosen for this auspicious job was David Neagle, the man in the federal courthouse who had wrested the knife from the hands of an enraged David Terry in the incident that led to Terry's incarceration for contempt.

Neagle was an interesting choice for bodyguard. Though the courtroom altercation had demonstrated his bravery, Neagle's probability of success in a physical one-on-one with Terry was limited. Neagle was only five feet five inches tall and weighed 135 pounds. Terry, on the other hand, was a comparative Goliath. Standing six feet three inches tall and weighing 220 pounds, he had proven to be a physical force of significance. He was also passionately angry. He was not likely to be physically subdued by a man of Neagle's stature.

Neagle had other credentials, however. He had been a Sheriff in the rough town of Tombstone, Arizona, during the days of Wyatt Earp. He had managed to keep order with his fast draw and accurate shooting. He was really good with a gun.

In the early morning of August 14, 1889, Field and Neagle were on a train bound from Los Angeles to San Francisco when the train stopped in Fresno to pick up and let off passengers. Neagle saw that the Terrys got on the train at that stop, although it was unlikely that the Terrys knew that Field was also a passenger. The train continued on to the small town of Lathrop, and Justice Field decided that he wanted to have breakfast in the dining room at that train station. Neagle allegedly made a serious effort to discourage him, but Field acted obliviously and insisted he would prefer the breakfast in the dining room. Later, pro-Terry reporters would opine that Field intentionally set up what was to follow.

Accounts consistently indicate that Althea immediately saw Justice Field when the Terrys entered the dining room. Neagle claimed he then watched her run out of the dining room believing she left to get her black satchel and gun. While she was gone, Terry did not appear to notice Field right away, but when he did, he walked up to behind where Field was sitting and witnesses say he punched the Justice in the back of the head twice. How he was allowed to get that close or strike those blows was never explained. Field was supposedly stunned, but Neagle was not. He took out his gun and shot Terry dead on the spot.

Althea was back in the dining room when her husband fell down dead. She threw herself over his body and when she got up, she yelled to the crowd that her husband had been unarmed and had been murdered by Field and his deputy.

Though Neagle claimed that Terry was about to draw his knife, it was never determined that Terry even had a knife—none was ever found on his body. Field supporters argued that Althea removed the weapon when she threw herself over her husband's body; that conjecture was never proven.

Although Terry had physically assaulted Field with some punches, Field was virtually unscathed. There was consequently a legal case that excessive force had been used by Neagle. As was Althea's assertion, it was also argued that Justice Field had intentionally set up Terry for the shooting.

In the train station, Althea was a woman in despair who was demanding justice of the trainmaster. He consequently sent telegrams to the San Fran-

cisco area advising authorities about what had happened. When the train stopped in Oakland, California, a detective met the train to arrest Field and Neagle. However Field's friends anticipated what might happen, and arranged for the U.S. Marshall to also meet the train. Another federal/state showdown occurred, with the U.S. Marshall telling the Oakland detective that he would himself be arrested if he dared to seize Field.

Several days later, Althea was able to get warrants issued for the arrest of both Field and Neagle for the murder of her husband. Field arranged to submit to authorities in the federal courthouse, and accepted the service of the warrant for his arrest respectfully. He sat down and invited the sheriff to have a seat as well. The sheriff did as he was requested. A petition had already been drafted in anticipation, and a writ of habeas corpus (which in this case means an order to release the prisoner) was signed by the federal judge in charge within minutes. The writ was served upon the sheriff who had been sitting and waiting at Field's request and Field was never actually taken into custody. A day or two later, the sitting governor of the State of California asked the district attorney to drop all charges, and the matter never proceeded to any formal hearing.

Neagle was arrested, but custody was immediately taken by the U.S. Marshall. His case was quickly dismissed by the U.S. Circuit Court on the grounds that he could not be held liable for "an act done in pursuance of a law of the United States." The matter was appealed by San Francisco authorities, and the U.S. Supreme Court upheld the decision with two justices dissenting.

Justice Field presented Neagle with a solid gold watch the day after he was released from all charges. The watch was inscribed with a statement of "appreciation of his courage and fidelity to duty under circumstances of great peril…." Clearly, Field did not mourn the death of his former adversary.

This U.S. Supreme Court precedent stands today; *a U.S. Marshall cannot be held liable for "an act done in pursuance of a law of the United States" and is outside the jurisdiction of state courts*.(3) The precedent is still taught in criminal law classes, though few students know the story that gave rise to the decision.

The Final Days of Sarah Althea Hill

On Monday, March 1, 1937, an article appeared in *Time Magazine* with a brief summary of the story above. It began:

"In a Stockton, California, insane asylum last week died a fat old woman with wild white hair and a lame hip. She had been locked up for nearly half a century, happily certain that she was a great, rich lady, babbling endlessly about her memories. She could never keep her story straight, sometimes asserting that she had been married to President Lincoln and General Grant, or that the King of Italy was her foster father, or that she owned the Republic of Guatemala. But the daft old crone was not to be pitied, for she had lived greatly once and her true story was almost as fabulous as her imaginings."(4)

According to the *Time Magazine* article, two years after David Terry was killed, Sarah Althea walked out onto the streets of San Francisco "in a ballroom dress at high noon, eyes blank, lips babbling…." Votaw (2) reports that she was committed to the California State Hospital for the Insane in March 1892, and her commitment papers were signed by someone who had remained at her side through her final and complete descent into madness—Mammy Pleasant.

Note

1. Stephen J. Field and George C. Gorham, *Personal Reminiscences of Early Days in California with Other Sketches*, Dodo Press, (2007).

2. Dow Votaw, "Judicial Vendetta: California Style," *The Western Political Quarterly* 12:4 (1959).

3. *In re Neagle* 135 U.S. 1 (1890).

4. "Mad Memories," *Time*, March 1, 1937, online: http://www.time.com/time/magazine/article/0,9171,757303-2,00.html

Appendix C
The Constitution of the United States of America

Preamble

We the people of the United States, in order to form a more perfect union, establish justice, insure domestic tranquility, provide for the common defense, promote the general welfare, and secure the blessings of liberty to ourselves and our posterity, do ordain and establish this Constitution for the United States of America.

Article I

Section 1. All legislative powers herein granted shall be vested in a Congress of the United States, which shall consist of a Senate and House of Representatives.

Section 2. The House of Representatives shall be composed of members chosen every second year by the people of the several states, and the electors in each state shall have the qualifications requisite for electors of the most numerous branch of the state legislature.

No person shall be a Representative who shall not have attained to the age of twenty five years, and been seven years a citizen of the United States, and who shall not, when elected, be an inhabitant of that state in which he shall be chosen.

Representatives and direct taxes shall be apportioned among the several states which may be included within this union, according to their respective numbers, which shall be determined by adding to the whole number of free persons, including those bound to service for a term of years, and excluding Indians not taxed, three fifths of all other Persons. The actual Enumeration shall be made within three years after the first meeting of the Congress of the United States, and within every subsequent term of ten years, in such manner as they shall by law direct. The number of Representatives shall not exceed one for every thirty thousand, but each state shall have at least one Representative; and until such enumeration shall be made, the state of New Hampshire shall be entitled to choose three, Massachusetts eight, Rhode Island and Providence Plantations one, Connecticut five, New York six, New Jersey four, Pennsylvania eight, Delaware one, Maryland six, Virginia ten, North Carolina five, South Carolina five, and Georgia three.

When vacancies happen in the Representation from any state, the executive authority thereof shall issue writs of election to fill such vacancies.

The House of Representatives shall choose their speaker and other officers; and shall have the sole power of impeachment.

Section 3. The Senate of the United States shall be composed of two Senators from each state, chosen by the legislature thereof, for six years; and each Senator shall have one vote.

Immediately after they shall be assembled in consequence of the first election, they shall be divided as equally as may be into three classes. The seats of the Senators of the first class shall be vacated at the expiration of the second year, of the second class at the expiration of the fourth year, and the third class at the expiration of the sixth year, so that one third may be chosen every second year; and if vacancies happen by resignation, or otherwise, during the recess of the legislature of any state, the executive thereof may make temporary appointments until the next meeting of the legislature, which shall then fill such vacancies.

No person shall be a Senator who shall not have attained to the age of thirty years, and been nine years a citizen of the United States and who shall not, when elected, be an inhabitant of that state for which he shall be chosen.

The Vice President of the United States shall be President of the Senate, but shall have no vote, unless they be equally divided.

The Senate shall choose their other officers, and also a President pro tempore, in the absence of the Vice President, or when he shall exercise the office of President of the United States.

The Senate shall have the sole power to try all impeachments. When sitting for that purpose, they shall be on oath or affirmation. When the President of the United States is tried, the Chief Justice shall preside: And no person shall be convicted without the concurrence of two thirds of the members present.

Judgment in cases of impeachment shall not extend further than to removal from office, and disqualification to hold and enjoy any office of honor, trust or profit under the United States: but the party convicted shall nevertheless be liable and subject to indictment, trial, judgment and punishment, according to law.

Section 4. The times, places and manner of holding elections for Senators and Representatives, shall be prescribed in each state by the legislature thereof; but the Congress may at any time by law make or alter such regulations, except as to the places of choosing Senators.

The Congress shall assemble at least once in every year, and such meeting shall be on the first Monday in December, unless they shall by law appoint a different day.

Section 5. Each House shall be the judge of the elections, returns and qualifications of its own members, and a majority of each shall constitute a quorum to do business; but a smaller number may adjourn from day to day, and may be authorized to compel the attendance of absent members, in such manner, and under such penalties as each House may provide.

Each House may determine the rules of its proceedings, punish its members for disorderly behavior, and, with the concurrence of two thirds, expel a member.

Each House shall keep a journal of its proceedings, and from time to time publish the same, excepting such parts as may in their judgment require secrecy; and the yeas and nays of the members of either House on any question shall, at the desire of one fifth of those present, be entered on the journal.

Neither House, during the session of Congress, shall, without the consent of the other, adjourn for more than three days, nor to any other place than that in which the two Houses shall be sitting.

Section 6. The Senators and Representatives shall receive a compensation for their services, to be ascertained by law, and paid out of the treasury of the United States. They shall in all cases, except treason, felony and breach of the peace, be privileged from arrest during their attendance at the session of their respective Houses, and in going to and returning from the same; and for any speech or debate in either House, they shall not be questioned in any other place.

No Senator or Representative shall, during the time for which he was elected, be appointed to any civil office under the authority of the

United States, which shall have been created, or the emoluments whereof shall have been increased during such time: and no person holding any office under the United States, shall be a member of either House during his continuance in office.

Section 7. All bills for raising revenue shall originate in the House of Representatives; but the Senate may propose or concur with amendments as on other Bills.

Every bill which shall have passed the House of Representatives and the Senate, shall, before it become a law, be presented to the President of the United States; if he approve he shall sign it, but if not he shall return it, with his objections to that House in which it shall have originated, who shall enter the objections at large on their journal, and proceed to reconsider it. If after such reconsideration two thirds of that House shall agree to pass the bill, it shall be sent, together with the objections, to the other House, by which it shall likewise be reconsidered, and if approved by two thirds of that House, it shall become a law. But in all such cases the votes of both Houses shall be determined by yeas and nays, and the names of the persons voting for and against the bill shall be entered on the journal of each House respectively. If any bill shall not be returned by the President within ten days (Sundays excepted) after it shall have been presented to him, the same shall be a law, in like manner as if he had signed it, unless the Congress by their adjournment prevent its return, in which case it shall not be a law.

Every order, resolution, or vote to which the concurrence of the Senate and House of Representatives may be necessary (except on a question of adjournment) shall be presented to the President of the United States; and before the same shall take effect, shall be approved by him, or being disapproved by him, shall be repassed by two thirds of the Senate and House of Representatives, according to the rules and limitations prescribed in the case of a bill.

Section 8. The Congress shall have power to lay and collect taxes, duties, imposts and excises, to pay the debts and provide for the common defense and general welfare of the United States; but all duties, imposts and excises shall be uniform throughout the United States;

To borrow money on the credit of the United States;

To regulate commerce with foreign nations, and among the several states, and with the Indian tribes;

To establish a uniform rule of naturalization, and uniform laws on the subject of bankruptcies throughout the United States;

To coin money, regulate the value thereof, and of foreign coin, and fix the standard of weights and measures;

To provide for the punishment of counterfeiting the securities and current coin of the United States;

To establish post offices and post roads;

To promote the progress of science and useful arts, by securing for limited times to authors and inventors the exclusive right to their respective writings and discoveries;

To constitute tribunals inferior to the Supreme Court;

To define and punish piracies and felonies committed on the high seas, and offenses against the law of nations;

To declare war, grant letters of marque and reprisal, and make rules concerning captures on land and water;

To raise and support armies, but no appropriation of money to that use shall be for a longer term than two years;

To provide and maintain a navy;

To make rules for the government and regulation of the land and naval forces;

To provide for calling forth the militia to execute the laws of the union, suppress insurrections and repel invasions;

To provide for organizing, arming, and disciplining, the militia, and for governing such part of them as may be employed in the service of the United States, reserving to the states respectively, the appointment of the officers, and the authority of training the militia according to the discipline prescribed by Congress;

To exercise exclusive legislation in all cases whatsoever, over such District (not exceeding ten miles square) as may, by cession of particular states, and the acceptance of Congress, become the seat of the government of the United States, and to exercise like authority over all places purchased by the consent of the legislature of the state in which the same shall be, for the erection of forts, magazines, arsenals, dockyards, and other needful buildings;--And

To make all laws which shall be necessary and proper for carrying into execution the foregoing powers, and all other powers vested by this Constitution in the government of the United States, or in any department or officer thereof.

Section 9. The migration or importation of such persons as any of the states now existing shall think proper to admit, shall not be prohibited by the Congress prior to the year one thousand eight hundred and eight, but a tax or duty may be imposed on such importation, not exceeding ten dollars for each person.

The privilege of the writ of habeas corpus shall not be suspended, unless when in cases of rebellion or invasion the public safety may require it.

No bill of attainder or ex post facto Law shall be passed.

No capitation, or other direct, tax shall be laid, unless in proportion to the census or enumeration herein before directed to be taken.

No tax or duty shall be laid on articles exported from any state.

No preference shall be given by any regulation of commerce or revenue to the ports of one state over those of another: nor shall vessels bound to, or from, one state, be obliged to enter, clear or pay duties in another.

No money shall be drawn from the treasury, but in consequence of appropriations made by law; and a regular statement and account of receipts and expenditures of all public money shall be published from time to time.

No title of nobility shall be granted by the United States: and no person holding any office of profit or trust under them, shall, without the consent of the Congress, accept of any present, emolument, office, or title, of any kind whatever, from any king, prince, or foreign state.

Section 10. No state shall enter into any treaty, alliance, or confederation; grant letters of marque and reprisal; coin money; emit bills of credit; make anything but gold and silver coin a tender in payment of debts; pass any bill of attainder, ex post facto law, or law impairing the obligation of contracts, or grant any title of nobility.

No state shall, without the consent of the Congress, lay any imposts or duties on imports or exports, except what may be absolutely necessary for executing it's inspection laws: and the net produce of all duties and imposts, laid by any state on imports or exports, shall be for the use of the treasury of the United States; and all such laws shall be subject to the revision and control of the Congress.

No state shall, without the consent of Congress, lay any duty of tonnage, keep troops, or ships of war in time of peace, enter into any agreement or compact with another state, or with a foreign power, or engage in war, unless actually invaded, or in such imminent danger as will not admit of delay.

Article II

Section 1. The executive power shall be vested in a President of the United States of America. He shall hold his office during the term of four years, and, together with the Vice President, chosen for the same term, be elected, as follows:

Each state shall appoint, in such manner as the Legislature thereof may direct, a number of electors, equal to the whole number of Senators and Representatives to which the State may be entitled in the Congress: but no Senator or Representative, or person holding an office of trust or profit under the United States, shall be appointed an elector.

The electors shall meet in their respective states, and vote by ballot for two persons, of whom one at least shall not be an inhabitant of the same state with themselves. And they shall make a list of all the persons voted for, and of the number of votes for each; which list they shall sign and certify, and transmit sealed to the seat of the government of the United States, directed to the President of the Senate. The President of the Senate shall, in the presence of the Senate and House of Representatives, open all the certificates, and the votes shall then be counted. The person having the greatest number of votes shall be the President, if such number be a majority of the whole number of electors appointed; and if there be more than one who have such majority, and have an equal number of votes, then the House of Representatives shall immediately choose by ballot one of them for President; and if no person have a majority, then from the five highest on the list the said House shall in like manner choose the President. But in choosing the President, the votes shall be taken by

States, the representation from each state having one vote; A quorum for this purpose shall consist of a member or members from two thirds of the states, and a majority of all the states shall be necessary to a choice. In every case, after the choice of the President, the person having the greatest number of votes of the electors shall be the Vice President. But if there should remain two or more who have equal votes, the Senate shall choose from them by ballot the Vice President.

The Congress may determine the time of choosing the electors, and the day on which they shall give their votes; which day shall be the same throughout the United States.

No person except a natural born citizen, or a citizen of the United States, at the time of the adoption of this Constitution, shall be eligible to the office of President; neither shall any person be eligible to that office who shall not have attained to the age of thirty five years, and been fourteen Years a resident within the United States.

In case of the removal of the President from office, or of his death, resignation, or inability to discharge the powers and duties of the said office, the same shall devolve on the Vice President, and the Congress may by law provide for the case of removal, death, resignation or inability, both of the President and Vice President, declaring what officer shall then act as President, and such officer shall act accordingly, until the disability be removed, or a President shall be elected.

The President shall, at stated times, receive for his services, a compensation, which shall neither be increased nor diminished during the period for which he shall have been elected, and he shall not receive within that period any other emolument from the United States, or any of them.

Before he enter on the execution of his office, he shall take the following oath or affirmation:--"I do solemnly swear (or affirm) that I will faithfully execute the office of President of the United States, and will to the best of my ability, preserve, protect and defend the Constitution of the United States."

Section 2. The President shall be commander in chief of the Army and Navy of the United States, and of the militia of the several states, when called into the actual service of the United States; he may require the opinion, in writing, of the principal officer in each of the executive departments, upon any subject relating to the duties of their respective offices, and he shall have power to grant reprieves and pardons for offenses against the United States, except in cases of impeachment.

He shall have power, by and with the advice and consent of the Senate, to make treaties, provided two thirds of the Senators present concur; and he shall nominate, and by and with the advice and consent of the Senate, shall appoint ambassadors, other public ministers and consuls, judges of the Supreme Court, and all other officers of the United States, whose appointments are not herein otherwise provided for, and which shall be established by law: but the Congress may by law vest the appointment of such inferior officers, as they think proper, in the President alone, in the courts of law, or in the heads of departments.

The President shall have power to fill up all vacancies that may happen during the recess of the Senate, by granting commissions which shall expire at the end of their next session.

Section 3. He shall from time to time give to the Congress information of the state of the union, and recommend to their consideration such measures as he shall judge necessary and expedient; he may, on extraordinary occasions, convene both Houses, or either of them, and in case of disagreement between them, with respect to the time of adjournment, he may adjourn them to such time as he shall think proper; he shall receive ambassadors and other public ministers; he shall take care that the laws be faithfully executed, and shall commission all the officers of the United States.

Section 4. The President, Vice President and all civil officers of the United States, shall be removed from office on impeachment for, and conviction of, treason, bribery, or other high crimes and misdemeanors.

Article III

Section 1. The judicial power of the United States, shall be vested in one Supreme Court, and in such inferior courts as the Congress may from time to time ordain and establish. The judges, both of the supreme and inferior courts, shall hold their offices during good behaviour, and shall, at stated times, receive for their services, a compensation, which shall not be diminished during their continuance in office.

Section 2. The judicial power shall extend to all cases, in law and equity, arising under this Constitution, the laws of the United States, and treaties made, or which shall be made, under their authority;--to all cases affecting ambassadors, other public ministers and consuls;--to all cases of admiralty and maritime jurisdiction;--to controversies to which the United States shall be a party;--to controversies between two or more states;--between a state and citizens of another state;--between citizens of different states;--between citizens of the same state claiming lands under grants of different states, and between a state, or the citizens thereof, and foreign states, citizens or subjects.

In all cases affecting ambassadors, other public ministers and consuls, and those in which a state shall be party, the Supreme Court shall have original jurisdiction. In all the other cases before mentioned, the Supreme Court shall have appellate jurisdiction, both as to law and fact, with such exceptions, and under such regulations as the Congress shall make.

The trial of all crimes, except in cases of impeachment, shall be by jury; and such trial shall be held in the state where the said crimes shall have been committed; but when not committed within any state, the trial shall be at such place or places as the Congress may by law have directed.

Section 3. Treason against the United States, shall consist only in levying war against them, or in adhering to their enemies, giving them aid and comfort. No person shall be convicted of treason unless on the testimony of two witnesses to the same overt act, or on confession in open court.

The Congress shall have power to declare the punishment of treason, but no attainder of treason shall work corruption of blood, or forfeiture except during the life of the person attainted.

Article IV

Section 1. Full faith and credit shall be given in each state to the public acts, records, and judicial proceedings of every other state. And the Congress may by general laws prescribe the manner in which such acts, records, and proceedings shall be proved, and the effect thereof.

Section 2. The citizens of each state shall be entitled to all privileges and immunities of citizens in the several states.

A person charged in any state with treason, felony, or other crime, who shall flee from justice, and be found in another state, shall on demand of the executive authority of the state from which he fled, be delivered up, to be removed to the state having jurisdiction of the crime.

No person held to service or labor in one state, under the laws thereof, escaping into another, shall, in consequence of any law or regulation therein, be discharged from such service or labor, but shall be delivered up on claim of the party to whom such service or labor may be due.

Section 3. New states may be admitted by the Congress into this union; but no new states shall be formed or erected within the jurisdiction of any other state; nor any state be formed by the junction of two or more states, or parts of states, without the consent of the legislatures of the states concerned as well as of the Congress.

The Congress shall have power to dispose of and make all needful rules and regulations respecting the territory or other property belonging to the United States; and nothing in this Constitution shall be so construed as to prejudice any claims of the United States, or of any particular state.

Section 4. The United States shall guarantee to every state in this union a republican form of government, and shall protect each of them against invasion; and on application of the legislature, or of the executive (when the legislature cannot be convened) against domestic violence.

Article V

The Congress, whenever two thirds of both houses shall deem it necessary, shall propose amendments to this Constitution, or, on the application of the legislatures of two thirds of the several states, shall call a convention for proposing amendments, which, in either case, shall be valid to all intents and purposes, as part of this Constitution, when ratified by the legislatures of three fourths of the several states, or by conventions in three fourths thereof, as the one or the other mode of ratification may be proposed by the Congress; provided that no amendment which may be made prior to the year one thousand eight hundred and eight shall in any manner affect the first and fourth clauses in the ninth section of the first article; and that no state, without its consent, shall be deprived of its equal suffrage in the Senate.

Article VI

All debts contracted and engagements entered into, before the adoption of this Constitution, shall be as valid against the United States under this Constitution, as under the Confederation.

This Constitution, and the laws of the United States which shall be made in pursuance thereof; and all treaties made, or which shall be made, under the authority of the United States, shall be the supreme law of the land; and the judges in every state shall be bound thereby, anything in the Constitution or laws of any State to the contrary notwithstanding.

The Senators and Representatives before mentioned, and the members of the several state legislatures, and all executive and judicial officers, both of the United States and of the several states, shall be bound by oath or affirmation, to support this Constitution; but no religious test shall ever be required as a qualification to any office or public trust under the United States.

Article VII

The ratification of the conventions of nine states, shall be sufficient for the establishment of this Constitution between the states so ratifying the same.

Amendment I

Congress shall make no law respecting an establishment of religion, or prohibiting the free exercise thereof; or abridging the freedom of speech, or of the press; or the right of the people peaceably to assemble, and to petition the government for a redress of grievances.

Amendment II

A well regulated militia, being necessary to the security of a free state, the right of the people to keep and bear arms, shall not be infringed.

Amendment III

No soldier shall, in time of peace be quartered in any house, without the consent of the owner, nor in time of war, but in a manner to be prescribed by law.

Amendment IV

The right of the people to be secure in their persons, houses, papers, and effects, against unreasonable searches and seizures, shall not be violated, and no warrants shall issue, but upon probable cause, supported by oath or affirmation, and particularly describing the place to be searched, and the persons or things to be seized.

Amendment V

No person shall be held to answer for a capital, or otherwise infamous crime, unless on a presentment or indictment of a grand jury, except in cases arising in the land or naval forces, or in the militia, when in actual service in time of war or public danger; nor shall any person be subject for the same offense to be twice put in jeopardy of life or limb; nor shall be compelled in any criminal case to be a witness against himself, nor be deprived of life, liberty, or property, without due process of law; nor shall private property be taken for public use, without just compensation.

Amendment VI

In all criminal prosecutions, the accused shall enjoy the right to a speedy and public trial, by an impartial jury of the state and district wherein the crime shall have been committed, which district shall have been previously ascertained by law, and to be informed of the nature and cause of the accusation; to be confronted with the witnesses against him; to have compulsory process for obtaining witnesses in his favor, and to have the assistance of counsel for his defense.

Amendment VII

In suits at common law, where the value in controversy shall exceed twenty dollars, the right of trial by jury shall be preserved, and no fact tried by a jury, shall be otherwise reexamined in any court of the United States, than according to the rules of the common law.

Amendment VIII

Excessive bail shall not be required, nor excessive fines imposed, nor cruel and unusual punishments inflicted.

Amendment IX

The enumeration in the Constitution, of certain rights, shall not be construed to deny or disparage others retained by the people.

Amendment X

The powers not delegated to the United States by the Constitution, nor prohibited by it to the states, are reserved to the states respectively, or to the people.

Amendment XI (1798)

The judicial power of the United States shall not be construed to extend to any suit in law or equity, commenced or prosecuted against one of the United States by citizens of another state, or by citizens or subjects of any foreign state.

Amendment XII (1804)

The electors shall meet in their respective states and vote by ballot for President and Vice-President, one of whom, at least, shall not be an inhabitant of the same state with themselves; they shall name in their ballots the person voted for as President, and in distinct ballots the person voted for as Vice-President, and they shall make distinct lists of all persons voted for as President, and of all persons voted for as Vice-President, and of the number of votes for each, which lists they shall sign and certify, and transmit sealed to the seat of the government of the United States, directed to the President of the Senate;- The President of the Senate shall, in the presence of the Senate and House of Representatives, open all the certificates and the votes shall then be counted;- the person having the greatest number of votes for President, shall be the President, if such number be a majority of the whole number of electors appointed; and if no person have such majority, then from the persons having the highest numbers not exceeding three on the list of those voted for as President, the House of Representatives shall choose immediately, by ballot, the President. But in choosing the President, the votes shall be taken by states, the representation from President shall act as President, as in the case of the death or other constitutional each state having one vote; a quorum for this purpose shall consist of a member or members from two-thirds of the states, and a majority of all the states shall be necessary to a choice. And if the House of Representatives shall not choose a President whenever the right of choice shall devolve upon them, before the fourth day of March next following, then the Vice-disability of the President. The person having the greatest number of votes as Vice-President, shall be the Vice-President, if such number be a majority of the whole number of electors appointed, and if no person have a majority, then from the two highest numbers on the list, the Senate shall choose the Vice-President; a quorum for the purpose shall consist of two-thirds of the whole number of Senators, and a majority of the whole number shall be necessary to a choice. But no person constitutionally ineligible to the office of President shall be eligible to that of Vice-President of the United States.

Amendment XIII (1865)

Section 1. Neither slavery nor involuntary servitude, except as a punishment for crime whereof the party shall have been duly convicted, shall exist within the United States, or any place subject to their jurisdiction.

Section 2. Congress shall have power to enforce this article by appropriate legislation.

Amendment XIV (1868)

Section 1. All persons born or naturalized in the United States, and subject to the jurisdiction thereof, are citizens of the United States and of the state wherein they reside. No state shall make or enforce any law which shall abridge the privileges or immunities of citizens of the United States; nor shall any state deprive any person of life, liberty, or property, without due process of law; nor deny to any person within its jurisdiction the equal protection of the laws.

Section 2. Representatives shall be apportioned among the several states according to their respective numbers, counting the whole number of persons in each state, excluding Indians not taxed. But when the right to vote at any election for the choice of electors for President and Vice President of the United States, Representatives in Congress, the executive and judicial officers of a state, or the members of the legislature thereof, is denied to any of the male inhabitants of such state, being twenty-one years of age, and citizens of the United States, or in any way abridged, except for participation in rebellion, or other crime, the basis of representation therein shall be reduced in the proportion which the number of such male citizens shall bear to the whole number of male citizens twenty-one years of age in such state.

Section 3. No person shall be a Senator or Representative in Congress, or elector of President and Vice President, or hold any office, civil or military, under the United States, or under any state, who, having previously taken an oath, as a member of Congress, or as an officer of the United States, or as a member of any state legislature, or as an executive or judicial officer of any state, to support the Constitution of the United States, shall have engaged in insurrection or rebellion against the same, or given aid or comfort to the enemies thereof. But Congress may by a vote of two-thirds of each House, remove such disability.

Section 4. The validity of the public debt of the United States, authorized by law, including debts incurred for payment of pensions and bounties for services in suppressing insurrection or rebellion, shall not be questioned. But neither the United States nor any state shall assume or pay any debt or obligation incurred in aid of insurrection or rebellion against the United States, or any claim for the loss or emancipation of any slave; but all such debts, obligations and claims shall be held illegal and void.

Section 5. The Congress shall have power to enforce, by appropriate legislation, the provisions of this article.

Amendment XV (1870)

Section 1. The right of citizens of the United States to vote shall not be denied or abridged by the United States or by any state on account of race, color, or previous condition of servitude.

Section 2. The Congress shall have power to enforce this article by appropriate legislation.

Amendment XVI (1913)

The Congress shall have power to lay and collect taxes on incomes, from whatever source derived, without apportionment among the several states, and without regard to any census or enumeration.

Amendment XVII (1913)

The Senate of the United States shall be composed of two Senators from each state, elected by the people thereof, for six years; and each Senator shall have one vote. The electors in each state shall have the qualifications requisite for electors of the most numerous branch of the state legislatures.

When vacancies happen in the representation of any state in the Senate, the executive authority of such state shall issue writs of election to fill such vacancies: Provided, that the legislature of any state may empower the executive thereof to make temporary appointments until the people fill the vacancies by election as the legislature may direct.

This amendment shall not be so construed as to affect the election or term of any Senator chosen before it becomes valid as part of the Constitution.

Amendment XVIII (1919)

Section 1. After one year from the ratification of this article the manufacture, sale, or transportation of intoxicating liquors within, the importation thereof into, or the exportation thereof from the United States and all territory subject to the jurisdiction thereof for beverage purposes is hereby prohibited.

Section 2. The Congress and the several states shall have concurrent power to enforce this article by appropriate legislation.

Section 3. This article shall be inoperative unless it shall have been ratified as an amendment to the Constitution by the legislatures of the several states, as provided in the Constitution, within seven years from the date of the submission hereof to the states by the Congress.

Amendment XIX (1920)

The right of citizens of the United States to vote shall not be denied or abridged by the United States or by any state on account of sex.

Congress shall have power to enforce this article by appropriate legislation.

Amendment XX (1933)

Section 1. The terms of the President and Vice President shall end at noon on the 20th day of January, and the terms of Senators and Representatives at noon on the 3d day of January, of the years in which such terms would have ended if this article had not been ratified; and the terms of their successors shall then begin.

Section 2. The Congress shall assemble at least once in every year, and such meeting shall begin at noon on the 3d day of January, unless they shall by law appoint a different day.

Section 3. If, at the time fixed for the beginning of the term of the President, the President elect shall have died, the Vice President elect shall become President. If a President shall not have been chosen before the time fixed for the beginning of his term, or if the President elect shall have failed to qualify, then the Vice President elect shall act as President until a President shall have qualified; and the Congress may by law provide for the case wherein neither a President elect nor a Vice President elect shall have qualified, declaring who shall then act as President, or the manner in which one who is to act shall be selected, and such person shall act accordingly until a President or Vice President shall have qualified.

Section 4. The Congress may by law provide for the case of the death of any of the persons from whom the House of Representatives may choose a President whenever the right of choice shall have devolved upon them, and for the case of the death of any of the persons from whom the Senate may choose a Vice President whenever the right of choice shall have devolved upon them.

Section 5. Sections 1 and 2 shall take effect on the 15th day of October following the ratification of this article.

Section 6. This article shall be inoperative unless it shall have been ratified as an amendment to the Constitution by the legislatures of three-fourths of the several states within seven years from the date of its submission.

Amendment XXI (1933)

Section 1. The eighteenth article of amendment to the Constitution of the United States is hereby repealed.

Section 2. The transportation or importation into any state, territory, or possession of the United States for delivery or use therein of intoxicating liquors, in violation of the laws thereof, is hereby prohibited.

Section 3. This article shall be inoperative unless it shall have been ratified as an amendment to the Constitution by conventions in the several states, as provided in the Constitution, within seven years from the date of the submission hereof to the states by the Congress.

Amendment XXII (1951)

Section 1. No person shall be elected to the office of the President more than twice, and no person who has held the office of President, or acted as President, for more than two years of a term to which some other person was elected President shall be elected to the office of the President more than once. But this article shall not apply to any person holding the office of President when this article was proposed by the Congress, and shall not prevent any person who may be holding the office of President, or acting as President, during the term within which this article becomes operative from holding the office of President or acting as President during the remainder of such term.

Section 2. This article shall be inoperative unless it shall have been ratified as an amendment to the Constitution by the legislatures of three-fourths of the several states within seven years from the date of its submission to the states by the Congress.

Amendment XXIII (1961)

Section 1. The District constituting the seat of government of the United States shall appoint in such manner as the Congress may direct:

A number of electors of President and Vice President equal to the whole number of Senators and Representatives in Congress to which the District would be entitled if it were a state, but in no event more than the least populous state; they shall be in addition to those appointed by the states, but they shall be considered, for the purposes of the election of President and Vice President, to be electors appointed by a state; and they shall meet in the District and perform such duties as provided by the twelfth article of amendment.

Section 2. The Congress shall have power to enforce this article by appropriate legislation.

Amendment XXIV (1964)

Section 1. The right of citizens of the United States to vote in any primary or other election for President or Vice President, for electors for President or Vice President, or for Senator or Representative in Congress, shall not be denied or abridged by the United States or any state by reason of failure to pay any poll tax or other tax.

Section 2. The Congress shall have power to enforce this article by appropriate legislation.

Amendment XXV (1967)

Section 1. In case of the removal of the President from office or of his death or resignation, the Vice President shall become President.

Section 2. Whenever there is a vacancy in the office of the Vice President, the President shall nominate a Vice President who shall take office upon confirmation by a majority vote of both Houses of Congress.

Section 3. Whenever the President transmits to the President pro tempore of the Senate and the Speaker of the House of Representatives his written declaration that he is unable to discharge the powers and duties of his office, and until he transmits to them a written declaration to the contrary, such powers and duties shall be discharged by the Vice President as Acting President.

Section 4. Whenever the Vice President and a majority of either the principal officers of the executive departments or of such other body as Congress may by law provide, transmit to the President pro tempore of the Senate and the Speaker of the House of Representatives their written declaration that the President is unable to discharge the powers and duties of his office, the Vice President shall immediately assume the powers and duties of the office as Acting President.

Thereafter, when the President transmits to the President pro tempore of the Senate and the Speaker of the House of Representatives his written declaration that no inability exists, he shall resume the powers and duties of his office unless the Vice President and a majority of either the principal officers of the executive department or of such other body as Congress may by law provide, transmit within four days to the President pro tempore of the Senate and the Speaker of the House of Representatives their written declaration that the President is unable to discharge the powers and duties of his office.

Thereupon Congress shall decide the issue, assembling within forty-eight hours for that purpose if not in session. If the Congress, within twenty-one days after receipt of the latter written declaration, or, if Congress is not in session, within twenty-one days after Congress is required to assemble, determines by two-thirds vote of both Houses that the President is unable to discharge the powers and duties of his office, the Vice President shall continue to discharge the same as Acting President; otherwise, the President shall resume the powers and duties of his office.

Amendment XXVI

Section 1. The right of citizens of the United States, who are 18 years of age or older, to vote, shall not be denied or abridged by the United States or any state on account of age.

Section 2. The Congress shall have the power to enforce this article by appropriate legislation.

Amendment XXVII (1992)

No law, varying the compensation for the services of the Senators and Representatives, shall take effect, until an election of Representatives shall have intervened.

Index